# *Col Elliott*
## IN BETWEEN THE LAUGHTER

First published 2014
This edition published in 2016.

ISBN: 978-1-63173-824-1

Copyright © Col Elliott 2014

Col Elliott has asserted his right under the Copyright, Designs
and Patents Act 1988 to be identified as the author of this work.

All rights reserved. No part of this publication may be reproduced, stored in or introduced into a retrieval system, or transmitted in any form, or by any means (electronic, mechanical, photocopying, recording or otherwise) without the prior written permission of the author. Any person who does any unauthorised act in relation to this publication may be liable to criminal prosecution and civil claims for damages.

Cover design and typesetting: Chameleon Print Design

This book is sold subject to the condition that it shall not, by way of trade or otherwise, be lent, re-sold, hired out, or otherwise circulated without the author's prior consent in any form of binding or cover than that in which it is published and without a similar condition including this condition being imposed on the subsequent publisher.

For more about Col Elliott, visit www.colelliott.com.au

Col's albums are available from iTunes and other major online services

*To my wife Karen, for her patience, understanding, love and loyalty.*

## TABLE OF CONTENTS

| | | | | |
|---|---|---|---|---|
| 3 | **PART ONE** | | 41 | **PART TWO.** |
| | **THE EARLY YEARS.** | 3 | | **THE NAVY YEARS** |
| 4 | Don't think, just do it. | | 45 | Just a bit off the sides please. |
| 4 | The Separator | | 47 | The Lesson |
| 7 | The Move to Lyndale | | 48 | The Window |
| 10 | Kings of the Road | | 51 | Flying Saucers |
| 13 | The True Patriot | | 53 | At the double Sailor |
| 13 | Tour de Lyndale | | 55 | Candid Camera |
| 17 | A 'foul' drive in. | | 56 | Big Guilie |
| 19 | The Stocktake | | 57 | The Georges |
| 20 | The Woggle | | 62 | Off to the Fleet |
| 21 | Wiped out | | 65 | HMAS Sydney |
| 22 | Take it off | | 66 | Learning the hard way |
| 23 | New Arrivals | | 69 | Climbing the Corporate Ladder |
| 24 | The Sceptic | | | |
| 24 | The Lyndale Cold Case | | 72 | Navy Speak |
| 27 | Learning to ride | | 73 | Vietnam |
| 28 | Cindy | | 77 | Alongopo |
| 28 | Hi-Ho Bobby | | 79 | When in Rome |
| 30 | The Fish and Chips Saga | | 81 | Dodgy Rum |
| 32 | Paper Boy (Dangerous Gig) | | 84 | Couldn't drink ... Couldn't vote ... but OK for war. |
| 33 | I was only trying to help | | | |
| 34 | Cindy's new home. | | 88 | Disaster at Sea |
| | | | 92 | Text of US Navy Commendation |
| | | | 96 | Back home |
| | | | 98 | The Sharpies |

v

| | | | |
|---|---|---|---|
| 102 | Pretend sailors | 199 | **PART THREE** |
| 105 | Back to Sea | | **BACK TO CIVVY STREET** |
| 108 | The New Band Member | 202 | Thru' A Looking Glass |
| 114 | Not A Good Call | 204 | Fast Glass |
| 118 | My Shout, 'Ralphie' | 204 | Sad Times |
| 122 | Dear John ... Col | 205 | Shell Shocked |
| 124 | The Marathon Swim | 208 | Fast Cars/Women? |
| 125 | The Frank E Evans' Disaster | 208 | Mr Cool |
| 128 | In the 'Ship' again. | 211 | KAZ – A New Beginning |
| 131 | Here we go again ... More 'Ship' | 211 | Mr Cool Again |
| 134 | Short Back and Sides | 214 | The Brew Masters |
| 137 | Ship's Driver | 215 | Jack Mills |
| 140 | Pay Attention or Die | 217 | My 'New' Wheels |
| 146 | The Snapshots | 218 | The Destroyer on Wheels |
| 147 | Changi | 220 | Kimbo Arrives |
| 149 | When in Doubt ... Improvise | 221 | It's all Greek to me |
| 151 | Don't let me down Elliott | | |
| 154 | My Friend The Queen | 225 | **PART FOUR** |
| 157 | HMAS CERBERUS | | **SHOWBIZ** |
| 160 | Recruit School Instructor | 229 | Looking for an outfit |
| 161 | I Did It My Way! | 230 | And the winner is ... |
| 162 | D.A.D.F.A. | 232 | The Honorary Bikie |
| 183 | The Chief Brewmaker | 235 | Actors' Equity |
| 185 | Crossed Teaspoons | 237 | My hero |
| | — Coster's Choice | 240 | Debt free at last! |
| 188 | Getting Restless | 242 | The Rep |
| 189 | Insurance, Hastings Style | 244 | Grog |
| 191 | Fresh Bread | 245 | Gee Up |
| 192 | 'ARRY | 246 | The rag trade |
| 193 | The Keys to the Lolly Shop | 247 | The pancakes |
| 195 | Opportunity Knocks | 248 | The Curse of Assumption |

| | | | |
|---|---|---|---|
| 249 | Jodie | 307 | If it looks too good to be true!!! |
| 249 | The Crayfish | | |
| 256 | Dying gracefully | 307 | Willy the Hill |
| 258 | Touring | 309 | Tom T Hall |
| 259 | Turning Pro | 310 | A new floor manager |
| 259 | Wally | 313 | I didn't exist |
| 260 | Free Meal? | 315 | False teeth and Hearing Aids |
| 263 | Out of work | 317 | Jack Mills moves in |
| 265 | Are You being Served? | 320 | Gotta give the Grog away |
| 268 | Getting straightened out | 330 | Cassie |
| 273 | The Wowser | 330 | Qld |
| 285 | Ernie | 331 | The Strip-o-Gram |
| 285 | Bootlegged!!! | 332 | Back to the Old Dart |
| 287 | Holy Smoke Max!! | 334 | Chooka |
| 291 | The Land Baron | 336 | Decisions, decisions! |
| 293 | "Maybe" | 337 | Denny's |
| 294 | Boots and all | 340 | The Punters |
| 295 | The Tip Wallower | 340 | Home sweet home |
| 296 | Footlighters | 341 | Stranger than fiction |
| 298 | Little big man | 344 | Kim's Poem |
| 299 | Paul Hogan show | 345 | in conclusion |
| 303 | E.M.I. | | |
| 304 | "We bloody well did it!" | | |

# PART ONE

## THE EARLY YEARS

**E**very time I heard the postman I would race outside. Sometimes I would be waiting for him ... any day now.

I was sweating on that all important envelope bearing the letters OHMS (On Her Majesty's Service). It would determine the course my life would take. It would mean my ticket out; I just had to be accepted into the Royal Australian Navy.

I felt I needed to leave, to get away from my father. All I had ever known him to do was sit at the end of the kitchen table and drink. I was over it.

I needed to go.

He could be very bad tempered, a totally selfish man. He kept my mother poor and treated her more like a servant than a wife. Not that he was unique in the area where we lived. It seemed there was an inordinate amount of drunks up our street, some mean, some not, and some in fact made us laugh.

My brother and I used to bet on how many times Mr O'Shea would bounce off our side fence on his way home from the pub. It was hilarious. "Eleven, I won," Ralph would yell. A great source of entertainment.

I had spent my life up to that point trying to please my father. It was an impossible task. He never showed any real interest in me or my siblings. He would just sit at the end of the kitchen table by the street window, dictate his wants, rave on to anyone who would listen; usually poor Mum, and drink! He had drunk himself to death by the time he was 49.

I had at times, on reflection, thought his nature and attitude could have been because of his war service in the English Navy during WW2.

Having met so many other returned men who had been through

as much and were good men, I realised this was just the type of man he was ... end of story.

Weeks before, I had sat all the Navy exams; maths, English, general knowledge, aptitude tests, health and psychological. (God knows how that went.) It was full on, but I walked away with the feeling that I had done well.

It was a fairly comprehensive range of exams and boys aged from 15 to 16 from all over Australia had applied and were probably feeling exactly the way I was right now.

George McRob, the elder brother of a girl I had gone to school with, had gone to train as a Junior Recruit in Perth the year before and had written to me telling me all about the training. It sounded like it was just what I needed. I was willing to sign away 12 years of my life. No problems. I had left school before I turned 15, half way through 3rd form. It wasn't that I couldn't do the work; it was just that I had grown so bored with it all.

I couldn't see the point. It's a problem in life I have always had ... impatience, I fight it all the time ... don't mess about, do it now.

It doesn't always give you the best outcome but I guess it's part of who I am. I think I have mellowed a little over time but it's still there. My wife Karen (Kaz) can attest to this, she only has to say "Hey Col, Greece would be nice to visit one day". Before her arse hits the ground, she's standing in front of the Parthenon with a souvlaki in her hand.

Kaz has been the levelling influence in my life and between us we seem to get a good balance.

Caution versus impatience = compromise = balance.

Back to 1964, I had gotten a part time job as a separator at the local stables. A separator separates the horse poop from the straw and I couldn't see any chance for advancement in the job. The next step up was an apprentice jockey and seeing as how they weren't racing draught horses any time soon, I thought I would move on ... that's when I found the Post magazine ... in the outhouse at the stables. There was a half-page advertisement espousing the incredible opportunity being offered for a 'life on the waves' in the RAN. A life of total adventure!

I got a job at McEwans, a local general-type store, to fill in till I could get a shot at the Navy. It finally came. Mum gave me the letter as I walked in from work. "Good luck love," Mum said as she handed it to me. I felt the apprehension as I opened the letter.

"It gives me great pleasure in advising you that you have been accepted into the RAN and will need to report" ... "YES" ... I let out a yell. Mum cried.

The Junior Recruit training scheme was adopted by the RAN in 1960 and went through to 1984. The idea was loosely based on Nelson's day when the British Navy used boys to man their fighting ships. The Australian Navy was basically a clone of our English counterpart. I was to become one of those 13,000 boys that would pass through this system. Some of these boys would see active service in the Indonesian conflict and Vietnam. I was sent to Vietnam in 1967. I was 17. This would not happen today.

Many of the boy sailors rose to senior positions in the Navy.

Vice Admiral Russ Crane, Chief of the Navy is one of our boys, as is Rear Admiral Brian Adams (Rtd). They joined in 1968 and 1970 respectively. I don't know of any of my J.R. (Junior Recruit) mates today, who don't boast of their achievements. We are very proud of them and of the many others that rose through the ranks to senior positions in our Navy.

The elation I felt at getting that letter was totally overwhelming and then I looked up and saw the sadness in my mother's face.

Mum and I had grown close as I grew into a teenager. She had taught me the Marriott Edgar poems that were made famous by the English comedian and actor Stanley Holloway. 'Albert and the 'orses 'ead 'andle', 'Sam, pick up thy musket','The Cockney in Court' and many more.

We would stand at the kitchen sink doing the dishes and she

would recite them all, using all her wonderful accents and natural comic flair. She taught me so much and the ability I have today to use accents on stage comes from those early times with her. She was in the Land Army in London during the blitz. She saw so much destruction, chaos and death and would always say that humour was a big part of their ability to survive.

Her party piece was Burlington Bertie from Bow, an old music hall piece made famous by Ella Shields in 1915. It's a classic and Mum would perform it at the drop of a hat. It's got me buggered how she got stuck with the old man. He was such a miserable sod, not at all interested.

Mum loved to perform and had joined the local amateur players when we settled in Australia. She was a natural as they say and I had no greater fan in later years. She would have made a great theatrical performer had she been given the chance. I say that without bias, even if I am talking about my own mum. She was a talent and that's the truth of it.

She had told me that when she was a little girl, she contracted whooping cough and that it had left her with a slight turn in her right eye. This made her lose her self-confidence and she felt she wasn't that attractive. When she told me this I really had to look twice. I had never noticed it ... amazing! I guess that's why she settled for the old man; he was definitely no great prize.

We had arrived in Australia from England in 1951; my elder brother Ralph, elder sister Carol, Mum, our maternal grandmother and myself. I was the youngest at 20 months. We have two more in the family now, but Michael didn't arrive for another 12 years and Wendy four years after that.

We went to live in Rosebud on the Mornington peninsula in Victoria. It is a beautiful spot with a great foreshore and a real laid-back feel. Mum had her two elder sisters already settled there, so it was an inbuilt support system.

It was a year before our father could come out and join us as he had to finish his Navy service in England. Turned out that it was the best thing he ever did for the family ... bring us to Australia.

## THE MOVE TO LYNDALE

When I was five, we moved to a commission house estate in North Dandenong. It was a little satellite suburb called Lyndale. It was truly diverse. There were people from all over Europe who had immigrated after the carnage that was WW2. It was a new beginning for many. Europe was a mess.

How they built the commission houses in Lyndale was quite unique; nothing like building today. They used to erect the concrete walls with teams of draught horses. I would stand and watch fascinated for hours. Our sister Carol would be over petting the horses at every chance. Her passion for horses has lasted all her life and to this day she still rides in dressage competition. We share many memories. She has the best sense of humour; a great sister.

The oldest of Mum's sisters was Auntie Celia; she was 12 years older than Mum. She and her husband had bought an apple orchard at Red Hill just outside Rosebud. Some of my earliest memories were of the visits to them. They had two Alsatian dogs, Smokey and Silver. I ran and played with them for hours. Uncle Harold would put me on his lap and let me steer his old tractor around the orchard. They had two children, Brian and Jill, both blessed with a lovely nature.

They worked hard and carved out a good life for themselves. They always made me feel very special and I have never forgotten their kindness.

Mum's other sister was our protector, Auntie Phil. Her nickname was 'Nobby'.

The sound of her name would strike fear into the old man. She took no prisoners and we loved her. She and Mum were very close. She was so protective, but she couldn't be there all the time ... more's the pity.

Her own story was tragic. Her two children, Roy and Nicky both died early. Roy killed in a mining accident, Nicky a drug overdose.

Auntie Nob and her husband Ralph, had divorced not long after coming to Australia. Uncle Ralph was an alcoholic and had been in the Royal Navy during the war. He would turn up at our place when he was broke. Mum always took him in. He could always charm her. He was a loveable rogue and she would tell him "Ralph, this is the last time," but the last time never came. Mum could never turn him away.

Uncle Ralph was a very gifted piano player; in fact he played everything from saxophone to guitar, but made his drinking money playing piano in local hotels. We loved this man, he was a charmer, a story teller and when he came to stay, he would bunk in with my brother and me and would have us in fits of laughter.

He was great until his pension came in, then he would break out on the grog. He would give my brother and me two bob (20 cents) each to pass the plonk in to him through the bedroom window. We would be sworn to secrecy. It was so much fun and I felt so important. Then he'd be smashed for a couple of days, run out of money and sober up. All the time telling Mum, "This is the last time ... promise Joanie".

I was his favourite. He taught me how to spit-polish my shoes, how to laugh. He gave me the time of day. He was everything my father wasn't ... he took me on the only holiday I ever had.

He was playing piano at a guest house in Healesville, a beautiful little country town in Victoria and I stayed with him for a week. The owners were lovely people and treated me like family. I revelled in the attention. I must have been eight or nine and that week was one time in my life that I still remember as special.

Uncle Ralph bought me my first pair of long pants. Uncle Ralph had a great sense of humour. He was a stirrer and loved nothing better than to give the 'old man' a bit of curry. My father would sit at his window seat every day where he could survey the street and pass judgement on all those that passed ... and drink.

Weeks earlier, my brother and I had received a gift from friends in Rosebud. We each received a Davey Crockett hat, complete with the fake-fur raccoon tail. Davy Crockett was all the rage at the time and we sang the Fess Parker hit song incessantly, till the old man would go off the deep end. Uncle Ralph would have us crouch under his window and we would sing at the top of our voices. The longer we could sing, the more money we got ... we made good money and copped a few back-handers.

Money was scarce in those days so we collected beer bottles and could make up to 10 pence (10 cents) a dozen. We also had a thriving business in horse and cow manure, selling to those neighbours who were into their gardens.

Some of my mates and I would use the cow pads as flying saucers, or would have shit fights in-between bagging the stuff. One afternoon I became a hero in the eyes of my mates when a gang of older guys came over to give us a belting. As they came toward us I threw a cow pad at them. It's surprising how hard cow dung can become, especially in the summer. I hit the kid nearest to me square in the mouth and it stopped him in his tracks. He stood there holding his face, bleeding and crying in pain. We ran like hell, pulling our billycart and laughing. I guess it was a case of ... shit happens.

Funny how important memories stay with you!!!

When we first arrived in Lyndale, Ralph and I began getting our bearings, exploring the neighbouring streets, checking out the locals and generally getting a feel for the place. The local teen hoods would hang on the street corners near the shops, smoke and whistle at the passing girls, hoping against hope that someone would notice them. We gave them a wide berth, but occasionally if Mum had sent us over to the shops to get something or other, we had to cross their path. Eyes down and moving fast I would try and get past without making eye contact, making myself as small as possible. Sometimes I would get past, sometimes I wouldn't. It was part of the routine. My brother Ralph learnt early that if you became a victim you would always be a victim. He was a lot smaller than most of these guys but in the end they had a great respect for him. He learnt to fight early … a right little dynamo.

Houses were still being erected all over the place, it was a gold mine for us kids; we would play in the half-built houses. Ralph and I couldn't wait to be off every morning.

## KINGS OF THE ROAD

One morning we had made stilts out of used round paint tins, by punching holes in the bottom of the tins and threading old twine through. We would then loop the twine, hold onto it and lift our right and left foot in turn and walk on the tins … great fun … until round the corner came the Redmond boys, all ten of them! I could be exaggerating here. There mightn't have been ten … there were ten kids in the Redmond family alright, but I think three were girls.

The trouble is the girls were tougher than the boys. Anyway, there was a heap of them, the biggest, Johnny, also one of the eldest, demanded we hand over the stilts. Our reaction of course was to tell them to "get stuffed". Their reaction was to punch me in the face. I went down for the count. I looked up, head spinning, eyes watering and blood pouring from my nose to see Ralph still trying to fight them off. He was getting hammered. They ran off with our stilts after telling us we were in their territory and could expect this on a regular basis. We went home to re-evaluate. We had met the Redmond's; they ran the street.

One of the first things the local council did was to erect a set of see saws and a set of kids' swings across the road from our place. It was like a central park … well not so much a park as a paddock, but it was an area set aside for kids to kick a football and hang out.

One night after school Ralph and I were on the swings, it was just on dusk and we had to get home before dark or risk a belting from the old man. We were just about to jump off the swings when we were surrounded by the Redmond boys.

"WHEN YOU COME OFF THOSE SWINGS," Johnny called out, "WE'RE GONNA BELT THE CRAP OUT OF YOU'SE."

My first reaction was to get the old legs moving again and keep that swing happening. Christ, what will we do? Ralph and I kept pumping, then Ralph made a life-changing decision. He knew we were stuffed either way. If we were late home we had to contend with the old man. If we got off the swings, we had the Redmonds to deal with. Both outcomes were bad.

Even today I try and find a positive in any situation. I mean even if you're getting your arse kicked, technically you're still in front ... right? Anyway, the problem at hand had to be solved. As we swung ever higher, Ralph told me his plan. It wasn't so much of a plan as picking the best alternative to our situation. He said, "Col, when I say jump, we do it together — I will go hell for leather at Johnny, you thump his brother as hard as you can and don't stop, they won't expect that and we just might get a couple in.

Now, on the count of three ... one ... two ... three."

We literally flew off the swings, legs running in mid-air. Ralph hit Johnny hard and down he went. Ralph was punching, yelling and screaming like a banshee. In the meantime I had hit Johnny's brother ... he backed away proclaiming innocence of the whole thing but I kept going like my brother told me. By this time Johnny was crying and begging for it to cease, the others were running down the street. They fair dinkum filled their pants, literally. There was definitely a rancid waft in the air.

I think that's what stopped the fight ... the smell of defeat and fear. With no one left to hit, we headed for home. We would have given each other a 'high five' but they weren't invented yet.

We got home late and copped a back-hander each as we came in the front door but it was worth it.

It was now our street and Ralph revelled in ambushing the Redmonds at every chance; on the way to school; on the way home from school; even during school. Finally Mrs Redmond, a typical Aussie mum, knocked on our door to have a word with our mum. She asked Mum if she could stop her boys from being belted. We were told to stop belting the Redmonds, but Mum had trouble with the maths. "Ralph," she said, "didn't you say there are ten of them ... that can't be right."

"Well Mum, there's only seven that we belt," said Ralph. "The sheilas would kill us."

The Redmonds were part of our growing up and they turned into great friends; a typical battling Aussie family.

We made our own fun in those days, and because of the lack of funds, the kids in the neighbourhood would trade. If a kid in your area got a truck say, for Christmas, you could bet through a series of trades, you would eventually get hold of it. Then you would trade it on. That's how my brother Ralph and I got the ping-pong set. It consisted of two balls, two paddles and a portable net. We were so excited to get this that we set it up on the kitchen table and started playing after Mum and the old man went to bed. We were having such a great time that we were oblivious to the fact that it was 2am.

Suddenly the kitchen door flew open. The old man was off his head. We had woken him. He swung at me; I ducked and got out under his arm through the kitchen door. Ralph copped a backhander and smashed his head on the wall. It was a slab concrete wall and he went down ... I think that frightened the old man and he backed off a little. We were told to get to bed.

The next morning he took us in the back yard and made us chop the ping-pong set into pieces. I had the axe and when he told me to start I nearly lost it. I will never forget Ralph saying to me, "It's OK Col, I'll buy you another one, one day." With tears in my eyes, I set to it. I hated my father at that moment.

In those early days the old man would go away with his work in the Public Works department. Sometimes he would stay away for up to two weeks at a time. He was the foreman of a team that would lay asphalt in country schools. Life was better when he was away.

## A TRUE PATRIOT

The other great trade was the slug gun. I am counting this as part of my war service. I will explain. Brother Ralph had traded a slug gun along with slugs for some other treasure. We can't remember what, but we will never forget the gun.

A slug gun is an air rifle. This one was not powerful enough to do too much damage but could inflict enough pain as to be wary of. We had a ball setting up targets under the house. I became quite a marksman if I do say so myself. I was about ten, Ralph three years older and I believed everything he told me. The local men of the area would go to work on bicycles; there were not too many cars around in those days. One particular chap would ride past our house every night on his way home from work. He was married to a Japanese lady and Ralph had convinced me he was a traitor and needed to be shot up the arse as punishment ... sounded reasonable to me.

Every night for a week I pinged his bum from the cover of being under our house. I felt it was my duty. He would jump off his bike, rubbing his arse yelling that he would find us. He never did.

He lasted a week and never rode our way again. I figured he either learnt the error of his ways and divorced, or just opted for a less confronting route ... anyway I still count it as service to my country.

## TOUR DE FRA... LYNDALE

The other local bloke in the area that I did some damage to was Al Smith who lived in the house directly behind ours. His side fence was our back fence and the path to his front door was running alongside that fence. Upon reflection of this incident I feel maybe it was karma that got 'Uncle' Al Smith, as we called him. This is how it transpired.

I desperately wanted a bike. There were only a few kids in our street lucky enough to own one and I would hang with them as much as possible in the off-chance they would give me a ride.

Mum knew how much I wanted a bike and by hook or by crook somehow she was going to make it happen. There was just no money left over from the meagre allowance the old man gave her, so she would go out 'charring' as she would call it. It meant scrubbing floors, babysitting, washing and cleaning for our local doctor and others, and saving every penny.

There was no way she could afford a new bike but Uncle Al had convinced her that he was an expert on bikes and if she gave him ten pounds, a veritable fortune in those days, he would get the parts and build me a fantastic bike.

The way he talked you would have thought that he'd ridden in the Tour de France. She needed it for Christmas Eve. He promised to deliver.

Christmas morning arrived and I was up early; it was 2 am Mum told me years later. There was the bike, in the middle of the lounge room; a semi racing frame, green in colour, handle bars down, left and right clutch hand-brakes. I was beside myself with excitement. It was the coolest present I could have wished for.

Mum stood in the doorway beaming. She had worked so hard to make it happen, and my excitement was all the reward she needed.

I couldn't wait for the sun to come up. I was out the door with the bike.

It even had racing toe clips, I had never seen them before, and I put my toes in them while Mum steadied the bike. I tightened the strap. My feet were now anchored to the pedals, so that meant you just had to keep moving forward or you would fall over. My feet were stuck. Mum gave me a push start and away I went.

The other problem I had was that the bike was what they called a 'fixed wheeler'. That meant the rider couldn't stop pedaling and rest, or even pedal backwards as most bikes do ... oh no ... on my 'Uncle

Al Special', the pedals were fixed to the sprocket which was attached to the wheel. If you got any speed up, your legs were moving up and down at the speed of light ... end result ... you were knackered within half a block and your arse was nearly churned to butter!

I was going around and around the block and every time I passed our kitchen window, I would try and signal to Mum or the old man to come and catch me. They thought I was just waving. Mum told me later she thought I just wanted to keep riding. It was hard to stop anyway because the first time I applied the brakes the brake rubbers shot out ... they had been installed back to front!

Lunch time came and went, by this time my balls were like footballs with the constant chafing. I couldn't feel my toes; the blood had been cut off from them in the beginning. I finally rolled to a stop when one pedal stem came away from the bike. I didn't lose it though; the stem was still attached to the pedal, which in turn was attached to my foot. At the same time the chain broke. I finally stopped and fell over, heartbroken ... but still firmly attached to the bike.

I watched as Uncle Al 'adjusted' the cotter pin with a hammer. I could tell he wasn't pleased to have his Christmas dinner interrupted. "The mongrel won't come out again," he muttered, half pissed, hammering harder and harder on my bike. He said it was only a minor problem and the bike was just 'wearing in'.

The bike never stopped wearing in and Uncle Al finally told me after two or three weeks of constant repairs, not to bring the bike back any more or he'd foot me up the arse.

Here's where the karma comes in.

I persevered with that bike and learned to fix the constantly breaking chain on a daily basis. If the chain didn't break it just came off because the wheels were not aligned. But the point was that I had a bike, no matter how it worked. There were days when I just got fed up putting the chain back on, so I used the bike like a scooter.

I decided to make a bike shed to protect it from the elements. I achieved this by making a kind of lean-to out of corrugated iron; it was against the back fence. Unfortunately, the roof of the structure hung over the top of the back fence — over the path to Uncle Al's front door.

About seven o'clock on a Friday night there was a desperate banging on our front door, Mum opened the door, let out a scream; the old man even left his chair and joined her. There was Uncle Al, blood running down his face and dripping off the end of his nose, with a huge bloody bald patch on top of his head. He was 'full as a boot' after spending the afternoon in the pub and he was screaming blue murder. He had walked into the roof of my lean-to. He had nearly been scalped. Geronimo couldn't have done a neater job.

I got a good hiding and had to dismantle the bike shed. I remember pulling the roof off my shed and seeing Uncle Al's hair hanging off the end. The thought crossed my mind to put it in a box and return it to him, but decided not to push my luck.

The toe clips on my bike nearly spelt my demise one afternoon. A bunch of local kids and me decided to ride our bikes to the local swimming hole about five miles from home. It was tough going for me, as I was the only one with a fixed-wheel bike. I was trailing behind because of the effort to keep pedaling. I could see my mates drawing ever further away.

All of a sudden a bunch of hoods turned up beside me in an old FJ Holden.

They slowed to my pace, with their windows down. They were all swigging on beer bottles with cigarettes out the side of their mouths and greasy black hair slicked back. This didn't bode well. There was nowhere for me to go. I was sandwiched between them on my right and the open water-filled ditch on my left. The ditch was more like an open storm drain and was flowing quite fast. It was the overflow of the river system we were heading to.

"Having a good ride mate?" one said, leaning out the window.

"Yes thank you," I replied, naively thinking manners might work for me in this situation.

"Pretty hot work, pedaling like that young fella, bet you're thirsty; fancy a swig?" one said, as the others laughed. He held out his bottle to me.

"No thanks," I said and tried a smile. I started slowing up, but they stayed with me.

"So you won't drink with us then?" he said with a feigned hurt look on his face.

I just smiled weakly, not knowing how to respond.

It was a 'cat and mouse' situation. What was coming, I had no idea. Then the car started to pick up speed. The guy in the back tried to grab hold of my handle bars to drag me along but couldn't quite do it ... the car slowed down again.

They must have gotten bored with this game and they started to drive off.

The hood in the back leaned out the window and called out "See ya," and belted me fair in the back of the head. My bike wobbled and I went into the ditch.

I was struggling to keep my head above water as it cascaded over me. I couldn't undo the bike clips. I began to swallow water. I thought I was going to drown, then all my mates were around me pulling me out — still attached to the bike.

I have never used bike clips since and by the way; today I am the proud owner of an eight-speed free wheeler, Malvern Star of course. I can even pedal backwards ... eat your heart out.

### A 'FOUL' DRIVE-IN

To make ends meet, we kept a dozen chickens. They gave us eggs and the old man would bump off a couple for Christmas. Mum would boil them up in the old copper in the laundry and when they were done we would sit on the back step and pluck all the feathers. It was a fairly big operation back then but a chook for Christmas was a big deal. In those days you only ever got chicken once a year. Today it's once a week. As they say ... times have changed.

At one stage we were desperate for money, so Mum bought some old bunk beds for us kids and moved Carol in with Ralph and me.

That created a spare room, which she rented out to a boarder. His name was Ebb, I think short for Ebenezer. He was Ukrainian and it was hard to understand his thick accent. He was very quiet and shut his door at night and only came out for meals. Ebb owned an old Ford, the best way to describe it was that it looked like an Elliott Ness-type car from the TV series. For all I know it was a 1920 vehicle. It was his prize possession. He kept it parked in the back yard.

There was a girl who boarded across the road. Her name was Val and Ebb was keen on her. He asked her out to the local drive-in movies, but she said she would only go if he took us kids in the back seat. We couldn't believe our luck. We were the chaperones.

We arrived at the drive-in and were treated to some lollies. The movie started. Ebb was moving closer to Val. After a while, he made his move and tried to kiss her. We began to make slurping sounds. He tried again and Ralph made a farting sound. We got a warning (in Ukrainian I think) then he settled down. A little while later he tried to move in on Val again ... we started again. He completely lost it and tried to belt us all over the back seat. Ralph didn't duck quickly enough and copped a beauty. We scrambled out of the car and ran around the back.

We were falling about laughing, then we became even more hysterical when we saw half a dozen chickens sitting on the back bumper-bar. They had been roosting there and had hung on all the way to the drive-in ... about five miles. Their eyes must have been watering.

Ebb was not amused. By this time Val was crying with laughter as well. Ebb's amorous intentions were totally shot. We had completely lost it. Ebb drove home in stony silence. We never lost a chook ... we never went to the drive-in again either.

## THE STOCKTAKE

Life back then was simple. We lived basic and because we were kids, we didn't miss what we didn't have. Every chance we got we would head into the surrounding countryside. We had secret cubby houses and a secret club. We would buy or steal cigarettes from our parents and it was always an adventure.

We would leave at first light and would not get home till just on dark. It was an innocent time. Our parents never worried or locked their doors. We had nothing of value to steal. People were more likely to break in and leave stuff.

I can remember Carol, Ralph and myself armed with Mum's saucepans, wandering the open fields mushrooming or blackberrying. Then we'd get home with our faces blue from the juice. Mum would make pies for us out of what was left. Great simple days!

I always get that same feeling of those innocent times when I watch that classic movie, Stand by Me, starring the late River Phoenix and Corey Feldman. They managed to capture the essence of young innocence and adventure. It was like that for us. Great memories.

The commission houses were all concrete which meant they were stinking hot in the summer and freezing in the winter. When it was steamy, condensation would stream down the walls.

In those days, there was no sewage system or septic. We had the outhouse in the back yard. It was of wooden construction with a hinged flap door at the back for the removal of the cans by the 'dunny-can man'. He must have had job satisfaction because I distinctly remember him whistling as he came in the back gates. He had a leather shoulder pad on and he would swing a 50 gallon can onto his shoulders with one fluid movement, take the full one to the truck and replace it with an empty. I guess he was happy with his lot. At least he was working, many weren't, but I guess his was the only job that would stipulate that he had to take shit from everybody.

Ralph and I would wait till one of our mates was in the dunny doing some serious business. We would lift the flap door at the back and touch their arse with a stick ... their reaction was incredible ... we would fall about laughing. Now that was funny stuff and we never tired of it.

One afternoon the dunny-can man was heading out the gate; he had a full can on his shoulders. I had just ridden up on my bike and I leant it against the gate; it fell over as I walked away. He tripped over it, staggered a few feet and dropped the full can. It was everywhere ... we heard the noise it made and looked out the window. There he was on his hands and knees. Ralph said, "He must be doing a stock-take." My brother swears this is a true story ... ain't too sure ... but it sure is funny eh!

## THE WOGGLE

Collecting beer bottles was a great source of pocket money for us and we would stack them up against the side fence. When they reached the point of collapsing, we would get in touch with the 'Bottle-o'. He would come around with his truck and crate them, then pay us. He was coming Saturday afternoon.

On the Wednesday night that week, I had been invited to come to a meeting of the local Cub group that had started up in the area. Cubs were the junior lead-up to Scouts and the two kids across the road were members. I remember watching them leave home each week to go to their group and being so envious of their uniform, especially the woggle.

The woggle was a wolf's head, with a hole in the middle to pull their scarf through. I wasn't interested in anything else, but I was in desperate need of a woggle; it was the coolest thing I had ever seen.

I went to the meeting with the other kids and watched and listened as they did their special chants "dib dib dib and dob dob dob," chants led by the lady leader of the group. They called her Arkela. It was all a bit confusing to me, but I would learn their ways if it meant getting a woggle.

She announced me as a prospective new member and welcomed me to the group. They gave me a round of applause.

Arkela told the group that the following weekend would be a 'bob-a-job' weekend and also a beer bottle drive. All money raised would go to the Cubs. I was to go with the bob-a-job group. The way it worked was that we would canvass the area and ask if we could do any jobs for people for a bob a job. (One shilling or ten cents today.)

## WIPED OUT

Some people took it literally and bloody near worked you to death and at the end only gave you a bob. I worked so hard that weekend and made around twenty-five bob. I thought the woggle was 'in the bag'. I got home just before dark, so tired that I was falling asleep at the table. Mum casually mentioned that the Bottle-o had come by and taken all my beer bottles ... I had completely forgotten ... "How much did I get Mum?" I asked. "I don't know love, he was with the Cubs and he paid them," she said. I was devastated. I hadn't given them MY bottles! ... how did this happen?

I didn't find out 'till the next Cub meeting. It turned out that Brian Craig, a mate of mine, told the group he was with on the bottle truck, that "Col has got a heap of bottles" ... that's all it took ... they wiped me out. I was bankrupt.

I explained the mix-up to the Arkela and asked for the return of my money. I had my exercise book with me, all ruled up with the appropriate column and totals. Plonk bottles, beer bottles, flagons etc. Arkela turned out to be an 'Arsola'! She flatly refused to reimburse me and then had the cheek to ask how much I made on the bob-a-job team. I told her "twenty five bob and you ain't getting any of it unless you give me my bottle money back," ... end result, I was drummed out of the Cubs at my second meeting. They wouldn't even entertain the thought of giving me a woggle as a parting gesture.

As a footnote to this story, last year while visiting Brian Craig some fifty-five years after the event, he presented me with a profound apology and a WOGGLE! Brian stayed with the scouting movement for many years and rose to the rank of Deputy Commissioner of Queensland. He is a great bloke and a great Australian ... and I treasure my woggle!

## TAKE IT OFF

A big event in our lives was the Dandenong show. It was an annual event not to be missed by us kids; the octopus ride, fairy floss, side show alley, and the horse events. It was such an exciting time and Ralph and I would spend all our time there when it was on. We saved our money for weeks before the show was due. I loved to watch the spruiker on the stage at Jimmy Sharman's boxing tent drum up business. I guess that's where that expression came from, 'drum up' because that's what they did. They had a bloke on a big bass drum belting it to draw attention, while the spruiker worked the crowd.

A good percentage of the fighters lined up on the stage were Aboriginal blokes and they were good. It was great entertainment.

All the locals would be egging their mates on to fight and the spruiker would bait them as well. In the end some would fight to save face. Once they had a full card they would charge one and sixpence to come inside and watch. I loved the boxing and looked forward to it every year.

We had a dilemma one year. Ralph was about fifteen so that would make me twelve. We had spent all of our money, except for enough to get into the boxing ... or ... now here was the thing ... I was keen to see the Dance of the Seven Veils which was about to get underway in the next tent. The girls were being displayed on the stage out the front, pretty much the same way as the boxers, except they were wearing less. I was starting to take an interest in 'boobs' at the time, so I was leaning toward getting into the strip tent.

"Well come on you dirty little bugger," said Ralph, "we'll try and get in."

It was two and sixpence a head to see the strippers, but Ralph convinced the spruiker that because I was so short and wouldn't see much anyway, we should get a discount. I gotta say at this point, I like to watch my 'bro' operate ... he's good!

The spruiker saw the reason in this and let us both in for a total of two bob.

The tent was packed. The music started, I was craning my head to see. I eventually shoved my head in between two big 'cow cockies'. They looked at me, shrugged and then they were back into the show. Blokes were whistling, the atmosphere was electric and the genuine 'Arabian Princess' was thrusting, gyrating and moving to the scratchy music being played. "Take it off," they yelled ... even I was yelling.

She teased and danced for what seemed to be forever, all the veils were now gone. She had her back to us now and her plump arse was only just covered by the tiniest knickers, "take it off," we yelled, my shorts ever tighter. She was undoing the back of her bra. Here come the boobs I thought ... my excitement was at a peak.

She turned to face the audience holding a board across her boobs that read CENSORED.

"AW FUCK," the crowd yelled.

"We'll be going to Jimmy Sharman's next year," Ralph said to me as we walked out of the tent ... my hands were in front of my tight shorts.

### NEW ARRIVALS

I was twelve when Mum had Michael. He was a beautiful baby and we were all excited. Four years later, our baby sister Wendy, arrived. I was in the Navy when Wendy came along. Nothing changed for the old man; it didn't affect him or his drinking. He never gave Mum any more money, she had to make do.

Michael was nicknamed 'Miffy', and we still call him that today. He was nine when the old man died. Wendy, our baby sister, was only four.

## THE SCEPTIC

I am a little bit skeptical when it comes to clairvoyants but I have to confess to this particular incident. I was told by a teacup reader that Wendy was 'on the way'.

I was on weekend day leave and staying with my friends in Perth, Mum and Dad George. I will tell their story a little later on ... but this is what happened.

Mum George was right into this spiritual thing and we would have long discussions on the subject. I was inclined to 'take the micky' out of her so one day she dared me to have a reading.

Away we went to Fremantle and the teacup reader. I was given a cup of tea, (no bikkies), and when I finished she read the leaves. I was trying not to laugh as I was only being condescending in the first place. Then she told me I was in the Navy ... guessing I thought ... then she said, "You will get a call from your mum, she is a long way away." She hadn't been told that Mum was in Victoria ... still guessing ... maybe. She finished the 'read' by telling me Mum would tell me she was having another baby and it would be a girl. "Thank you," I said, wanting to get out of there before I started laughing. I took the micky out of Mum George all the way home. Two days later, I was told to report to the gangway to receive a phone call from my mother!

## THE LYNDALE COLD CASE

In Lyndale we always left the windows open to our bedrooms with never a thought of burglaries. This was how we all got in the house at night ... not one of us kids used the front door. Ours was a sort of half-way house for a lot of the kids in the neighbourhood. Whenever there was a 'blue' on at their homes, or for others, nowhere else to go, some would end up at our place. Mum would always find something for them to eat.

Talking on old times with her years later, she would say it was very tough. She was on poverty allowance from the old man and there were no social networks in place to help as there are today.

Sometimes I would wake up in the morning and find a kid in the other end of the bed; it was the norm in those days.

My mum was so good to some of those kids and many never forgot her kindness. They would constantly visit her and check on her until she died of heart failure in 2006. They loved 'Mrs E'.

As I stated before, our windows stayed open and only once did it cause a problem. When our maternal grandmother came to stay, my brother and I would vacate the bedroom and sleep in the lounge. We had been doing this for years and all the kids knew that Gran was at the Elliott's, so no sleep-overs.

At this point, I need to move forward to my coming home on leave from the Navy. I was around 19 at the time. Gran was staying, so I was on the couch ... you can guess what's coming, but it's now Elliott folklore.

Jim Craig, Brian's brother, was a great mate of ours growing up and is still our mate to this day, in fact I am Godfather to his eldest daughter Narelle.

Anyway, I came home on leave. Jim was playing lead guitar in a local band, so we went to the gig and after the show, we hit the town. We were both a little ... well more than a little, socially excited; quite pissed actually. Jim drove me home, dropped me off and headed to his place.

His dad was waiting for him, saw the state of Jim, took his car keys and threw him out of the house.

Naturally, Craigie heads to my place and through the window

he goes, sits on the edge of the bed, and manages to get one boot off when Gran wakes up screaming "rape". Jim nearly has a heart attack, fell forward smashing his head into the wall, just as Gran grabs her ever-trusty walking stick and with uncanny accuracy, belts Jim right down the middle of the back. The walking stick broke in half. Gran kept screaming as Craigie dived out the window and headed for home or the hills; whichever was closer. I slumbered on.

Mum ran into Gran who, by this time, was basking in her triumph. Mum came and woke me, told me what had happened and asked me to call the police. When the police arrived, they interviewed all of us and went into the bedroom. They came out with a single size 10 Beatle boot, all the fashion at the time. I explained that it wasn't mine and the copper made the comment that the rapist must've been a fairly big bloke, judging by the size of the boot.

The police left and we settled down to a cuppa as the sun was coming up.

About 8 o'clock that morning the phone rang. "Col, it's me, Craigie, how's Gran?"

I thought, "Shit, word spreads quick around here ... how did you know about it?" I said.

"Cos' it was me," said Jim.

I said, "You tried to rape Gran?"

"No," said Jim," I thought it was you!"

"You tried to rape me?"

"No ... no ... no," said Jim, and then went on to tell his side of the story. I was crying with laughter but Jim didn't seem to think it was funny at the time. He said he thought he had something broken in his back and that it hurt when he breathed; that and a gigantic hangover which wasn't helping.

I convinced Jim to come over as Gran hadn't recognised him as the intruder; it was too dark. Reluctantly he agreed.

When he walked into the kitchen Gran said, "Oh, hello Jimmy, did Col tell you what happened last night?" (Gran was very fond of Jimmy.) I saw Jimmy sigh with relief and then I watched his face as Gran gave him a blow-by-blow account of the incident. I was standing behind Gran facing Jim; I had to leave the kitchen. I was trying hard to stifle an insane fit of laughter. We couldn't tell Mum or Gran what actually happened, we were in too deep.

In the lounge room, Jim and I sat re-telling the night's events. I didn't think I could laugh any more till Jim stood up and said, "I'd better get my other boot." I was on the floor.

Craigie never did retrieve his boot. We have always maintained it is one of Australia's oldest 'cold cases'. It was twenty years later that Jim and I told Mum the truth ... she wet herself.

## LEARNING TO RIDE

As we settled into our new lives at Lyndale, each of us kids made our different friends and hung out with those in the area of our own age.

Ralph played football and cricket; Carol hooked up with the local horse scene. She became a very accomplished horsewoman and her weekends were spent at the local stables riding track work for Charlie McCompskie an ex-jockey turned trainer. Carol would go on to become a strapper. She revelled in her work.

Charlie had three daughters and they lived on a property of 100 acres, complete with training track. It had two great dams and it was mostly unfenced. Charlie agisted horses from the locals and at any given time there would have been a herd of 30 or 40 of them running free on the property.

My mates and I started sneaking up to the place, swimming in the dams, trying to catch the horses and out-dare each other by getting on the back of any horse we could get near. We would kick them into a gallop and ride bareback, no bridle, just hang on to their mane and hope for the best.

After a while these horses knew what we were doing and would take off as soon as we were sighted. We needed a new approach and I devised the perfect solution.

My mates would drive the herd through an opening on the far side of the track. They had to slow down to pass through a series of open double gates. At one point there was a large fig tree overhanging the path. I would hang on to a branch and as they passed underneath, I would drop onto the back of one of them. Invariably they would spook and break into a gallop or on occasion, start bucking, depending on the horse you landed on. Either way it was stupid and dangerous, but as they say, kids are 'bullet-proof'.

This is how I learnt to ride and I grew to love horses, both caring for and riding them.

## CINDY

Carol's greatest wish was to have a horse of her own and when she was 14 the old man managed, through a series of shady trades, to get hold of an unbroken two year old filly. She was wild eyed and terrified when she was unloaded off the truck straight into the backyard of our commission house. The old man wasn't too bright.

Carol was over the moon. She had such a way with horses. In no time at all she had gentled her and was on her back. She named her Cinders. It was soon shortened to Cindy. Carol would ride her to and from the stables which were about 5 kilometres from home.

Cindy was 14.2 hands high and solid. In the end you could do anything with her. She was a beautiful gentle animal in every way, until she saw a truck. She was terrified of trucks or any large vehicles; it must have been fear from that very first trip.

## HI HO BOBBY

One afternoon we were all over at the park. Carol was on Cindy and Bobby Cavanagh, one of the local lads, was asking Carol if she would let him ride her by himself. Carol had been giving pony rides to all the kids for sixpence a ride. She would lead Cindy around ... "next kid."

"I know how to do it by myself," said Bobbie.

"Better not," said Carol. But sixteen year old, macho Bobbie, would not be put off. "I know how to ride," he said. He just wouldn't stop nagging. He was swaggering about trying to impress all the kids.

"Ok," Carol said, finally relenting, "but don't pull on her mouth and if you see a bus or truck ..." Bobbie gave her a kick before Carol could finish and Cindy jumped forward just as the coal truck turned into the street.

Hi ho Bobbie.

Cindy was in pure fright, galloping in the opposite direction. Bobbie was screaming ... but not for long ... Cindy was on a collision course with a lamp post. She swerved to miss it at the last moment ... Bobbie didn't!

Bobbie lay at the base of the lamp post screaming in pain ... both arms broken.

As the ambulance arrived to take Bobbie to hospital, we went to look for Cindy. She had crossed all the major roads, with the traffic swerving to miss her and finally came to a stop at the gates of a farm, two miles up the road. It was hell for Bobbie in Lyndale after that. As we went passed him we would call out "Hey Bob, fancy a ride?" or, "Hey Bob, how's the lessons coming along?" ... or, "Hi ho Bobbie" ... he hated that one.

Most of the areas we rode in were open rolling hills so the truck problem only happened occasionally, but when it did Cindy would bolt, blindly galloping in the opposite direction. When I rode her in the early years, I had no chance of pulling her up, she was so strong. I would just hang on and hope for the best. We rode bare-back and that's how I learnt.

On the weekends, Carol would be out on Cindy riding with her friends. By that time Charlie had let her keep her horse at his place.

When she had finished her ride, she would come home, hand me the reins and get me to take her back to Charlie's. She was using me and I knew it but I got a chance to ride. It was a great arrangement; we were both winners.

I got to know Charlie and his family. He was a tough-talking, take-no-prisoners type bloke; always yelling and bitching. His girls and his wife, Mrs Mac, were great people. I eventually worked part time in his stables and became part of the scene. By observing Charlie, taught me so much about horses and their care. It was a part of my life I will always think back to with fond nostalgic memories.

## THE FISH AND CHIPS SAGA

Charlie had an apprentice jockey, Dave Bolsh, who lived at the stables. He was 17 and an easy-going type of bloke. I envied Dave; I would have loved to have been an apprentice, even under Charlie. Dave and I became good mates but he was a little afraid of Charlie. Dave had trouble keeping his weight down and Charlie would be constantly on his back. I can still hear Charlie lecturing Dave.

"We got Rosedale coming up in two weeks, so you make sure you eat right, I'll be watching," Charlie would say.

Dave absolutely loved fish and chips, but seldom got the chance to indulge. Once when he did sneak some, Charlie literally smelled them on him and chased Dave down the paddock, alternately footing him up the arse and swinging a heavy leather halter at him ... not too much union involvement in those days.

Dave was cured for a time but the temptation was too great. He came up with a plan and was sure he could get away with it. There was an old bike at the back of the stables, so after Charlie had gone back down to the house for the night, Dave and I went to the far side of the track, lifted the bike over the fence and headed off to the fish and chip shop in Lyndale. He would 'dink' me on the handle bars.

We came back with the contraband tightly wrapped in newspapers. We headed for the middle of the training track, stripped down to our underwear so as not to get the smell on our clothes and proceeded to gorge ourselves. It was the middle of winter but we were desperate, or at least Dave was. We buried the wrappings. Dave even insisted we wash up in the dam just to make sure.

The next morning I was mucking out a stall, when Dave ran past at top speed with Charlie close behind, swinging the halter and screaming blue murder ... the bastard had the nose of a bloodhound. The element of danger added such a great taste to those chips, the likes of which I have never tasted again.

At 18 my sister Carol had married her boyfriend Jack. He had emigrated out from Manchester when he was 18 and was sponsored by his elder sister and her husband. Jack's biggest interest in life is pigeons. He is still breeding and racing them to this day. He is a top 'fella' with a great sense of humour. Carol and Jack are like the proverbial 'Darby and Joan'. Jack and I have become great mates. Many years later Jack would be part of my touring team and we would often sit and reminisce about our time together on the road.

At the time they got married, I inherited Cindy. I was 13 and spent every spare minute riding through the hills with a bunch of local kids, all horse mad. Life at home wasn't too good so I spent more and more time at the stables.

While I was still at school I had gotten a job Saturday mornings at the local grocery store stacking shelves and packing groceries. It paid 10 bob ($1) for four hours' work and if they needed me to work back I got paid in broken biscuits. It sounds lousy of them but I enjoyed the sweet biscuits. I always made sure I dropped the packets that were my favourites. I felt justified. The money I saved would keep my horse shod; a set of 'slippers' or worn second-hand horse shoes would set me back a pound ($2).

## PAPER BOY (DANGEROUS GIG)

I needed more money than the grocery store was giving me and I 'lucked' out one Saturday afternoon. A mate of mine asked if I could fill in selling the Herald newspaper and the Sporting Globe at the local drive-in. The kid who normally did it was going away with his folks and could I take over the gig for a fortnight.

It was the best job and paid well. We sold papers every night after school as well. I worked one of the main intersections; one kid on one side of the road, me on the opposite corner. There were six of us doing different areas. The owner of the Chick-Inn was our boss, long before there was such a thing as Red Rooster. He and his wife ran this little takeaway and had the paper contract as well. They would often give us a few chicken wings to take home.

Food ... always a plus with me; I gave them total loyalty.

Saturday nights we hit the drive-in. We got to sit near the takeaway canteen after the papers were gone and eat chips and hamburgers that they gave us before throwing them out ... then we would watch what was left of the movie.

As luck would have it, the other kid didn't come back. The job was mine.

"HEEEEARRRDA HERALD AN DA SPORTIN GLOBE," was my cry ... I was now in the big league.

The corner I worked was outside the Stamford hotel. The kid that sold in the bar had it made. The blokes in the bar would buy a paper and tip big. He was the top paper boy and had got me the job in the first place. He would get rid of his papers in a third of the time it took the rest of us.

I turned up for work after school one night and the boss told me to go to the pub, apparently my mate had broken his leg.

I settled in to the pub routine quickly. It would be hard going back to the road when my mate came back. I was being spoilt ... heaps of tips and less time on the job ... then disaster struck.

I had sold half my papers in the main saloon when I approached a guy at the bar. I hadn't seen him before; he was in a loud conversation with someone else and had his back to me. "HEEEEARRDA HERAL" ... that's all I got out. He turned toward me and punched me fair between the eyes.

I woke up with two blokes leaning over me. "You OK son?" one said.

The bloke that hit me was laying on the floor, bloody nose and fat lip ... he was out to it. The boys had taken care of him.

I sat up. Someone passed me a drink, raspberry I think. "How many papers you got left son?" one asked, as I got shakily to my feet. "Drunken bastard," he muttered as he moved away with my papers under his arm. The boys in the bar sat me on a stool and told me to finish my drink, all the time rubbing my head and saying, "We'll fix this ... don't you worry." They sold all the papers before the raspberry had gone, then one bent over the guy on the floor, pulled two quid out of his wallet and along with the paper money, put it in my pouch. "Here's an extra tip son."

It was my biggest night yet ... I got three quid in tips ... and two black eyes. I have no idea why this bloke hit me ... maybe it was my cry. "HEEEARRDA HERALD", it could have been annoying ... oh well!

## I WAS ONLY TRYING TO HELP

I was in my last few months of high school when I was approached by our headmaster, Mr. Monroe, asking if it was possible if I could give pony rides at the school fete that was about to be held. I agreed and said I would be there at 9 am sharp. The morning of the fete arrived. I was riding down the hill towards the school. I could hear the sound of bagpipes. The local highland dancers were putting on a display. Kids had made toffee apples, cakes and pies. Parents had made up handcraft to sell; stalls were everywhere, all proceeds going to the school.

Just as I was adjacent to the school gates a Grenada's bus came around the corner. I felt Cindy tense up; she was like a coiled spring. I had nowhere to go and no chance of keeping control. She bolted in fright. She headed straight through the school gates and was on a collision course with the highland dancers.

All I could see were people diving from the stage, bagpipes, kilts and swords flying through the air. She didn't stop. We demolished at least five stalls in our path. People were running, screaming, kids crying ... I just hung on and went with the flow.

She was still galloping when we got to the other side of the sports field which was bordered by a market garden. She sailed over the barbed-wire fence and headed into a paddock of cabbages, finally pulling up on the far side, blowing hard and shaking ... we both were.

A bunch of teachers, including the headmaster had gathered at the fence as I trotted back; they were all yelling at once. I couldn't get all that was said, just bits and pieces like, "You'll have to pay for the damage to the stalls, someone could have been killed, what a stupid thing to do, all that food demolished, typical of you Elliott ... blah, blah, blah." They spun on their heels and still cursing, left. I called out, "Does this mean it's not 'on' for the pony rides?" ... no reply.

## CINDY'S NEW HOME

I had to report for induction into the RAN in early October. It was now the beginning of September and the old man was pressuring me to sell Cindy. He figured she was worth 80 pounds and if I couldn't find a buyer, she would have to go to the Dandenong sale yards.

I had ridden horses in the ring for the auctioneer on occasion for a few bob pocket money. In fact, it was held on Fridays and I would 'wag' school to do it, so it was always a great day. Sadly many of the horses would end up at the knackery, especially the broken down racehorses. Now and again they would stipulate 'no slaughter' for owners looking for a home for a pony that a kid had outgrown.

That's where I and a few other kids came in. We would talk to the owner. They would tell us what we could and couldn't do with the pony and we would display the animal to its best advantage. Sometimes they would sling us a few extra bob. I would have done it for free anyway; any chance to get on a horse's back. Some of the horses we rode probably would have been better off going to the knackery. I had been bitten and kicked many times.

Some of these poor animals, sadly, had been mistreated ...they were head-shy and jittery. I never witnessed it but it was understood some animals had been sedated to get them through the ring. Pity help the poor buyers when the drugs wore off.

I had completely run out of time and the old man wanted his money. I rode her down to the market. It was a really tough time for me but I was out of options. I got to the sale yards early and saw old Tom the auctioneer. He was a nice old cow-cocky and he promised me he wouldn't let her be sold to the knackery. Even when it was stipulated 'no knackery sales', there had been times when they had caught knackery agents posing as private buyers. Tom promised to be vigilant.

I was brushing Cindy down half an hour before she was due to go through the ring, when a middle-aged man leaned on the rail and spoke to me. He had a ten-year-old boy with him and he began to ask me about my horse. I told him why she was being sold and all about her, even how she bolted at the sight of a bus or truck. That didn't seem to worry him too much. He had me stand on her back; crawl between her legs; pick up her feet; hang around her neck; all the time this was happening the boy looked on and hung on every word.

The boy was his son and they lived on a farm in Gippsland and he needed a good solid pony that the boy could ride for mustering. "Could the boy have a ride," he asked? "Sure," I said. With no hesitation the boy vaulted the fence and scrambled onto her back. He picked up her reins and trotted her around the enclosure. Clearly the boy could ride.

I knew he liked her and I could tell his father did too. The boy stood patting her and she gently nudged him back.

His father did the normal routine of checking her teeth and legs then he turned to me.

"I could go in and bid for her," he said, "but if you've got a reserve on her we could do the deal out here, strictly cash, up to you young fella ... and by the way, she'll be going to a good home and be well looked after, you can come and see her any time you like, guaranteed."

That clinched it for me so I told him I wanted eighty five pounds and wouldn't take a penny less and at that price she was a bargain.

Old Tom made out the receipt and even though he was technically entitled, he wouldn't take a commission.

I headed for home with the wad of notes. "Here it is Dad, eighty pounds," I said. His eyes lit up and I am sure the bastard was dribbling. I left him in the kitchen counting the cash.

I kept the odd five pounds for a couple of days and then gave it to Mum. I knew she wouldn't have had a chance in hell of seeing any of the other money. It was our secret.

She had been doing it tough for a while now. The old man was paying off an old car and took half the payments out of her allowance even though he never took her anywhere. In fact, when she needed a ride to go and do domestic work at the doctors, he charged her petrol money. This bloke was 'one out of the box' as they say.

*Aged four, with "Silver"*

*From left, Mum, Auntie "Nob" and showgirls*

*Ralph, Carol, me and Mum*

*Ralph, Mum and me*

*At fourteen*

*Uncle Ralph and Auntie Nob*

*Mum and Gran*

# PART TWO
## THE NAVY YEARS

The day arrived for me to leave. Mum wanted to come into Melbourne and see me off at Spencer Street station. A neighbour, Mr. Robertson, had offered to drive us into town. He was an ex-Chief Petty Officer and he loved nothing better than to talk about his days in the Navy. I did odd jobs for him and his wife and when I told him I was waiting to go into the Navy, he kind of took me under his wing.

I walked into the kitchen to say goodbye to the old man. He was in his usual place, beer in one hand, cigarette in the other. I knew there was no chance he would be coming into the station with us but I guess I was hoping against hope that he just might. At that stage, I guess I was still in there swinging.

He had lectured me a few days before about the importance of sending my mum an allotment from my pay as he said he had done when he was in the Navy. He made me feel that it was expected and that I would be less than a good son if I didn't.

"Well I'm off Dad," I said, feeling a little awkward.

"Alright boy, keep your nose clean and remember your mother's allotment," he said.

I moved forward to give him a kind of hug that never quite worked and headed out the door.

Mum and I jumped into Mr. Robertson's car and we were off.

We arrived at Spencer Street station and joined a bunch of mums, dads and boys gathered around some men in Navy uniform.

We answered a roll call and I can remember being assembled in a large room and raising my right hand and being sworn in, pledging allegiance to Queen and Country. With tears in her eyes, Mum waved me goodbye.

I remembered a couple of the guys that had sat for the exams on the same day as I had. We re-introduced ourselves and settled into our seats on the train. It was a three day journey to Perth with a stop in South Australia along the way to pick up some more boys. We sat up all the way. It was second-class travel; that's the way the Navy did things in those days.

Many of the guys I met on that very first day were to become lifelong friends. We share a bond that has lasted nearly 48 years and I enjoy our bi-annual reunions more and more. The stories we tell, get more and more embellished and outrageous as the years go by.

We were picked up by Navy buses at the Perth station and driven to what was to become our new home for the next twelve months, HMAS Leeuwin.

The next three days were a blur, inoculations, uniform issue, basic drill to show us our left foot from our right; we doublemarched everywhere. We were taught how to iron our different uniforms, creases in the right places, even the Navy way to fold your kit and make your bed. While all this was happening, we were being constantly yelled at by the instructors and being told we were "The biggest shower of shit that God had ever shovelled guts into."

One memory that has stayed with me all these years is being assembled in the drill hall and being addressed by the Chief Drill Instructor, Chief Petty Officer/Quarter Master Gunner Owens. When we were all lined up in a semblance of order, he attempted to teach us two basic movements, how to come to attention and how to stand at ease.

I was in the front row and he was directly opposite me screaming and yelling at our incompetence. Our eyes met; direct eye contact was the mistake I had made. He moved in front of me his face inches from mine. Spittle was flying all over my face as he screamed how useless I was. My feet were NOT 15 degrees at the angle and was I just trying to be a smart arse, or was I deaf or just stupid. He wanted an answer. "Just stupid," I said thinking it was the best response of the three choices he gave me.

"JUST STUPID ... WHAT?" He roared.

"Just stupid ... I guess," said I.

"JUST STUPID CHIEF PETTY OFFICER OWENS," he yelled in my face.

"JUST STUPID CHIEF PETTY OFFICER OWENS," I parroted back.

And with that, he kicked my feet from underneath me. I fell hard. I got to my feet as quick as I could, as he was walking away bemoaning, "JESUS CHRIST, WHAT HAVE THEY SENT US ... GOD HELP THE FLEET."

## JUST A BIT OFF THE SIDES PLEASE

Our first haircut was an eye opener, I had joined with shoulder length hair as it was the fashion of the day; the Beatles and the Stones were the choice of music of our generation and we dressed accordingly. Pointy-toed Beatle boots, tight-pegged corduroy pants, psychedelic shirts ... at least some of our mob did anyway.

My turn came. I sat in the Barber's chair. "A little bit off the top and just trim the ends please," I said as the barber grabbed a handful of my hair and laughed.

I walked out of the barber shop with a small strip of hair down the middle of my head. "Bloody hell," someone said, "Col looks like a mohawk" ... and that was what I got to be known as from then on ... Mohawk Elliott ... a nickname that has stuck.

To this day, my Navy mates know me as Mohawk. In fact, there are those that I served with who didn't know what my real name was, until I got into show biz many years later.

Every now and then at a gig I hear from the audience "HEY MOHAWK" ... I know where it's coming from.

We were Marks division, named after Commodore Marks and we were the 13th intake. We were split into classes, 1, 2, 3 and 4. I was assigned to Marks 3 which meant I would receive not only sufficient school subjects, Maths., English, Physics, but also mainstream Naval subjects like Navigation, NBCD (Nuclear Biological Chemical Defence and Damage Control), and Naval Indoctrination, as well as practical seamanship instruction. It was full on. All this was done with a strict eye to discipline. There were 104 of us that started the year ... 84 finished and went into the fleet.

There really were only 101 that actually got to Leeuwin, we lost three on the way ... deserted ... we don't know where. I'd love to know, but I guess they will never show up at our reunions. Mind you, they'd be welcome. After all they were a part of our story. They don't know what they missed.

We became part of the pecking order. There were three divisions senior to us, the most senior doing their last three months. They had been training for nine months and were bigger, fitter and had an incredible arrogance about them. They tried to put it on us at every opportunity.

Bastardisation was a part of our time there, but I believe it didn't become an issue with many of us, because we didn't let it happen. If you fought back, in most cases you were left alone. Never be a victim, I had already learnt that lesson. Some of the boys though, had come from nurturing backgrounds. They hadn't been exposed to anything as confronting as this before and I believe it was too much for some of them. They were more vulnerable. I can still remember laying there after lights out, listening to quiet sobbing.

After lights out at 9.30, senior recruits would raid the divisions junior to them and gather boys to 'run the gauntlet'. They would line their dormitory either side and make an aisle. They armed themselves with pillow cases filled with boots, books or anything that would hurt. They made their victims run from one end of their dormitory to the other, down the middle as they were beaten.

## THE LESSON

To my knowledge, many in our donga (barracks) never succumbed. We protected our weak and stood up to the idiots, even to the point of copping a hiding. I have never forgotten the backup I got from one of my best mates at Leeuwin. We had hit it off right from the start. We were both from Victoria and sat together on the train over to Perth.

Chris Williams was from Echuca and we had so much in common. We loved the Beatles and we became the best of friends. His nickname was 'Taffy'; his bunk was the next one up from mine.

On one occasion, we were polishing our boots and were the only ones in the donga at the time.

All of a sudden I noticed a bunch of seniors coming towards us. "There he is," one called out, "that's him," he said pointing to me.

I recognised him from an incident that had happened the day before at the canteen. I had gone there to buy something or other and on my way out he demanded I give him my cigarettes. I told him to get lost and started to move away. He grabbed the back of my shirt. I spun around and shoved him. He wasn't expecting retaliation and fell over backwards. I shaped up to him. He wasn't game and backed off telling me I would 'cop it' later.

It was normal for seniors to hang around the canteen and intimidate the younger ones into giving them money and cigarettes. They believed it was their rite of passage. After I walked away I thought no more of it.

I looked up as they approached, there were seven of them. Two quickly grabbed my arms and shoved me up against my locker. Two of them were big blokes, obviously they were enforcers. They didn't need to do the gang-up thing because either one of these two bigger blokes could have beaten the crap out of me anyway. They worked on the principle of strength in numbers. They were calling me a 'jack' which is Navy speak for 'smart arse' and they were going to teach me a lesson.

They started slapping me about when all of a sudden Taffy flew across the bunk, arms flailing, screaming "weak mongrels" and he was connecting. I broke free and did the best I could. At this point I could say we cleaned them up. It would make a good story, but the truth is they beat the crap out of us. We both were a sad and sorry sight when they left. We compared our 'shiners' and headed off to the sickbay because Taffy thought he might have a broken rib.

Of course when asked by the sickbay attendant on duty what had happened ... of course, we had both fallen down the stairs together ... it was the code.

About a week later we were playing a senior division at Aussie rules. The ball came towards me; I looked up and saw one of the gang that had belted Taff and me. He was running toward me. I dropped the ball and then dropped him. Mind you, he wasn't one of the bigger guys, but I bent over him and told him to tell his mates we were coming for them. I was bluffing but I saw the shock in his eyes. It wasn't supposed to happen like this. Another week went by and I shirt-fronted another in the drill hall. That was enough. We were left alone after that.

Taffy and I remained great friends until his sudden death from a heart attack in 2001. He was just fifty-two ... I still miss you Taff.

## THE WINDOW

We were housed in old wooden dormitories and given a locker with a small desk attached. The donga was bleak and bare of comforts, except our wire beds. No posters, photos or decorations allowed. There was no heating or air-conditioning, but the roof didn't leak. The buildings were left over from WW2, but they did the job.

I woke up one morning and I could feel a light breeze blowing over me, there was copious amounts of sand on my bed. I looked up and noticed the window above was missing. I figured out later that one of the older recruits had somehow broken his window and decided to replace it with mine.

We were having a kit muster and general inspection that morning. I thought I would ask for a new window when the divisional officer came to inspect my kit, which was now laid out meticulously on my bed.

We came to attention at the end of our beds as the bosun's whistle sounded to pre-empt the officer's presence. They duly arrived at my bed. A gust of wind had just deposited another film of sand over my freshly laid-out kit.

It was too late to attend to it. I took a deep breath and blurted out "Junior Recruit Elliott ready for inspection, sir." I said this in a somewhat shaky voice. The officer was accompanied by our Divisional Chief, Chief Petty Officer Thurlow.

The officer looked at my kit and then back at me. He looked a little peeved.

Chief Thurlow turned to me, "Elliott why is your kit covered in sand?"

"It blew in from the window Chief," said I.

He looked up "WHAT HAVE YOU DONE WITH THE WINDOW ELLIOTT?"

"It just disappeared Chief," I said.

"Naval windows don't just disappear Elliott, you stole that window and sold it didn't you?" He was enjoying this.

"No Chief, I just woke up and it was gone," I said.

Taffy was standing at attention next to me. He was losing it, trying to stifle the laughter.

"You find this amusing Williams," the Chief asked?

"No Chief," Taffy stammered.

"Are you pair in cahoots with this window sale?"

"No Chief," we both said in unison.

"So you stole it on your own Elliott?"

"No Chief."

"So you admit Williams was in on it?"

"No Chief, Taffy had nothing to do with it," I said.

"So you take sole responsibility for the missing window then Elliott?" he said.

"Yes Chief," I said, thinking I was protecting my mate.

"How clever was that?" I thought, "No wonder he's a Chief."

"You will be charged with misappropriation of naval goods and the cost will be deducted from your pay. Report the missing window to stores."

"Yes Chief," I said, hardly believing my ears.

This was going to hurt. Our pay as a first term junior recruit was around four and a half pounds a fortnight ($15). The money was banked and we were given about $1.50 pocket money to get our toiletries and cigarettes with. I had already started Mum's allotment of a pound, so things were going to be tight.

I subsidised my pay by collecting empty 'goffa' (soft drink) bottles.

They were like gold. We would cash them in at the canteen. It was a top little earner, for a while any way, then one kid got caught stealing them from the back room of the canteen. He would take them around the front and re-cash them in. I don't know what happened to the culprit but stealing in the Navy is one of the worst crimes you can commit. It would have been a really big deal at the time. Hard to believe but stealing even at that level was a huge offence.

I also got two cigarettes a pair for 'spit-polishing' boots. Taff and I had a great little set-up with the boots. We traded some of the cigarettes for extra food. We were constantly hungry. Not that we were not getting enough good food, it was the sheer physical effort of our training that kept us ever hungry.

I particularly loved the food. Up until I joined the navy I had never had a piece of steak or bacon; that type of food was reserved for my father. He would let Ralph and I eat the bacon rinds that he had left over on his plate after his breakfast, but never a full-on piece of bacon. Cigarettes for bacon were a great deal as far as I was concerned.

There was always plenty of fruit which was another commodity we saw little of as kids.

I always remember when we were kids, my brother Ralph came across a peach at someone's house he was visiting. He was overawed by it. He came home and described it to me "Col," he said, "it's like a suede apple."

## FLYING SAUCERS

I was given the job of Mess man at the Petty Officers' Mess one weekend. There were two of us to do the job, Allan Easter and myself.

Al was a little guy, fifteen years old and quiet; a nice guy.

Our job was to make sure there was clean cutlery put out, the Mess tables had all the condiments and were set up for all meals.

It was a weekend, so there was probably only four or five POs on board. We set up three small tables. It was an easy gig.

Sunday afternoon we had to put out plates of butter and slices of fruit cake ... a standard fare that was fed to the crew.

The Navy used hard plastic plates; they were light green and unbreakable.

We had just started to put the cake out. Allan went to the cold room to get the butter. He put a block of it on a plate. He said, "This looks a bit off, Mohawk," and put his nose near it to smell.

"YOU LITTLE SHIT," a voice screamed out "YOU LICKED THAT BUTTER DIDNT YOU?" ... A Petty Officer stood swaying by the galley door.

"No sir, I was just seeing if ..." said Allan, but he was drowned out by the now out of control PO ... this guy had a skin full.

The Petty Officer had come through the galley and was clearly 'off his face'.

He was staggering and lurching towards the table where Al was standing, still holding the butter.

"EAT IT YOU DIRTY LITTLE PIG... EAT IT," he kept on screaming.

He shoved Al's face into the butter ... "EAT IT."

Al was terrified. This guy was going berserk. Al started to eat the butter; he was starting to heave. The jerk had hold of the back of my mate's head.

I lost it ... I screamed out ... "HE WAS JUST CHECKING IT ... YA BASTARD ... LET HIM GO." He let Al go and made a move to me. I had a knee-jerk reaction and threw the plate I was holding. I didn't actually throw it at him but it was like a flying saucer. Bang! Right between his eyes ... he crashed into the table and lay on the floor moaning. Al looked at me ... "RUN," I said and that's what we did, straight back to our donga.

We sat on my bunk and looked at each other.

"What are we 'gonna' do Mohawk?" Al asked nervously.

"Well he's pretty pissed, we'd better sneak back to see if he's not dead or something," I suggested.

We snuck up to the Mess window and peered in. He wasn't there.

We crept back inside. I was thinking maybe he'd staggered back into the pantry and died in there ... nothing in the pantry.

I looked at the tables and there was evidence that two people had eaten some cake, had a cup of tea and left it for us to clean up ... so we did. We went back to our donga and waited nervously for something to happen ... nothing did.

We came back for tea. Two Petty Officers were in there having a discussion and ignored us. We set them up for tea and waited.

After they left, we cleared all the plates and cutlery, mopped the floor, turned off the lights and left.

I wish there was a great tag to this story but the truth is we never saw the guy again. We were looking for days for some PO with two black eyes or a broken nose, but we never found him. Best I could come up with was that he was visiting from another ship or depot or maybe he was a 'Rocky' (Naval Reserve). They sometimes came into the Mess on a weekend to play 'pretend sailors'. We didn't exactly put out the 'welcome mat'.

Kaz and I attended the fifty year reunion in 2010 at Leeuwin and as we stood on the parade ground I casually looked up to where the Petty Officers' Mess used to stand. All new buildings now but the thought crossed my mind, maybe the wounded PO crawled underneath the floor space. That was the only place we didn't look.

I wondered if the demolishers found any old bones. (Keep this to yourself.)

## AT THE DOUBLE, SAILOR

Life at Leeuwin was never dull. You were on the go from 5.30 am till 'Lights out' at 9.30 pm. You were never allowed to walk anywhere. Everything was done 'at the double'. You could never 'rubber neck'. "Find out where you want to go and go there." They were the rules. There is no such word in the Navy vocabulary as procrastinate and no excuses.

I never had trouble with the early rising bit, in fact 5.30 was a bit of a lay-in to me, after the stables. But for some, it was the middle of the night.

The punishment for lying-in was simple. The offender had to run around the parade ground with their mattress and bedding on their head. It was effective.

Punishment was handed out for the least infringement. Running late for a parade, being too slow at carrying out an order or being sloppy in your dress; any insubordination was never tolerated and was dealt with quickly.

If you were put on 'chooks', (Navy speak for punishment), life became really difficult. We were already pushed beyond belief but doing chooks at the same time was really tough.

MUPs (men under punishment) would be up working an hour before everyone else and put to work cleaning or scrubbing out pots in the galley. All breaks were cut in half. You worked through most of the lunch break. This was a punishment in itself, as many times you didn't have time to eat. We were growing lads and forever hungry.

After knock-off, a JR on chooks would fall in on the parade ground for extra drill. This was at the discretion of the duty Petty Officer in charge. Drill meant marching around with .303 rifles but that sort of drilling meant the Petty Officer would have to constantly give orders. Too much trouble for some, and I guess they didn't want to be there in the first place so they would give us one drill movement ... 'double march'.

In single file we would run around the perimeter of the parade ground, dubbed 'the bull ring', your rifle on your shoulder. The P.O. could then casually watch us while having a smoke. The 303 weighed about three and a half kilos. After a few laps the going got tough.

Another punishment was the running kit muster. It meant lining up at the gangway (entrance gates) where the duty Petty Officer or officer would have us run back to our donga and dress in whatever uniform he would designate.

He would call out "full blues", which was our dress uniform ... "go".

We would have five minutes to cover a kilometre, dress and be back at the gangway. No sooner than you got back, puffing and blowing, the officer would call out "Number sixes ... go," This would go on until we had donned at least ten different uniforms. This punishment was sometimes meted out to entire divisions if they were noisy after lights out. We'd all sleep well that night.

On one occasion, the Depot Commander (second in command) had the whole of Marks division on the parade ground in pyjamas, bunny hoppin', hands above our heads, back and forth across the parade ground. He kept this up for an hour and although we were fairly fit by that stage of our training, it proved to be a bit too tough for us. We had to walk backwards down stairs for a week after.

I did the bunny hops with a 303 above my head one night when a half-pissed officer decided to give us a bit more to think about during our chooks run. He had wandered down from the Ward Room

(Officers' Mess) with a glass of wine in his hand and an evil twinkle in his eye. What could the Petty Officer do but let him take charge. It nearly killed us. When he tired of this sport, he staggered off into the night.

Most of the time we were given 7 days' chooks but there were occasions when we copped 14.

I ran quite a few chooks in my time. I wasn't a bad lad per se; I would say that I was just adventurous. I tried to buck the system, just a little. I was punished for a diverse number of reasons; being caught out after lights out; swimming in the officers' swimming pool; being caught hiding in a cupboard instead of doing PT (physical training); being caught drinking alcohol down an alley in Perth with a bunch of mates. That was a 'biggie'.

Drinking age was 21 in those days.

## CANDID CAMERA

Skulking early morning PT sessions became an art form in Marks division. Like all young blokes, early morning exercise was a pain. We would devise places to hide, like hanging onto the back of a toilet door while it was half ajar, so that at a glance it would appear to be an empty cubicle.

Yelling instructors with their sticks banging on doors and lockers would stream through the blocks to make sure all were on the parade ground, hard at it. Anybody caught hiding would be dealt with severely.

But the most ingenious hide has got to be the one devised by Col McVea, a guy with a great sense of humour and creativity.

Col's bed had a distinct sag in the middle; it had been in service since Menzies was a boy. Col would have one of us make his bed over him while he was still in it; hospital corners, his head was under the pillow; ... the full bit. It was brilliant. You just couldn't pick it.

Col did this trick successfully many times.

It all came undone after about two months of this ruse. Col was lying very still, listening to the instructors come through. All of a sudden he realised they were in his actual section, he could even hear Lt. Burns' voice ... "unusual" Col thought, "he never joins in the searches." He then heard a definite camera being clicked ... "Strange," Col thought. Then a voice said, "OK McVea, up and at 'em."

With that the cover was pulled back and the camera went click ... before and after shots had been taken, although they were smiling ... seven days chooks.

How did they topple to it? Did we have a traitor in the ranks?

Somewhere in a shoe box; maybe under a bed or in a shed are those photos. Please send them on for the archives.

## BIG GIULIE

Eddie Giuliani is still one of my closest mates. He joined the Navy with me from Victoria. We became fast friends and he has been the source of so much our shared memories of our time at Leeuwin. I guess he could be likened to the Shaman of the village; the Keeper of the faith; the Teller of the stories ... a great memory.

His nickname, Big Giulie (pronounced Julie) suits this man. He is big in so many ways ... a big laugh, a big size and a big heart ... and the greatest memory for detail I have ever come across. These days he is a walking history book on world politics and events. It's quite amazing.

I believe he has trained his brain to remember and retain, but there was a time when he screwed up big time. It happened like this.

Taffy and I decided one wintery morning to hide in a space between the walls in the new accommodation block instead of going to PT. Now this space was really just for the heating pipes and maybe two feet wide. It was incredibly hot in there but we would only have to bear it for around 45 minutes while the other mugs were out on the cold parade ground doing exercises. Most of the time the PTIs (physical training instructors) didn't do a roll call but it was a small chance we were prepared to take. There was a door to this space but it could only be opened from the outside with a special handle that we had fashioned. It was Big Guile's turn to lock Taff and me in the space and let us out when he came back from PT.

Taff and I were listening to all the guys run out for PT, then there was silence. We heard the instructors check the building for stragglers, or any lazy buggers trying to skulk, (us).We kept quiet and still till they left. Bloody hell it was hot. We alternately put both our feet up on the wall opposite to give them a rest from the hot water pipe we were forced to stand on. If you left your feet on the super-heated pipe there was a good chance of not only cooking your feet but a distinct possibility of melting your Navy issue runners.

We were starting to sweat profusely. Then we heard everyone come back.

We waited for the space to be opened. Then we heard them all leave for breakfast.

"Guile you bastard, where are you, let us out." .... nothing ... bloody hell it was hot!

We stayed still and kept quiet as we could hear our divisional officer Lt Burns and Chief Thurlow discussing divisional business in the office directly below ... bloody hell it was hot!

Big Giulie went to morning parade then on to classes at the education block, some three hours after we first entered the space. At the start of a navigation lecture the instructor decided to do a roll call.

"Elliott ...Elliott... Ell..."

Big Giulie jumped up and ran screaming from the class, the instructor screaming at Giulie.

Big Giulie was yelling over his shoulder "Sorry sir ... no time to explain."

He ran the kilometre in record time. Olympic Champion, Ben Johnson, with a bucket of steroids couldn't have beaten him. He ran full pelt into the block, past the office. The DO was demanding he explain himself. "No time," he yelled as he bounded the stairs, three at a time.

Big Giulie stood puffing and panting fumbling with the improvised handle all the time saying, "Sorry fellas, are you guys alright?"

Bloody hell it was hot! Apart from losing about 3 kilos each, we also lost a month's leave and ran seven days chooks to boot. All l can say is, "Bloody hell it was hot!"

We did all our training and parades with the Lee Enfield 303 rifles. We were taught how to maintain them and how to use them. Many of our boys were great shots. Some were from the bush and quite exceptional. A few earned their cross-rifles badge first time out. I was OK at shooting someone up the bum from under the house with a slug gun, but the 303 was another issue. It wasn't my choice of weapon, although I scored enough on the range to pass my weapons training.

It is interesting to note that the 303 rifle with fixed bayonet was over five foot long. At the start of the year some of our boys weren't quite that tall.

Naval training and discipline was a real eye opener for many of the boys who signed on. Some didn't cope but many more grew and embraced the system.

I believe my time at Leeuwin helped shape my life. Sure it could be tough, but it taught me the benefit of focus and self-discipline and of teamwork. The Navy helped me with self-esteem issues.

I found that I wasn't as useless as I had always been portrayed and told by my father.

In the final exams we sat on passing out of Leeuwin, I topped the division in the seamanship exams. To this day I still feel pride in that achievement. My name is still on the honour roll.

At the passing-out parade I marched forward, stood to attention in front of the Admiral, saluted and accepted my prize ... a book entitled The Australians. I have it to this day.

Much of my important formative years were spent in the Navy, I was mentored by some great people in those early years and for that I will always be grateful.

Part of our training was to spend two weeks aboard HMAS Diamantina, stationed at our wharf just outside the Base. It would give us a taste of the practical side of seamanship. She was a river class frigate and was used in the South Pacific during WW2. Her role was as an anti-submarine vessel.

She had a proud history and took the surrender of the Japanese forces in Nauru, Ocean Island and Bougainville. Their surrender was signed on board.

All the guys were very excited at the prospect of going out in a real 'warrie'.

We were taken on board and issued our hammocks. I couldn't find a place to hook mine, so for the first couple of days I slept under the Mess deck table. I could have handled that but the amount of blokes that got violently seasick made it a lot more uncomfortable.

I had to wash out my gear every day.

I think a few of the boys were starting to doubt their choice of careers after that little foray into the fleet. Personally I loved every second of it. That feeling has never left me.

The Diamantina is now in a dry dock at South Bank in Brisbane and is part of the Maritime museum there. I have taken my grandchildren to see her on several occasions. They are fascinated and I get a little of the old buzz as well.

## THE GEORGES

Over the course of the junior recruit training, the Navy, along with local Rotary and RSL clubs, ran a sponsorship scheme. It was a system introduced to give boys some respite from the intense training regime.

Local families that had been screened would take a lad or two home overnight on weekends and give them a little family life.

The boys were able to chill out so to speak, have a home-cooked meal and interact on a personal level with the family. Many of these good people sponsored boys year after year, and many lifelong friendships were born.

I found my family over a chance meeting at the gangway, one Sunday morning. I was on a MUP work detail. Dick Gough, a mate, came over to talk for a minute. He was being picked up by his sponsors, Rod and Shirley George.

They had sponsored Dick's brother the year before when he was a JR.

While we were talking, the Petty Officer in charge strode over, gave me a bollicking and told me to stop slacking and to get back to work. He sent Dick on his way quick smart. Shirley had seen what had happened and asked about me. "That's Mohawk; he's on chooks," said Dick. It must have brought out the mother in her. Dick came back that night with a cake she had baked for me and an invitation to come out for a Sunday roast when I got off punishment.

Two weeks later on a Sunday morning after church parade, which was compulsory, the Georges, along with their seven year old son Bruce, picked Dick and me up at the main gate.

I had the best day; no pressure, lots of laughs with the nicest people I had met in a long time. I addressed them as Mr and Mrs George. It felt disrespectful any other way, but they insisted on a less formal approach. Rod and Shirley was OK with them.

We were treated to a tour of their area of Subiaco and were told how Subiaco was the best football team in WA, then back to their home for a Sunday roast. The meal was laid on the table, I was about to start when I noticed Rod bowed his head to say grace, I felt awkward but duly bowed my head. I had never seen this done before … amazing.

That night we were driven back to the Base. Leave expired at 10pm.

I thanked them for a wonderful day and went to say goodbye. Shirley then asked me if I would like to make it a permanent arrangement ... being my sponsors. This would only happen, Rod butted in, if I promised to barrack for Subiaco in Aussie rules ... done deal.

I came to know them as Mum and Dad George. Rod and Shirley somehow wasn't right. Dick and I got to know all of their extended family and whenever possible, were included in all of the normal birthdays, outings and family get-togethers.

Rod was an ex-digger, a returned man; he was the gentlest man I had ever met. He had a great sense of family; he loved a good laugh and loved music.

He played saxophone in a jazz quartet for many years until a degenerative disease withered his right arm. It broke his heart. He was a member of the local RSL and understood how young people such as us would benefit from this surrogate family scheme. He always called me 'Mo' and we became lifelong friends.

Shirley loved life; she was loquacious in the nicest way. She could talk in shorthand and had an incredible bubbly personality. They doted on their son Bruce; he had been adopted by them when he was a baby. They had been told for some reason they could never conceive, but as happens in many cases, Shirley fell pregnant 10 years later and gave birth to a beautiful little girl, Amanda.

Shirley would ring my mum and keep her up-to-date with my progress, and they became fast friends. Many years later they would come to visit us all in Victoria.

All through my Navy years, when any of my ships would pull into Perth, there they were on the dock waiting to greet me. In later years as an entertainer, while on tour in WA, I would set them up in the best seats available, with everything laid on and Shirl would proudly announce to anyone in ear shot, "He's our boy, you know." Shirley passed away with dementia at the too-young age of sixty-seven. Dad was lost without her.

Through their kindness they demonstrated how a family should be and I feel so fortunate in having them in my life.

They got to meet my wife and our three children and embraced them as they did me. Karen (Kaz) and I were fortunate enough to be able to visit Dad just before he passed away in 2010. We walked into the nursing home and he looked up and said, "G'day Mo … and hello Kaz," as she bent to kiss his cheek. A little while later, he began to fade and slowly he drifted away, but his initial recognition brought a tear to my eye.

I flew to Perth to attend his funeral along with many of his extended family and friends; they welcomed me as usual as one of their own.

## OFF TO THE FLEET

The year at Leeuwin passed quickly. On reflection, the last three months were exciting; exams, revision, constant study and trying to decide in what area of the Navy we would work. Some of the guys knew from the start what they wanted. They had been influenced by family members or they had joined with a definite idea in mind. We were to list our preferences, first, second and third and an internal selection board would make the decision.

In my case it was a chance to change my life for the better and I wasn't that fussed with what branch I got. It was said that the Navy Board in Canberra would let our selection board know how many of each branch they needed. Quotas had to be met. Aptitude was supposed to be the main criteria.

Somehow I was given marine engineer. Thinking about it now, I must have listed it as a preference sometime during the process, because that's where I was put. I know absolutely nothing about engines. Either that or it was a typo.

Being a marine engineer meant working in the engine room as a stoker.

I accepted the situation at the time, but on my first ship, the troop carrier HMAS Sydney, I lasted two shifts. Luckily I was able to change to sonar operator ... a seaman branch, which was, I believe, where I should have been placed in the first place. After all, I did top the seamanship exams didn't I? Fresh air was what I craved, not the smell of diesel.

How stokers ever got used to the unbearable heat, noise and smell I will never know.

We had our passing-out parade. Many of the WA boys had friends and family in attendance. Mum and Dad George were there for Dick and me on the big day and we had sandwiches and tea in the Drill Hall afterwards. It was time to say goodbye to these good people and head into the next phase of our navy service ... the fleet.

Many of our division, including myself, were to be drafted to HMAS Sydney.

Originally she was a British aircraft carrier, laid down (constructed) as HMS Terrible, one of six Majestic class light aircraft carriers. We acquired her in 1949. She was our first aircraft carrier. She went on to have a proud history of service in Korea and the Far East. In 1958 she ceased flying aircraft and became a training ship. Then from 1962 till 1972 she was classed as a troop transport. On 24 occasions she took our troops to serve in Vietnam. My brother Ralph was with 1 RAR. He did the trip on her in 1968. He went on to fight in the Battle of Coral/Balmoral that year. He, like many others, came home a changed man.

After we left Leeuwin we were given a month's leave and were then to report to the Sydney, where she was berthed at Garden Island in Sydney.

I was excited to get home and catch up with everyone.

Ralph was managing a rock band called The Swingin' Margates. They were made up of local lads, Jimmy Craig was playing lead guitar and they were starting to make good in-roads into the music scene in Melbourne. The band was getting live spots at all the top venues. Live rock was the scene in those days. There were some great gigs; Springy Rock, The Thumpin' Tum, The Havana Coffee Lounge, Croxton Park and Pinocchios. They were also getting some valuable exposure with television on shows like Komotion and Go.

They constantly worked with artists like John Farnham and his band Strings Unlimited, Normie Rowe, Billy Thorpe, Bobbie Bright and Laurie Allen, Pat Carroll and Olivia Newton-John and many others. The then 16 year old Denise Drysdale danced and performed on Komotion. The boys would occasionally work with her as well. Denise is one of the nicest people in the business, and I have worked with her on many occasions since. She's a top lady ... what you see is what you get.

I went to all the gigs with Ralph and Jim over that leave break.

Mum wasn't any better off and my father hadn't changed at all. It just reinforced why I left in the first place. It was the right decision.

I found out later that Mum never received any benefit from the money I sent her, my father took the same amount off her weekly allowance.

Ralph was really getting into the management roll of the band when the Government introduced National Service. It was done by drawing numbers out of a barrel. The numbers corresponded with birthdays. Both Jim and Ralph's numbers came up, as did Normie Rowe's ... so they said.

Jim was deferred, as he was still doing a mechanic's apprenticeship, but Ralph was called up. He went into the Army as a Rifleman in 1967.

1968 saw him in Vietnam. Normie Rowe was a casualty of the call-up. He was a huge star and in the middle of his popularity. It has been alleged the Government of the day used him for political purposes ... Vietnam was a very unpopular conflict, and Normie was a casualty in more ways than one.

Interestingly enough, Ralph went on to serve for a further 14 years ... must have been the food!

## HMAS SYDNEY

My leave came to an end far too soon. I was having a ball. I caught the Southern Aurora train to Sydney. I was looking forward to seeing the city of Sydney; I had never been to NSW.

I caught up with a few of the Victorian boys and we duly reported to our new ship. I was issued a set of fighting irons (knife, fork and spoon), a small locker to stow my kit, some bedding and a hammock. There were no bunks aboard, save for the senior sailors and officers.

I never minded sleeping in a hammock. Once you got used to sleeping on your back it was fine. At least you never fell out with the motion of the ship. The worst part of it was the routine. At 6am every morning you would wake to the voice of the Bosun's mate on the PA, "Wakey, wakey, wakey …Lash up and stow, lash up and stow." It meant you had to lash your hammock into the shape of a banana and stow it in a big open 'hammock bin' at one end of the Mess.

Then after rounds (inspection) at night, you could hang it up again on the hooks attached to the deck head (ceiling).

The biggest problem with sailors was coming back from being ashore a little worse for wear and trying to hang their hammock with a skin-full.

The clever ones had a mate who was staying on board put it up for them.

Many a night you would find a sailor asleep in the hammock bin … myself included. If you were caught you would face a charge, 'absent from place of duty' … back on chooks!

We were now officially Ordinary Seamen, the lowest rank aboard the ship. We were really starting all over again, back to basics. The lowest of the low.

There was a huge adjustment to make. We had been used to calling everybody 'sir' when we were JRs. Even Able Seamen who were in reality only one rank above us were addressed that way at Leeuwin.

Now, in the fleet the only person you addressed as sir was an officer. The senior sailors only just tolerated us, but if you kept your head down and did your work you got by.

## LEARNING THE HARD WAY

I went for a shower early one morning. There were a few sailors having a dhobey (shower). I stepped into the cubicle, turned on the water and heard a loud bellow. A big hairy, burly sailor leaned into my space and punched me square in the face. I fell to my knees, blood dripping from my nose and being washed away with the running water.

"You just burnt my arse, son," he screamed. "Next time you call out 'BACKS' before you turn on water ... got it?"

With that he strode away.

Another young sailor came over to ask if I was OK. "I see you just met Whitey," he said. "It might be a good idea if you kept out of his way."

He told me that this Whitey character had been in the Navy 18 years and was still only a Leading Hand. I wondered if his lack of promotion had anything to do with anger management ... apparently he had a 'weed on with the world'. That's Navy for not being a 'happy camper'. My new friend also told me that I must always say "watch your backs" or "backs" very loudly, before I turn on any water. It warns the sailor in the cubicle next to you to step away from the water, so as not to be scalded.

I was learning fast and I must say that particular lesson has stayed with me even today. I still say "backs" as I get in the shower at home. Even when I am in a motel by myself, I call out "backs" ... how sad is that?

*With Dick Gough and our adopted family, the Georges*

*Marks 3*

*The seamanship award*

*HMAS Sydney*

*Big Julie (today) — keeper of the stories*

## CLIMBING THE CORPORATE LADDER

I was given my own department on the Sydney; I became the 'Fwd (Forward) Heads (Toilets) dodger' ... sounds impressive ... well that's Navy jargon for bog cleaner up the front of the ship. Navy would call it ship's husbandry but let's face it, I was a toilet cleaner. Mind you I took pride in my work and anyone who served with me in those days will attest to the fact that it was an honour, nay, a veritable privilege to lay a 'cable' in my crapper.

Our main boss was the Chief Bosun's mate, Chief Petty Officer Irwin, a WW2 veteran and as tough an 'old salt' as you could hope to find.

Chief Irwin was to give me one of my very first lessons in naval improvisation. I was standing by the heads' door, awaiting rounds by the Officer of the Day and Chief Irwin. I saw the Bosun's Mate and heard him blow the Bosun's whistle to announce the imminent arrival of the inspection team.

I had worked really hard and had gotten all twenty four crappers spotless ... well nearly ... one was totally blocked and it just wouldn't flush. I had discreetly put the lid down on that one cubicle and slightly adjusted the door the tiniest bit, just so it would look like it had moved naturally with the roll of the ship.

I felt quite sure it wouldn't be noticed. It was usually a cursory glance at best, as most times the duty officer would want to get rounds over and done with as quickly as possible, so that he could get back to the wardroom for a few more night caps.

As they approached I came to attention. I snapped up my smartest salute and reported. "Ordinary Seaman Elliott sir, Fwd heads ready for inspection sir."

I said this with all the pride I could muster, I felt sure I would get a "Well done Elliott," ... alas it wasn't to be. The officer made a beeline straight to the offending bog. It was like he had a built-in crap sensor ... he lifted the lid, turned to the Chief and said, "Attend to this will you Chief," and with that, spun on his heel and strode off with the Bosun's mate shrilling his whistle heralding his next inspection.

He never even glanced in my direction. The Chief Bosun's Mate beckoned me over. I looked at the mess in the bog, then casually looked above my head to see if there were any fans.

"What's this Elliott," says he.

"Crap, Chief," says I.

"Whose is it?" says the Chief.

"Not sure Chief," says I.

"It was left here for you Elliott, so it must be your property now ... well?" said the Chief, awaiting my answer.

"It's my crap Chief," said I.

"What's it doing here then?" says he.

"Just sort of lying there," says I.

"Why is that?" says he.

"Because it won't flush Chief," I said, wondering where he was going with this.

With that, the Chief rolled up his sleeve, put his whole forearm in the crapper. Seconds later he withdrew it with a hand full of shit and paper. "Hold out your hand Elliott," he said.

He dumped the whole lot in my hand and stared hard into my face.

"Do you feel any pain son?" he asked.

"Not really Chief," I said in between heaves.

"Then we have established one thing," he went on.

"It seems that shit is relatively harmless but I must inform you Elliott, it does have the ability of doing a lot of damage to an Ordinary Seamen's leave pass that is of course if the said shit is found in the wrong place at the wrong time. Do you understand Elliott?"

"Yes Chief," I mumbled; still heaving.

"Where is this mess supposed to be right now Elliott?" said he.

"In the sea Chief," said I.

"Now we are getting somewhere, he said. So in fact the shit is absent from place of duty and when that happens, it's the job of the next highest in rank ... which happens to be you, to get it to where it is supposed to be, at any cost. Would you agree Elliott?"

"Yes Chief," says I.

"Then in future, if you get your shit together, you won't have to take any shit from me. Do I make myself clear?"

"Crystal clear Chief," I said.

"Right, get it in a bucket and over the side," he called over his shoulder, as he finished washing his hands and strode off.

At this point, I would love to say after relating this story ... "only kidding," ... but I can't. Names have been changed to protect the innocent.

## NAVY SPEAK

I absolutely loved being at sea; it felt very natural to me. Some of the boys didn't like it at all and couldn't wait to get back into port.

I especially liked being on watch at night, whether it be as a 'look-out' or doing a 'trick' as Helmsman. It was never dull for me; it was more of an adventure than a job. Those of you who sail or cruise know that special feeling. It seems I have taken so much of the Navy way of things back into civilian life but the love of the sea, I think, must have been there in my DNA from the start.

Navy speak or jargon is quite unique and is used every day by sailors without a thought, but upon reflection it must sound ridiculous to a civilian.

A 'dhobey' is a wash. To do your 'dhobeying' is to do your washing.

A 'tiddlie oggie with jippers' is a pastie with sauce; 'scran' is a meal.

The name for different meals would probably put civvies off their meal. Tomato au gratin was 'train smash' to us; hard boiled eggs became 'bum nuts', mince on toast became 'shit on a raft', 'piss strainers' were kidneys, 'corned dog' was corned beef, RN (Royal Navy) steak was lambs fry or liver, 'duff' is dessert. Our cooks were referred to as 'Fitters and Turners' by the sailors. They would 'fit the food into the pot and turn it into shit' ... not that it was ever said to their face; there were some tough old boys in the galley.

Some of our cooks went on to become master chefs in civilian life. I guess there wasn't too much room for experimentation for our cooks in those days though.

As an ordinary seaman it was common-place to be pulled out of the 'scran' queue by the duty cook and be shanghaied into either serving the queue of hungry sailors, or scrubbing the pots and pans and mopping out the galley. It was an unwritten law for the cooks to do this and you wouldn't dare complain. I didn't mind too much. It meant extra food and that has always been a plus with me.

I guess I didn't know it at the time but I had changed a great deal since I first joined the Navy, not just physically but mentally as well. I had come to realise that I could shape my own life. I was getting to see the world and be paid for it at the same time. It was very exciting. I felt that I had some direction for the first time in my life. Not that I was knuckling down that much, or not pushing the boundaries any more ... far from it. We partied hard.

As ODs (ordinary seamen), and under 18 years of age, we were still on 'Cinderella' leave, which meant we had to be back on board by midnight. Many a night I and a few of my 'stepping oppos', (mates), would be brought back to the ship via Shore Patrol. ... back on chooks ... Ah well!

In fact I hate to admit it, but it took me 6 years to get my 4 year good conduct stripe. ... I guess that's in my DNA as well.

## VIETNAM

Our time on the Sydney was going along as planned. When we finished our time, we would draft off and be replaced by the next lot of ODs. We were to be given a month's leave and then report to our assigned Bases to do our Branch courses. Once the courses finished we would emerge as Able Seamen; in my case, Able Seaman/Under Water Control. All of us were excited at the prospect.

Along with a few of my mates, I would report to HMAS Watson, situated at Watson's Bay NSW. Our particular course as sonar operators would take around six months and then we would be drafted back to the fleet. Only a few short months to go ... and then an unexpected interruption.

I was about to step off the ship with Rick Anderson, another of my mates from Leeuwin, when we were called to report to the Officer of the Day. We were told we must report at once to HMAS Hobart, she was sailing for Vietnam and were two crew short.

"But sir," I said, "we were going on leave and," "DID YOU HEAR WHAT I JUST SAID, ELLIOTT," he bellowed.

I think we got across to the Hobart on the strength of his breath ... how did this happen?

Rick and I reported to the gangway of the Hobart, She would sail within two hours. Hobart was to be under the command of the American Seventh fleet and would be the first Australian ship to go into combat in Vietnam.

HMAS Hobart was the pride of the fleet; our latest destroyer. She was the first of three Perth class guided missile destroyers, built for the RAN. She was based on the United States Navy's Charles F Adams class destroyers. Her sister ships were HMAS Perth and HMAS Brisbane.

The Hobart was built by the Defoe Shipbuilding company in Bay City, Michigan and was commissioned into our service in 1965. She cost our taxpayers $45 million. She was state of the art. She spent eight months in work-up trials round Hawaii and then headed back to Australia. It was March 1967 and we were off to Vietnam.

The Hobart could do 35 knots; she got us out of trouble many times in combat. Hobart's main armament was a Mark 13 missile launcher which fired Tarter missiles, two Ikara (aboriginal for throwing stick), anti-submarine missile launchers; two 5inch/54 calibre mark 42 guns; two twin Mark 32 triple torpedo tube sets; and an armoury full of small arms ... and of course me. We certainly came prepared for anything they could throw at us.

After the initial shock in my change of fortune, I realised it was the start of another adventure. Certainly it was daunting in a way, but at the same time I felt the exhilaration of being on a fighting ship.

It was a total turn-around to being on a carrier; the Sydney seemed like a floating hotel compared to the Hobart. It wasn't the amenities so much as the space. Everything seemed so compact.

I was even given a bunk. How cool was that. Although when we were at sea I must admit I missed my hammock.

The crew of the Hobart was about half of the original crew that commissioned her. I was the youngest on board. Rick, my mate, was a month older than me. We were both seventeen. I turned eighteen two months before I came home from Vietnam. In fact that birthday will never be forgotten by me. It was the day the USS Forrestal, a carrier, was to be racked by explosions killing 134 sailors, injuring another 161. We were sent to help; a little more of that later.

The Hobart was in work-up mode getting ready for our role in the Seventh Fleet. The crew were real 'pros' and knew what they were about, so Rick and I had to learn our part and learn quickly.

We weren't the only ODs on board but the others were adult entry sailors and although they were in their twenties and we were still only seventeen, we had been in the Navy a lot longer. These guys were just out of recruit school, having only just finished three months at HMAS Cerberus in Victoria.

At sea in peacetime, the Navy of my day ran on a four watch system, which meant as well as your eight hour day working on ship's husbandry or whatever detail you were given, you would keep another two or four hour 'watch' in that twenty-four hours as well. For instance you might knock off work at 1600 (4 pm) and then get the first watch, which was from 8 pm till midnight.

The next night you would have midnight till 4 am. We called that watch 'the guts' (all night in with the guts kicked out).

We had two short two hour watches we called the 'dog' watches. They ran from 4 pm till 6 pm, then 6 pm till 8 pm. This rotated the watches and ensured you never got the same watch every day. It sounds a little confusing but it works well. As a seaman I had to do these watches on a daily basis. In one four hour watch, I could be doing an hour (called a trick) on the helm, an hour as a lookout on the port or starboard bridge wing, be a 'gopher' on the bridge or be sitting by the sea-boat at the ready in case of an emergency.

The Hobart was preparing for our role in Vietnam and was put into a two watch system ... four hours on watch, four off. This system was laced with calls-to-action stations; practice drills being carried out all the time we were on our way to the US Navy Base at

Subic Bay in the Philippines. We would officially join the Seventh fleet when we got there.

Sometimes you would just hit your bunk and action stations would sound. By the time you got that over and done with, it was time to go back to work. It was the luck of the draw so to speak. We drilled hard day and night to get to action stations in the shortest time possible.

It was never quick enough for our skipper, Captain Guy Griffith. He was a hard task master but loved and respected by the crew.

From being fast asleep on your bunk, to your detailed place at action stations required the whole crew to be closed up (in place) within two minutes. There were times in Vietnam that we could go up to 19 hours without sleep ... but that was yet to come.

Eventually we achieved our skipper's goal and he announced a "well done" over the PA. ... the crew erupted in cheers. He kept the pressure up all the way. We all felt we had the reputation of the RAN on our shoulders and we were reminded of it constantly.

My action station was as an anti-aircraft lookout, exposed personnel. I wore a helmet, a flak jacket (bullet proof vest) and full cover anti-flash gear. I was stationed above the bridge, just aft of the fwd 5 inch gun. My job in general would be to report to the bridge the position of shore batteries firing at us in relation to our ship and the position of the shells falling around us.

In the two-watch system I was in the Mount 52 gun magazine as part of the crew loading shells and then when action stations was sounded, I raced to my AA position up top.

I must admit that being an AA lookout when we were under fire, was better than being in a magazine below the water-line, listening to shrapnel hit the side of the ship, when the shells exploded near us. At least I could see what was happening. My mate Rick was stationed in the aft magazine during action stations and he wasn't impressed.

But all of that was yet to come; first we would be briefed in the Philippines.

We duly arrived in Subic Bay.

## ALONGAPO

The American Naval Base was strategically close to Vietnam, some 750 miles west across the South China Sea. Just south of the Base was Bataan and Corregidor. Both of these places featured in heavy conflict during WW2.

Directly outside the Base was the city of Alongapo.

While the skipper was being briefed by the Commanders of the U.S. Seventh fleet, the crew were getting a series of lectures and being shown explicit films of the depraved vices and life found ashore. Those who gave the lectures tried hard to convince us that nothing but trouble and danger lay in wait for us in Alongapo.

The Naval Base itself had every facility available to the servicemen including restaurants and night clubs, which provided hostesses to dance and dine with, (but that's all). Every sporting interest was catered for on the Base but alas, it was far too tame for our sailors. We couldn't wait to hit town.

To get ashore you would line up at the gate. You were searched and once again told the basic rules. If you were seen on your own in town, you would instantly be thrown in the MP's (Military Police's) wagon and locked up for the night. These MPs were marines known as 'hard hats' and they didn't dispense with niceties, they used truncheons and you learnt very quickly not to back-chat. They roamed town all night. They were, in reality, there to protect us but we saw them as a pain in the arse ... party poopers, but not to be messed with. I know, I tried and it hurt! It wasn't that I back-chatted, it was just that they couldn't understand my Aussie accent and they thought I was taking the piss. It didn't help that I was two sheets to the wind as well.

You were also told never, under any circumstances to leave the main street. Murder was common, life was cheap and we were seen by the locals as an opportunity to make a quick buck.

During the lectures and films we were shown American servicemen actually being shot or stabbed in the main street. I thought ... who was filming this stuff? So it seemed even in the main street we were not safe.

While we were in port on one trip an American Junior Naval officer was murdered. His body was dumped out of a jeep, trussed up. His genitals were cut out and stuffed in his mouth. He had bled to death. This was a seriously dangerous place, but of course we were young Aussies abroad and bullet proof!

Once through the gates we crossed the Po river bridge, the most polluted stretch of water I had ever seen in my life.

It was more like an open sewer and kids would be in the water looking up and begging for coins to dive for. Poverty was rife.

From the time you left the gate, you were surrounded by people trying to sell you anything from a shoeshine to a short time with their girlfriend, sister, or mother… or brother, whatever your bent.

The local transport was a jeepney (old second hand jeeps left over from the war). They were painted with every colour of the rainbow, like something out of a circus and would converge on you at every chance. You had to climb over their bonnet when they hemmed you in.

The thing that hit you most was the smell of the place. It stunk to high heaven and took some getting used to. It was a sweet, sickly smell of incense, sweating bodies and decay; very hard to describe but I would come across that same smell in many of the poorer parts of South East Asia in the years to come.

Little kids would swarm around you, jostling, touching, tugging at you and all the time they were seeing if they could steal your wallet … if you were foolish enough to be carrying one.

I had learnt earlier from some of the 'old salts' never to carry a wallet or wear a watch or any jewellery ashore. A few years later in downtown Hong Kong, I helped a drunken American sailor get back to his ship. He had been mugged up an alley; they couldn't get a ring off his finger so they took both ... the ring with the finger attached.

In Alongapo, the main street seemed to go on forever, bar after bar, massage parlours, street vendors selling monkey meat on a stick; not a good idea to eat because you wouldn't have it for long.

There was one bar, The Aces and Deuces, which had a small pool out the front. The pool was covered with wire and inside a one metre crocodile lay skulking in the filthy water. A kid stood beside the pool selling live baby ducklings or chicks to drunken sailors to feed to the croc.

In the bars the girls would swoop on you as soon as you walked in "Hey John, I 'lub' you no shit ... you buy me drink?"

Everyone was 'John' and when they got to know we were Aussie's we were 'Ned Kelly, No 1'.

STDs were rife and we were told in no uncertain terms that if you took a chance of unprotected sex, your chances of coming down with 'a load' was a near certainty. During the lectures we got on arrival we were told of the diseases that were now immune to penicillin or any other treatment. There were American servicemen on the Base that were never allowed home again. Scary stuff but it didn't stop us still wanting to get ashore and check out the action.

## WHEN IN ROME ...

The segregation that was happening in the ranks of the American sailors seemed so foreign to us. At one point in Alongapo, because of an incident that was happening back in the States, they had white and black bars in different sections of town. They would work together at sea, but ashore they kept to their own.

I was in town one night with my mate Bill; we had been getting into the San Miguel, a local brew and just starting to get a little socially excited when we decided to move to another bar. We walked the drag for a while and Bill said, "Hey Col, this looks like a likely spot ... let's go in."

The joint was really swinging, the band was blaring out Love Potion No 9. The dance floor was full, lights were flashing, what a great atmosphere. Then the band stopped. You could have heard a pin drop ... what the? My eyes had adjusted to the light but still I had trouble picking out faces but I could clearly discern the white uniforms. Then it struck me; we were in a black bar. The tension in the room was palpable.

We were half way into the bar. "Bill," I said, "this is a black bar, we'd better get out ... quick."

"It's a Yank problem mate, not ours and besides I want a beer," he said as he started to stride towards the bar.

Like a stray dog I followed Bill, expecting the worst.

"Two San Miguels thanks mate," Bill demanded of the little Phillipino barman.

"Please sir, you must go quick," the barman stammered.

"Bill, for Christ's sake mate, let's go," I said with anxiety rising.

"Two San Miguel's mate," Bill said again, this time lifting his voice for more power of command.

The silence was broken by the scraping of a chair being pushed back. I slowly turned to my right and saw the biggest Negro I had ever seen in my life getting to his feet. He looked directly at me, then his face broke into the biggest grin as he announced to the rest of the room, "It's OK guys, these boys ain't white ... they's 'Orstraylian'."

The band started playing again and the big black guy slapped us both on the back and said, "This one's on me fellas."

We joined his table and met his friends; it was one of the best nights I ever had. We left with an open invitation to return any time we wanted. It was to become one of our favourite drinking holes.

During our time operating in Vietnam, Subic Bay was visited quite a few times. We came back for maintenance, one time to replace a melted gun barrel.

## DODGY RUM

We found our favourite bars, became street-wise and got to know a lot of the local girls; they always knew when our ship was in and after a while we felt we were, in some way, a part of the scene.

We made some great mates from the American ships we worked with in Vietnam and many times we would catch up in Alongapo.

At one bar we had a slush fund that we all contributed to. When we hit port we would all meet and party hard.

Partying hard turned into a terrifying run ashore for me on one occasion. My mates and I had met a bunch of our Yank mates in our designated bar.

On the way there I had bought a bottle of Manila rum from a hawker in the street. What a bargain, it only cost me two pesos ($1.50), I was saving a buck and felt I had bargained well.

We sat around drinking and laughing and generally having a great time. We only had a couple of days left and would be back on the gun-line so we were going for it.

The rum had a strange taste to it but I thought, "Ah well ... when in Rome." I had drunk about half the contents of the bottle and hadn't felt at all even slightly drunk which was unusual for me. Normally two beers and I was anybody's, as the saying goes. I was definitely a two pot screamer.

I reached across the table to pour myself another shot but my hand was paralysed. It wouldn't work, literally. I tried again ... nothing. "Hey guys, my hand won't work," I said, half laughing, but feeling a little uneasy.

The boys duly laughed and kept carousing, thinking I was messing about.

By this time my whole arm was useless. I picked it up with the other hand and dropped it on the table. It got a good laugh but inside I started to panic, I thought of heading to the toilets to wash my face.

The humidity always kept us on edge, maybe it had something to do with that.

I tried to stand ... my legs wouldn't work. I tried to tell the boys but my vocals had ceased. I was sitting there unable to move or communicate but I was aware of everything going on around me. I was using all my willpower to scream out for help but I physically couldn't do it.

After what seemed to be an eternity one of the boys made the suggestion that we move to another bar. All agreed.

"Hey Mohawk, let's go," Bill said, noticing I hadn't moved from the table with the rest.

"Mohawk's shattered, grab the other side," one said, as they lifted me to a standing position. The trouble was I couldn't stand.

"At least help us, you prick," Bill said, as they half dragged me through the door and into the main street.

I was going into a state of shock, of utter terror. The boys were pissed, I was ostensibly still sober and could see and hear all that was going on but my body was totally useless. It just didn't work. If you have ever seen the movie Weekend at Bernie's you would be able to picture this scene.

While all this was happening I was trying to will myself into movement. It wasn't working.

We moved into a new bar and I was shoved in a seat at the table. I fell to the floor. The boys laughed and dragged me back to a sitting position and somehow propped me there.

The bar girls swarmed in, "Hey John, I 'lub' you, no shit, you buy me drink," she said, as she tried to sit on my lap. I hit the floor again, this time face down, blood trickling from my busted lip ... the boys propped me back on my chair, still laughing. One wiped the blood away and looked full into my face ... "Mohawk, you're a funny bastard," he said.

At one point, in the second bar Bill asked me for a 'rubbers' (a loan) of twenty bucks and having gotten no reply or knock-back from me, he took it from my pocket with the promise of paying it back on payday. I duly noted the transaction.

They dragged me into two more bars, then a crazy ride back to the main gate in a jeepney and back to the ship, some three hours later. I was still unable to function.

I was carried over two Yank destroyers we were tied up to. On each gangway the boys fumbled in my pocket for my ID card, flashed it to the gangway staff and moved on. I was dropped twice before we reached our ship.

I was hoping against hope that they would take me to the sickbay but no, they dropped me on my bunk, fully booted and spurred after hitting what seemed to be every bulk head on the way down to our Mess. They were all pissed, hit their respective bunks and within five minutes I could hear snoring.

I figured it must be around 2 am. I was convinced I was going to die.

I lay there thinking how ironic. Here I was dying of whatever, after one half bottle of rum and my old man had been hitting it for years with no apparent side effects. I lay there for another two hours listening and wrestling with my thoughts.

I had just about resigned myself to my fate when I felt an involuntary movement in my right hand. Slowly I could move my right arm, then I could wiggle my toes, then my leg. I made a strangled sound and was able to utter a few words, probably "fucking hell", but then a feeling of great relief flooded over me ... the boys snored on.

When I regained full use of my body, I swung down from my bunk, and with shaky legs I headed for the ship's café. I knew I could get a hot cup of Kai, (chocolate drink, not unlike Ovaltine).

I sat there by myself pondering what had happened. I decided to head straight to the sickbay after 'Wakey, wakey'.

I met the guys at breakfast. I was copping a lot of flak from the night before but by the time I had given them a full description of our time ashore, including Bill's $20 rubbers … they believed me. Lesson learnt; no more street rum.

I was sent to the base hospital to be checked out. The doctor there told me of the dangers of locally made brews. He seemed to think the concoction I drank was laced with some sort of anaesthetic, probably stolen from a local hospital.

No two bottles tasted the same. I stayed on board the next night as I still felt a little shaky. The morning afterwards we headed back to the gun-line.

## SEVENTEEN … COULDN'T DRINK, COULDN'T VOTE, BUT OK FOR WAR

On reflection, my time in Vietnam was a life-changing experience. No longer did I think of myself as a lowly Ordinary Seaman. I felt I was an important part of a team, of something bigger. The entire crew came to realise we were involved in a dangerous theatre of war and we all needed to be on our game if we were to come away unscathed.

As a seventeen year old, I didn't have a total grasp of the politics involved in the Vietnam saga, except for the general assumption that it was to stop the flow of communist expansion. The theory that the 'domino effect' would happen, was the accepted line being touted; Laos, Thailand, Singapore, Malaysia and then eventually Australia. We were there to stop them. It sounded reasonable to me. Our government had sent us so it must be right. … Right?

Our skipper, Captain Guy Griffith, was the conduit between the powers that be in the Seventh fleet and ourselves. We revered him and relied on his incredible leadership. We were the first of the Australian ships to be used in combat since the Indonesian conflict and our skipper knew the eyes of the world were on us. We had complete trust in him.

When we were scurrying to action stations at all hours of the day and night, he would address us when he could, with details of the imminent action. After the briefing, there was always a final "good luck". Upon completion, he always gave us a detailed de-briefing.

Where possible we were kept in the loop and it proved to be a huge morale booster to the crew.

The start of our tour of duty was not what we expected.

Our first area of operation was south of the de-militarised zone and south of Da Nang. It was repetitive, mundane and tiring, but very essential.

We were giving assistance to the troops ashore and in between dishing out harassment and interdiction fire to the NVA (North Vietnamese Army) and Vietcong. We supplied suppression fire to beach landings for the marines and our troops. On many occasions we could watch the action ashore as it unfolded. All this seemed so surreal at the time, especially at night.

We were all feeling a little bored with the general routine, but satisfaction was gained in the knowledge that we had been an important part of many operations and we had saved lives in the course of our deployment. This was all reflected in the glowing signals that the skipper received.

He would always pass this information on to us.

This mundane existence wasn't to last. Within weeks, we were assigned to Sea Dragon operations. We headed into North Vietnam, on the 17th parallel of latitude.

Working north of the DMZ (de-militarised zone) was a totally different kettle of fish. We never came under attack down south; our only opposition was the possibility of a MIG (Russian-made aircraft) strike.

In North Vietnam, it was a totally different ball game. We were in their backyard and we were to find out how vigorously it was going to be defended. Our main role was to decimate their lines of supply and coastal communications, and to do that meant taking on their coastal defence sites.

We soon came to realise it was a dangerous area of operation.

Much of the time we had spotter aircraft from the carriers, giving us information as to where the WBLC (water born logistic craft) were hiding. The vessels would hide in the river mouths awaiting a chance to run down south where they would deliver troops, ammunition, weapons, food and medical supplies. Our spotter aircraft had many casualties. It wasn't a job for the faint hearted. The pilots were incredibly brave and daring ... some paid the ultimate price. Throughout history, it has been proved that any Army or combatants are only as good as their supply lines. The old saying stays the same "an army cannot march on an empty stomach".

Our job was to dry up those lines of supply ... starve them. It proved to be a full time enterprise.

The craft being used by the NVA and Viet Cong came in all shapes and sizes; from thirty foot junks or sampans, to ninety foot barges, and up to 100 ton trawlers or ferries.

In our time up north, we also attacked and destroyed ammunition dumps, fuel supplies, army installations, ferry terminals, bridges, radar installations, troop vehicles and their movement areas; much of this being done while duelling with shore defence sites.

When they locked onto us hovering in an area, they would move in extra fire-power. There was never really an element of surprise on our part; we were tracked constantly. We went in, did our thing and got the hell out the best way we could, firing back at their coastal defence sites as we were speeding away.

We would use a tactic of high speed runs-in to attack, all the time zig-zagging to avoid being hit as they opened up on us.

We were straddled by shore fire many times. During one operation, up to two hundred shells exploded above and around us and our partner ships. On record the closest to Hobart was 10 feet on the port bow. This happened when we were doing a high speed WBLC sweep from the Song Yen River to Hon Me Island. It was considered the hottest area in the Sea Dragon operations at that time.

A few years ago I was reunited with Bevan Stringer, a naval

photographer on board the Hobart during some of those actions. He was 'choppered' onboard to record our work on the line. He got some amazing shots while we were under fire. He presented me with a catalogue of those images forty-five years after the event. I look at them today and I still feel it seems like yesterday.

On average, we replenished our fuel and ammunition every three days, sometimes twice in a day. There were times when we would go to action stations up to six times in a twenty-four hour period and could get critically low on our needs, especially ammunition.

Underway replenishments were arduous work. This was done by transferring between supply ships and ourselves, while steaming side by side.

Unreps (underway replenishments) were carried out day and night, at all hours by High Wire and Manila Line between ships. All hands had to work, storing the 5 inch shells and cordite by hand.

The supply ship and the ship, or ships being replenished would be guarded by a destroyer during this procedure, in case of attack.

Ammunition and fuel were carried by separate supply ships and many times we would have to re-supply both commodities within hours of each other.

On most occasions we would head straight back into action or on patrol. It was exhausting work and it wore on the nerves.

While on operation we functioned on minimal sleep. Nineteen hours was the longest stint of sleep deprivation I can remember and all those on my watch suffered the same.

On that occasion the skipper took us out to sea, put a 'skeleton' crew on watch and gave us a few hours to catch up on much-needed rest.

Unlike some of the other units we operated with on our tour of duty, we were lucky enough never to have received a direct hit. That is apart from the shrapnel zinging about from anti-aircraft shells which were sometimes used when the North Vietnamese had run low on high explosive. How we escaped being hit is beyond comprehension. When you looked at the 'fall of shot' board after an action, it just seemed amazing. (See photo.)

The longer we operated north of the DMZ, the more accurate their defences became. We were becoming more and more of a problem to them. They increased their fire power in number and sophistication. The communist gunners were quickly re-equipped. They began using search and ranging radars which meant we became more vulnerable at greater ranges. They were no longer guessing. This in turn meant more direct hits to our ships.

The USS Du Pont had received a direct hit nine days prior to joining us for a gunfire support mission in the Cap Lay-Cua Viet River area.

One of her turrets had been hit, killing an officer and wounding nine sailors. As we went back into action with her, it brought home the possibilities to all of us.

Other American ships we were operating with, St Paul, Damato and Mansfield, all took direct hits for a loss of one sailor killed, three wounded and significant damage.

The Canberra was hit twice in ten days. We were all on our toes.

## DISASTER AT SEA

On July 29th, my 18th birthday, we were called to assist the USS Forrestal, a carrier on 'Yankee' station, some 95 miles away to the north. We had been operating with her aircraft in the Gulf of Tonkin. She had been racked with explosions with many dead and wounded. We closed on her and the sight that met us was unbelievable.

Fire and explosions were out of control on her flight deck. Planes were literally melting over her side. Crew members had to physically push planes over the edge of the ship. Bombs were exploding intermittently. Men had been blown off the ship. Some had jumped to escape the inferno. Destroyers were searching for survivors, 44 were found. The explosions tore great holes in her decks. Aviation fuel caught fire and leaked to the levels below. Many men were incinerated. We watched helplessly as the men of this mighty aircraft carrier desperately tried to contain the damage.

It transpired that the first bomb blast killed nearly all of the specially trained fire crew. Those that were left were forced to improvise.

On one side of the deck the fire crew that were left, were spraying foam to smother the fuel fires, the correct procedure. On the opposite side, crew members used seawater, which actually spread the fuel fire and helped it leak below with dire consequences.

When we first got the news of this tragedy we had only just taken mail by 'helo' transfer from a Forrestal chopper. It was being refuelled in flight by our task unit partner at the time, USS Chandler.

Our skipper recalled the chopper to Hobart and uplifted our doctor, Ship's Surgeon Barnett. He was transferred to the Forrestal to assist. It was reported later that he worked tirelessly and helped save many lives.

A short version of the cause of this disaster is that a MK-32 Zuni rocket, mounted on a Phantom jet ready for takeoff, was accidentally fired due to a power surge. It struck a wing-mounted external fuel tank on a Skyhawk. Its safety mechanism prevented it from detonation but the subsequent fuel ignited starting off an unbelievable chain of events. There were 134 men killed and 161 wounded that day.

Since this event, the biggest Naval disaster in the Vietnam conflict, the US Navy has put in place many more safety procedures and checks. The Forrestal incident is now part of every new sailor's curriculum.

As the Forrestal limped toward Subic Bay, we left her and returned to our patrol area. We carried out an H and I mission at 0430 the next morning. We were with the Chandler, firing on the coastal sites as we did so ... no time for contemplation ... I was numb.

As a footnote, one of the pilots escaped his jet as it was engulfed in flames, by jumping from its nose. The pilot was LCDR John McCain, who later was to become a US Senator and Presidential nominee.

Months later, not long after relieving us on the gun-line, the Perth was hit, wounding six of her crew. Then on June 17th 1968, on her second tour of duty, the Hobart was hit three times by 'friendly fire' with two crew being killed and seven wounded. R.I.P. Ord/Seaman R.J.Butterworth, Chief Electrician Hunt. The wounded were evacuated by helicopter to Da Nang.

That night the Hobart, Boston and Edson were attacked, as were US CGC.Point Dume, an 82 foot coast guard cutter and PC 12, a US patrol boat. Although the Boston also took a direct hit, only the Hobart suffered fatalities.

It appears these ships were attacked by US Air Force jets that had somehow mistaken them for enemy helicopters.

I was back home by then, but the news of these events was received by all of us with much sadness and understanding.

Many of the actions I was involved in have stayed with me all these years, but one incident is still very vivid. We were doing a high speed attack and were under fire. Things were heating up and getting hectic. I was starboard side at my action stations as an AA lookout above of the bridge. I was reporting shore fire.

I watched as their gunners started stepping their shells in toward the ship.

They had locked onto us. The shells were in a line, maybe fifty yards apart, each fall of shot getting closer to us. Although we were taking avoiding action, they seemed to be one step in front of us. I counted six splashes in line. I knew the next one would hit us. The Chief Gunner yelled "Hit the deck". I was already there. I thought "This is it", but luckily the shell exploded above us … we were peppered with shrapnel. Their last round was AA (anti-aircraft).

Had it been high explosive, all of us in the immediate vicinity would have been killed. I got to my feet and kept spotting. I would reflect later when I wasn't so busy.

I would often have dreams about this incident. I always sit bolt upright before the seventh shell.

We spent many days on patrol while in Vietnam, sometimes five or six weeks at a time. It was certainly intense and tiring. Our time in port was for upkeep, repairs and R and R. It should have been for sleep but that never happened ... all a little highly strung!

We were only away from our station for short periods; the most time in any port was six days, rarely more.

We visited Hong Kong, Taiwan, Japan and of course the Philippines.

Sea Dragon operations didn't totally stop the flow of supplies and troops to the south. It harassed the communists enough to find ulterior routes inland like the Ho Chi Min trail. It was much more difficult and time consuming. They were also forced to use smaller inland river systems to move their supplies. They would have to unload their vessels, carry the cargo to the next river complex and load up again.

I came home a different person; my life would reflect this in time. I had seen and experienced so much. I was now eighteen, I could legally drink back home ... I saw the irony of this. I could be shot at, but not allowed to drink ... underage drinking could do me harm!

We returned to Australia but were not welcomed home as heroes. It was not a popular conflict and many civilians made us aware that we were seen as part of the problem. Many returned men experienced much abuse. We got our share.

We were told not to wear our uniforms ashore so as not to antagonise the civilian population that was demonstrating.

I put my medals away and never wore them until a reunion of my shipmates some twenty five years later.

My shipmates and I were awarded a USN Commendation for our time in Vietnam. It was presented to us by the Commander in Chief United States Pacific Fleet, Admiral John J Hyland.

I proudly wear it today. It reads:

'The Secretary of the Navy takes pleasure in commending HMAS HOBART (D39) for services set forth in the following ... For Exceptionally Meritorious Service during the period 10th March to 20th September 1967, while engaged in Combat Operations in direct support of Free World Objectives in South East Asia.

As an element of Task Unit 70.8.9 HMAS HOBART provided Naval Gunfire Support for United States and Allied Forces ashore in the Republic of Vietnam, and as an element of Task Group 77.1 in the Gulf Of Tonkin, supported Naval Operations against North Vietnamese logistics groups and lines of communications.

Undeterred by frequent, vigorous, accurate enemy shore fire, HOBART was responsible for the destruction of numerous enemy installations, earning an enviable reputation as an aggressive, eager and dauntless member of the US Seventh Fleet.

The outstanding team work, courage and professionalism displayed by HOBART's officers and men reflect great credit upon themselves and the Royal Australian Navy and were in keeping with the highest traditions of the Naval Service.'
**(Text of US Navy Commendation.)**

*Stepping ashore "Up Top" (The Far East)*

*Just home from Vietnam*

*HMAS Hobart*

*Under fire, Vietnam 1967*

**AWM ID Number: NAVY13512**
Ordinary Seaman Col Elliott, R95102 passes powder cartridges from the after gun powder stowage room to the Mount 52 gun magazine and loading room. In the two watch system he is a member of the magazine crew for the after gun turret (Mount 52). When action stations are sounded, Col Elliott mans the starboard Target Designation Transmitter (TDT) binoculars on the AA control deck of HMAS Hobart.

**AWM ID Number: NAVY13476**
Sub-Lieutenant D N Peterson onboard the Guided Missile Destroyer HMAS Hobart during a respite from operations in the Gulf of Tonkin. He is holding a board which he used to plot the fall of shots as they splashed down near the ship. At the time, HMAS Hobart had been under fire from coastal defence sites. The straight line represents the ship and the crosses indicate the accuracy of North Vietnamese barrages.

**AWM ID Number: NAVY13463D**
A slinged pallet of fuzed ammunition arrives onboard the Guided Missile Destroyer HMAS Hobart during Sea Dragon operations in the Tonkin Gulf. A work party of sailors, hoist the ordnance which has been delivered from the ammunition ship USS Diamond Head partly visible in the background. Replenishment at sea ensured the ship could manitain a sustained period of operations on the gunline.

Photos by L/A Phot Bevin Stringer

## BACK HOME

After we arrived back in Sydney, Rick and I drafted off the Hobart and were given a month's leave. It was well overdue.

After our leave break, we would do our branch courses and become Able Seamen. All our mates from Leeuwin had already completed their training. They had been promoted and been sent back to the fleet. We were behind the eight-ball, but glad to be home in one piece.

An overnight train ride on the Southern Aurora and I was back in Melbourne. A bunch of us headed to Young and Jacksons for a beer. I was starting to enjoy a drink; maybe a bit too much in those days but for now it didn't seem to be a problem. All my service mates gave it a bit of a nudge, so why not?

*All together, home on leave*

I got out, paid the cab, looked up and there was Mum, coming down the steps of the house. With tears in her eyes, she gave me a big hug and welcomed me home. It was so good to see her.

I walked into the house, dropped my kit bag in the lounge and walked into the kitchen. Dad was sat in the same position as when I had left; it was like I hadn't left. I could see the irony of it, I remember laughing out loud. "What's up boy?" he asked.

"Just glad to be home," I said, searching for an excuse.

I noticed the new carpet in the lounge. Ralph had it done and Mum was as 'proud as punch'. As manager of the band, Ralph needed a phone so he had that connected as well. The place was a little more befitting a Band Manager. It looked really nice. Mum was so pleased.

Ralph and the band were still doing the rounds but he only had a little while left before he would be in the Army.

I caught up with all of my mates; it was great to see them.

Some of the boys I knocked around with before I joined the Navy were a couple of years younger than Ralph and Jim and his band. They too, had a group. I guess our common interest was music.

I went to a few of the dances they were playing at but I felt out of place.

It was a little disconcerting. It wasn't like it was before. Something was different; I didn't feel comfortable. I tried hard to recapture that old feeling that we all shared. Then I realised that my mates hadn't changed, I had.

I found it hard to talk about the things I had experienced. When we did talk, I realised that they couldn't or wouldn't understand or comprehend the type of life I had been exposed to in the Navy. Theirs was a different world to mine now and there wasn't any going back.

## THE SHARPIES

The band was playing at Saint Mary's Hall on a Friday night. I was at the pub and said I would come up for the last set.

When I arrived, I saw two skin-head-looking guys giving one of our mates a belting ... two on one. I jumped in to help him.

It was more shoving than punching when two cops arrived and broke it up.

They told us to move on.

We were looking in the grass for my mate's watch that had gone missing during the blue, when I noticed I was surrounded by a whole bunch of these skin-head looking guys.

It was a gang of 'Sharpies', a new phenomenon that had sprung up in Melbourne. They distinguished themselves by wearing very neat, wide baggy pants, square toed boots, short, almost skinhead haircuts and polo neck shirts.

They hung around in gangs and liked to kick people.

I had never seen them before ... fascinating.

"Fancy yourself do you mate?" their leader said. My mate was nowhere to be seen. "Let it go," I said, "it's all over" realizing as I said this, they had blocked all my exits ... bugger.

Their leader shaped up to me, his mates egging him on. I put my fists up and squared up to him ... then I was hit in the back of the head. I was on the ground and I was copping a kicking. Whatever happened to 'never hit a man when he's down', a code that we grew up with in Australia? Apparently there was a new set of rules.

I was trying to cover up as best I could. I could hear them almost baying, "Pull his hands down, pull his hands down," as they tried to get a clearer shot at my head.

It seemed to go on forever then they finally moved off. "That'll teach ya ... smart arse," one called back.

I started to get up and one came running back at me. I stood there swaying. He was small and skinny and I thought, "This is the runt of the litter trying to get a reputation." He looked into my eyes and thought better of it. He just yelled something at me and ran to join his mates. My head was swimming; I staggered over to the hedge and was violently sick.

I found a tap and washed my face and checked myself for damage; torn shirt, the knee out of my jeans and bloody. There were a lot of lumps and skin missing on the side of my head and my back felt as if it was going to snap. I was able to walk OK, so I knew it couldn't be too bad.

I walked back to the main street and caught a cab home.

I woke in the morning to Ralph in the opposite bed looking at me. "Col ... what the ..."

I told him of the night's adventures and he explained how things had changed.

That's when I found out these arseholes were called Sharpies.

The next week or so went by and my scrapes were starting to fade.

Ralph's band was playing the Havana Coffee Lounge in Dandenong and I said I would meet the guys there.

I walked up the street towards the coffee lounge. It was upstairs and there was a crowd of people grouped around the entrance. As

I got closer I spotted the 'runt' of the litter first and then the rest. Bugger, "here we go again," I thought, "I can't catch a break."

"Hey smart arse, back for more?" the leader said, more of a statement than a question. The rest started to close in. These jerks had the routine down pat. This time I maneuvered my back to the wall thinking "at least there won't be any surprises" ... then I heard Ralph's voice.

"What's going on Donnie?" he asked of the leader.

"This smart arse here needs another lesson," he said.

"Col, do you need a lesson?" Ralph asked, and then, "Oh Donnie this is my brother Col, just home on leave from the Navy."

Then Donnie was sitting on the footpath holding his head wondering what had happened. The band members were cleaning up his mates ... and oh yes, I managed to foot the runt up the arse as he turned to run. It would have been more effective had I been wearing a pair of their type of boots!

As luck would have it, Pam Bryce, a singer and one of our gang, was having a break downstairs. She saw what was unfolding and raced up and told the boys, "Col's in trouble."

They were in the middle of a set; but they 'downed tools' and headed downstairs.

I have known Pam since I was a kid. She went on to entertain in Vietnam and our daughters have all grown up together. I am Godfather to her eldest daughter Christie. Our families have shared many wonderful times together. In later years Pam and her husband Peter (a drummer) toured with me.

Pam tells this same Sharpie story but according to her it happened every weekend. Pam, it only happened once ... fair dinkum, but I love your enthusiasm.

After leave, I headed back to Sydney to HMAS Watson. I began my branch course in under water control, as a sonar operator. I would be working with the latest technology in detection of submarines. I was excited to start the course.

We were taught how to use a Bathythermograph, a bomb-looking device that measures temperature against depth. It gives a reading of the different temperature layers in the water and is a good indicator of how the sonar beam will bend in the different layers.

We also learnt how to operate and maintain depth-sounding equipment, and the workings of our latest torpedoes, and of course how to detect and track submarines.

It was a fairly intense course but I enjoyed it immensely.

When I had completed my course I was promoted to Able Seaman/U.C. (under water control). Finally I was starting to get somewhere.

At that stage I had been in the Navy for nearly two and a half years.

I was notified that I would be drafted to HMAS Stuart, a river class destroyer escort. I wouldn't be leaving Watson for another month or so as she was still up top (South East Asia).

In the mean time I would be on the gangway, watch-keeping. My job was to check ID's and general security work at the main entrance to the Base.

The gangway staff consisted of me as Bosun's mate and a Leading Seaman as Quartermaster; my immediate boss.

I accepted the situation. I mean there was no choice. You did what you were told — no questions asked.

The job itself wasn't hard, just boring at times, but I contented myself with the fact that it wouldn't be for long. I was going back to sea and looked forward to that.

To my surprise I was reunited with my old boss from the Hobart, Leading Seaman Martino.

Marty and I had been thrown together as gangway staff in all the Asian ports we had visited, while we were having our breaks from the gun-line in Vietnam. I was his Bosun's 'chop' (Bosun's mate).

Marty had, at that stage been in the Navy for sixteen years and worked in under water weapons. He had taken me under his wing. He had been my mentor, my sea 'Daddy' and was one of the nicest men I had ever met. He treated me with respect. We had become great mates. He was also a very funny bloke with a quirky sense of humour. He was a big fan of country music and we kept each other amused.

Marty taught me how to work the system and to have fun at the same time. He was a wealth of information; a great story teller. I learnt more about the Navy from this man than anyone else.

## 'PRETEND' SAILORS

On Thursday nights the Reserves would infiltrate the Base. They were what were known as 'weekend warriors'. Once a week they would gather, and play 'pretend sailors'.

The trouble was that they would have a brass band to march to on the parade ground and God they made a huge racket.

The members of the Reserves were civilians during the day but come Thursday night, bank clerks or a postmen could don uniforms and become Commanders or Captains. They would march the rank and file Reserve sailors around and around the parade ground. It was a bit like dress-up for them.

Most had never set foot on a ship and it used to rankle many of the ship's company. Standing orders stated that we had to salute their officers. It got up our noses. We felt they hadn't earned the right.

The biggest problem was that the parade ground was beside the accommodation blocks and the poor sailors who were on board couldn't sleep or even watch TV. Thursday nights were painful.

There was one 'would-be' who believed he was a real Commander and would strut about trying to be seen. He would often come to the Base early, so he could walk around and be saluted by the ship's company. It was quite pathetic and became a bit of a joke amongst the regular sailors. He would try and push the point to the gangway staff, especially if he was trying to impress someone in the car with him. Marty and I were getting quite incensed with this bloke. We hadn't long been back from the gun-line and here is this guy pushing our buttons; a civilian at that. He was a postal employee during the day.

As a car approached the entrance to the Base, my job was to check their ID, before letting them in. If it was an officer I would approach the vehicle and say "Good evening sir, may I see your ID please?" I would check the card. If their ID was verified, I would then stand aside, come to attention, salute and let them pass. Standard procedure.

This pretend officer would approach and before I would utter a word he would start to dress me down ... "Straighten your cap sailor," or, "Stand properly to attention when you're addressing a senior officer," or something else as ludicrous. He would do his best to intimidate. It was all I could do to contain myself, but I would ignore his comments until he produced the ID card and then, and only then, would I act on his order. This wasn't what he wanted. He was trying to impress and all he could get out of me was "ID please sir" ... them's the rules, as they say.

One night this Commander duly arrived at the gangway. He had his lady friend with him and had been invited to a dining-in night at the wardroom with our fair dinkum officers. We had been sending officers from our ships, visiting vessels and Navy Bases up to the wardroom all night. It was a huge affair.

The Commander turned up resplendent in his best uniform; his lady friend dripping in jewellery.

I stepped in front of the car "Good evening sir, may I see your ID?"

"You know who I am sailor, now move aside." he interrupted.

"I repeat sir, may I see your ID?"

He was now losing it big time and at the same time fumbling for his wallet, mumbling "Oh, for God's sake."

He produced his wallet and began a frantic search to find his elusive Reserve ID card ... guess what? ... It wasn't there!

"Bingo," I thought. "Excuse me sir," said I. "I will need to confer with the Quartermaster." With that, I hailed Marty.

"What seems to be the problem Able Seaman?" Marty enquired of me as he approached; a mischievous twinkle in his eye.

"It seems the gentleman here has no ID, Quartermaster," I said.

"You know who I am Quartermaster; now let me through," said the shaking Commander.

"I do apologise sir, but without an ID card that is quite impossible. Now if you could turn your car around sir and clear the Base it would be most appreciated," Marty said in the most dulcet tones.

"I DEMAND TO SEE THE OFFICER OF THE DAY," the Commander yelled.

"Quite impossible sir," Marty rounded, "he is at a wardroom function tonight and has left strict instructions not to be disturbed unless it is urgent naval business. If you have no ID sir, then this obviously is not naval business."

"I KNOW WHERE HE IS. I AM INVITED," he shouted back.

"Please remove your vehicle from the Base sir, or I will be forced to call the Naval Police," Marty said a little more forcefully.

The Commander screeched his tyres doing his U-turn and headed back down the hill.

"Enjoy the rest of your evening sir," was Marty's passing shot.

We were absolutely falling about when the phone rang. It was the Officer of the Day wanting an explanation as to what was going on. He wasn't happy.

Our 'mate', had gone down the hill and rang through to the wardroom from a pay phone outside the Base.

"He is coming back up Quartermaster, now you let him in ... got it?" said the Officer of the Day.

"Aye aye sir," Marty said ... and then to me — "as long as he's got an ID Card."

The car pulled up again, the Commander wound his window down and smirked at me.

Marty was next to me. "ID please sir," he said.

"THE OFFICER OF THE DAY TOLD YOU TO LET ME IN," he yelled back in pure frustration.

"Yes sir, he did, but I am sure he meant if you produce your ID," said Marty.

"I HAVENT GOT IT WITH ME AND…"

"I know that sir," Marty interrupted "this seems to be our problem, doesn't it"…

I noted the tad of condescension in Marty's voice.

"I DEMAND TO SEE THE OFFICER OF THE DAY," the Commander screamed.

"Impossible, I am afraid sir, he is at a wardroom function tonight and …"

The tyres screeched again as the Commander sped away.

Ten minutes later, the Officer of the Day, a young Sub Lieutenant, came down to the gangway obviously a little emotional. Marty was armed with the standing orders. "If you could look here sir…paragraph 4 page …"

"I know what standing orders state Martino." He was yelling as he strode away … just a little rattled.

Marty was threatened with retaliation the next day. It never came about. We did however hear through the grapevine that the young 'Subbie' received a severe reprimand for trying to contravene standing orders and trying to enforce an illegal order.

As Marty said, "They make the rules, just follow the prompts."

As for the Commander, well he kept pretty much out of our way from then on.

Marty taught me how to work the system.

Marty went on to serve a total of thirty-eight years in the Navy. He became a very senior Warrant officer and commanded huge respect in the RAN. He is now seventy six and we still re-enact the gangway routine at our reunions. It gets better every year.

## BACK TO SEA

I joined HMAS Stuart, a great ship and a great crew. I was reunited with mates from Leeuwin and new ones that I had completed my branch course with. I settled into the routine quickly and was given

Quarterdeck as my part of ship. This meant that the aft area of the ship would be where I worked on a daily basis.

The only real difference from being an Able Seaman (my new rank) and being an Ordinary Seaman was about $10 a week. The work was the same but you were treated as a professional instead of an apprentice. It was a happier existence all round.

Once again I revelled in being at sea.

It wasn't long before we were sent to the Far East. It was always exciting and in no time at all these exotic ports became like a home away from home to us.

It was about this time that I was messing about with a guitar.

Russ Le-Cren, a Leading Coxswain, had the bunk below mine. He played flamenco guitar and was a very gifted musician. He could play some mean rock and roll if we could 'con' him into it, but was of the opinion that anything but flamenco was not much of a challenge. I know of 'musoes' now that have that attitude. I guess it's fanaticism for a certain genre.

Russ gave me a few basic guitar lessons and I was away. What a great way to idle away the time at sea. Music ... I began to explore.

I enjoyed learning new songs and it was good that I did, because if you lingered too long on the same song there was a strong possibility you might end up wearing the guitar. Sixty blokes living in a small space does pose some 'in-your-face' type problems. I needed to be flexible with my practice times and what I was playing.

I started to write parodies to amuse my ship mates; it kept boredom at bay.

Before too long, a few like-minded souls and I formed a little group, Billy Binns, a fellow Messmate came up with our name. We became The New Nee Soon City Ramblers Jug and Jazz Band. We figured we wouldn't need a big set to open with ... just our intro would take a bit of time. Nee Soon was the village just outside HMS

Terror, the English Navy Base where we were berthed. It was about twenty five miles from Singapore.

We played everything from the Coney Island Washboard Roundup Blues, to Who put the Sand in the Vaseline, (a tear-jerker that I had been working on while on watch).

The whole idea of the group came about because we only got paid fortnightly.

We were all payday 'Barons', which meant when we were in port, we would spend up big-time for the first three days of the fortnight and virtually be broke till the next pay day. We figured if we had a band, we could play in the bars and would get paid in grog, mainly on off-pay weeks.

The group could swell from three members to ten, depending on who was desperate and broke at the time. The only requirement was you had to contribute musically in some form to the band.

Truth was you could count yourself in if you could hum and stand up.

We had at any given time, electric-comb, Mess deck spoons, home-made soap-box bass, and a wash-board which still had the Navy markings from a safety plaque that used to reside in the engine room. We had a guitar, a ukulele, a jug and various vocalists who became more vocal as the gig wore on.

We played all through the far east, Singapore, Hong Kong, Kuala Lumpur, Penang ... no port missed this unstoppable musical phenomenon.

We would get permission from the 'Mamma San' in any given bar that we deigned worthy and set up in the corner.

The deal was we would play to whatever customers they had, for free drinks and the occasional dim sim. If we could con the customers into buying the drinks, so much the better.

We operated a little bit like the bar girls, except we didn't get screwed ... well at least I know I didn't.

It was a win-win situation until we were all too pissed to play, but what top nights they were.

In between numbers, I would do a bit of patter, tell a gag or generally take the piss. On reflection, it was a great learning-ground.

At the time, I never thought that I would draw on those great nights and eventually it would lead me into a career as an entertainer.

We had been in Penang for six days and it was off-pay week. We had a large amount of band members in the corner of the bar where we were playing. The night was really starting to get underway. There were a few Yank ships in and some Air force blokes and their wives from the Butterworth Air Force Base. We had played in the bar for two nights and the word had spread. The joint was nearly full. The Mamma San was all smiles and giving us little nibblies. The grog was coming thick and fast ... and free.

## THE NEW BAND MEMBER

During the break, an American in civilian clothes came up and told us how much of a good time he was having. His name was Dick Beck. It turned out he wasn't a serviceman. He told us he was a teacher and that he was based in Bangkok and was having a little time off. He'd never been to Penang before and was enjoying his stay. He was heading back to Thailand in a few days.

The band adopted him. He sang with us and laughed along with us and said he had never experienced anything like this before. He played guitar and sang some great songs. We enjoyed his input and his company. We took him all over Penang in the next few nights; mind you he didn't party as hard as we did. He was a little more conservative.

Try as he might, 'Red' Johansen, our jug player tried to line him up with some of the bar girls but Dick would just say, "I'll wait in the bar with the other guys, you go ahead Red."

"You don't know what you're missing." Red would say as he sauntered off with one of the girls. Dick just laughed and waved him off.

Dick was from Wisconsin and had been teaching in Bangkok for three years. He could speak Thai and Tagalog, which is the dialect of the Philippines. He said he loved his work, but in another two years he would go back to the States.

Eventually we had to say goodbye to our new-found friend. We exchanged postal addresses and told him we would visit him when we hit Bangkok. What a top fella.

About three months later we anchored at Pattaya, near Bangkok. A bunch of us went ashore and headed for the capital. We would surprise Dick.

We had his school's address.

When we arrived at the school, we found the administration office and asked the young receptionist if we could see Dick. She made a phone call and spoke in Thai, then turned to us and said, "He will be over very shortly."

We were offered a drink of some sort and sat down to wait for Dick.

The office door opened, Red exclaimed ... "Jesus Christ". There stood Father Dick Beck in the robes of a priest.

I was, at first gobsmacked, then Dick looked at me and said, "How's it going Mohawk?"

Red was beside himself. He had been brought up as a strict Catholic and he looked like he was about to break into a few Hail Mary's.

Dick hadn't lied to us ... he was a teacher ... he just omitted the fact that he was a priest.

I am not religious and have never been, but Red's reaction was a sight to behold. The closest I came to religion was when Ralph and I became Young Soldiers at our local Salvation Army Group. We only signed up because after the service they let us go in the back room and play their drums.

I was ten and Ralph twelve.

We were thrown out of the Salvos because we collected beer bottles and the Major said we were making money from sin.

He gave us a choice at the time, God or beer bottles, ... it was a 'no brainer'… the bottles were paying. To a ten year old, God took a back seat.

Anyway, getting back to Dick Beck.

By the time he had consoled Red and told him he wouldn't burn in the fires of hell, I was starting to see the funny side of it all.

As Dick said, had we had known he was a priest, the fun would have stopped. He was dead right.

I know I would have changed the song list out of pure respect.

'How can I say I love you, when I can't breathe down here', would have probably been replaced with 'Blowin' in the wind' or something less confronting.

Dick went and changed into civvies and gave us a tour of the school, which in fact doubled as an orphanage.

The little kids just hung off Dick; clearly he was loved by them.

As we walked I felt a little hand slip into mine, I looked down to see the biggest brown eyes. She was about four and she stuck close as we walked. I looked around and noticed the other guys were being chaperoned as well.

That afternoon Dick took us into Bangkok for a feed. Red couldn't eat and was the quietest I had ever seen him.

A few days later our ship hosted a day for the kids. The skipper thought it was a great idea and the crew was fantastic. The cooks outdid themselves and made all sorts of treats for them. We thought they had been holding back on us!

Sailors took kids all over the ship and Dick was over the moon.

We caught up with Dick once more the next year, then he went back to the States. We wrote a few times and then lost track.

I have never forgotten this special man.

We arrived in Hong Kong — it was 1968 and still under British rule.

Hong Kong was ceded to Britain in 1841 and wouldn't return to Chinese control until 1997. Even then it retained its status as a free port and a capitalist enclave.

The British influence was everywhere back then. It was always a great place to pull into. We would hit downtown Wan Chai, a favourite district with all the sailors from visiting nations. It was the poorer side of town; street stalls, bars and short time hotels.

It seemed we were always broke. I guess we ran too hard and never made our money go the distance. One of the bars we hung out in was the Susie Wong bar and I tumbled onto a great way to drink for free. I still feel a little ashamed of this but ...hey, it was a long time ago. The statute of limitations must surely be up.

The bar itself was famous in its own right, as it had been used as the location in the 1960 movie starring William Holden and Nancy Kwan, *The world of Susie Wong*.

There was always a good crowd in there and it was a 'must go and visit' bar to the Yanks when they hit port.

The American sailors were under a totally different system to us. They would only be given their pay when they hit port. These guys were always loaded.

One night I was at the bar ordering a beer. I was charged $1 Hong Kong. The Yank sailor standing beside me bought the same beer for $2 Hong Kong. He was oblivious to what had just occurred. He walked away and I asked the girl behind the bar, "How come?"

"Yank have more money than Aussie ... he pay more," was all she said.

Red and I introduced ourselves to the Yank and his mate and got into a shout with them. We worked the scam ...

We always made sure we actually went up and got the beers.

Four beers $4 ... their shout, four beers $8. We pocketed the extra $4 and that paid for our shout.

We weren't actually stealing. I mean they would have paid $2 a beer anyway. They had the benefit of our great company ... cheap at half the price.

I have tried to justify this for all these years ... I can't, it was wrong and I still carry the guilt ... thieving little bastard Col.

In Hong Kong, there is a huge amount of tailors. There still is today.

The competition is tremendous and when we walked into a shop the service was way over the top.

Many of the sailors would do a 'tailor' run.

As you walked into the shop you would be sat down and offered a beer.

Then they would start to show you swatches and fabric, all the time trying to get you to commit to having something made.

By the time you reached the end of the street you might have visited a dozen shops and were getting a little tanked.

This in itself was OK but I always started to feel terribly guilty and after a dozen beers or so I would start to order stuff. Dinner suits, new uniforms, silk shirts etc. This was great for my conscience but when the tailors turned up at the ship a few days later ...

I looked so good in all my finery but I couldn't go ashore, the new threads cost me a fortune ... I was broke. We would invariably have a band meeting!

One particular night I ordered a set of bells (bell bottom trousers).

When the tailor brought them to the ship we all cracked up.

Instead of the pockets being in a flap at the waist in front, there were two pockets in the knees. I must have been pissed and confused the poor little bugger when I was describing what I wanted. I must have touched my knees sometime during the initial order.

I none the less paid him and we hung them up in the Mess as a warning not to be too demonstrative at the tailors.

HMS Tamar was the British Naval Base in Hong Kong. We came under their jurisdiction while we were there. We shared facilities and they had their Naval Police patrolling and maintaining order in the port. Often we would send two sailors over to assist in Shore Patrol duties, especially when there were a good number of ships in port.

It was a Friday and my mate Dan Sheldon (Shellie) and I were very surprised to see our names down for Shore Patrol duties. Whoever put us together on that duty roster wasn't paying attention, or they weren't playing with a full deck.

We couldn't believe it actually was written on Daily Orders; Able Seaman Elliott, Able Seaman Sheldon ... Shore Patrol. Surely they would rescind this duty call.

*Band practice "Navy style"*

*A reunion with Marty Martino — what a team*

*HMAS Stuart*

## NOT A GOOD CALL

They wouldn't send two rogues like us out on Shore Patrol together. We were usually brought home by Shore Patrol.

Shellie and I were party buddies … not to be put together in a situation like this.

We sweated all day and no one picked up this obvious mistake.

At 1600 hours, we left the ship to report to the regulating office at HMS Tamar. So far so good!

We were given white gaiters (ankle webbing), webbing belt, MP arm bands (Military Police) and a truncheon each.

We were told the area of patrol in Wan Chai and a briefing on protocol by their Duty Chief. We were told to call in every hour on the radio.

Then to our utter amazement he threw a set of jeep keys to Shellie. "You ok to drive?" he asked. "No problem Chief," said Shellie.

We floated out the door, all the time waiting for someone to yell out, "Ok you two, back to the ship, it was just a joke."

We headed down Hennessey Road into Wan Chai. We drove around a bit to savour the moment. We couldn't believe our luck. It was a sweet duty. After the first hour, we reported in over the radio. We thought we would stretch our legs. We headed into a bar. The Mamma San rushed up with two beers. They wanted to keep the Shore Patrol happy and it was good for business. Of course we were on duty and couldn't drink ... but hey, a beer each won't hurt.

After we reported in for the third time we were 'lit up'. A bar girl had my hat and arm band on. Shellie was dancing on a table with another girl, the truncheon between his legs, doing some dirty dancing moves and laughing. We couldn't remember where we last parked the jeep and I don't remember much after that. When they eventually found the jeep up an alley, the wheels and Base radio were gone, as were the seats; basically it was a shell.

The English Shore Patrol found us two hours later and we woke up in the 'slammer' at Tamar ... back on chooks. We shared the cost of the radio and wheels (two each). Shellie buried us deeper when he asked if it were possible to get three quotes for the tyres and seats.

It wasn't all 'beer and skittles' in the Far East. We were there for a reason. We operated with many other nations in joint exercises. Our presence was part of our Government's commitment to our security at the time. Officially we were on Far East Strategic Reserve. We were stationed in the area in case politically things flared up again. It was eight years after the Malaysian emergency which went from 1948 to 1960. Things were still a little delicate.

We spent a fair bit of our time at sea and were kept in a high degree of readiness so we tended to go for it when we hit port.

I wasn't the only Aussie sailor that took every opportunity to keep the party going.

At one time our ship had to leave port with crew still ashore in Hong Kong.

When a typhoon warning was given, all ships had to be ready to put to sea at a moment's notice. The rationale being that if ships were left in port, they could break their moorings and do immense damage drifting aimlessly within the harbour.

As I remember on this occasion, there were 7 or 8 Yank warships in port, three of which were Carriers, all on R and R (rest and relaxation). That meant up to 10 to 15,000 American sailors roaming the bars and streets. Add to that, 2 British anti-submarine frigates and ourselves, each carrying around 230 personnel.

The typhoon was building and heading towards Hong Kong. The standard warnings were put up around the city to warn the populace of the imminent danger. Yank Shore Patrols were out in force, ordering their sailors to get back on board and suggesting to us we might need to do the same.

The fleet of warships put to sea ... the 'wash up' was not one Yank sailor was left behind; the Brits left three. Surprise, surprise, 70 Aussie sailors from our ship; that's a third of our crew, went missing.

"I was asleep sir," was the standard reply ... no charges laid.

I rode out three typhoons in my time. It's very scary stuff. I had been caught on board on each occasion and never got to run with the boys ... bugger!

I guess I was one of the, shall we say more active members of the crew, but we were young and life was one big adventure. Our energy was boundless.

As far as my work on board was concerned, I was on the ball and applied myself to the job I was involved with in under-water control.

The stories I relate in this memoir occurred over a period of the seven years that I served in the RAN. What I am saying is, they didn't all happen at once. If that were the case, I would still be in the slammer!

They were my formative years and the memories are still vivid.

It was a huge part of my life and the lessons I learned became a definitive part of who I am today.

While in the Far East, we made our presence known and visited many ports. One of the most interesting ports of call was in Japan.

I went to Japan four times over the years and each time I found it to be more intriguing. I started to learn the language and culture and applied for a language course in the Navy. I was told Japanese was not in the curriculum but could study Malaysian on the course. I declined and taught myself from a book. I was becoming more fluent with each visit.

Today it's all but gone. Like they say, 'use it or lose it'.

I visited the war museum in Hiroshima and it had a profound effect on me. The graphic detail I found there was horrifying.

In July 1945, the American President, Harry S Truman and the allied leaders issued the Potsdam Declaration, outlining their terms of surrender for Japan. It was an ultimatum. Months earlier, Germany had capitulated and the war in Europe was over.

The Japanese were a fanatical enemy and ignored the ultimatum.

This fanaticism shown by the Japanese was being felt by the allied nations. Anti-Japanese sentiment was running high.

The Japanese military were brutal and had an horrific reputation for committing atrocities, not only on their prisoners but also civilians of the many areas of occupation.

It was hard to believe these same gentle, polite people that I encountered on my visits were of the same race.

Hiroshima was bombed on August 6th. This was followed by Nagasaki on August 9th.

These two events are the only time nuclear weapons have been used in history. Let's hope and pray it is the last.

Japan surrendered on August 15th, thereby ending the war in the Pacific and therefore WW2.

It was estimated that 90,000 to 160,000 died in Hiroshima and 60,000 to 80,000 in Nagasaki.

Half the people in both these cities died on the first day. Some died weeks later from burns and injuries. Many died years later from the effects of radiation-sickness and cancer.

The justification and the ethical question of these events are still being debated today.

Most of the people that died were civilians ... it's always the way.

## MY SHOUT, 'RALPHIE'

We had spent about seven months in the Far East; it was time to head back home. Two weeks later we were back alongside in Sydney and due for a bit of leave. I had planned to go home for a week to see Mum and then head back to Sydney and stay with one of my mates.

Mum had written to me every Sunday night while I was overseas. She never missed. Every now and then there was a scrawled note tacked on the end of Mum's letter from my father wanting me to pick up something or other. That was the only contact I had with him.

My brother Ralph and I had written to each other often. He was now in the Army, a Rifleman. He had finished 'boot camp' at Puckapunyal in Victoria, then his infantry course at Singleton NSW. He then completed jungle training at Canungra in Queensland.

He described the Canungra course, saying it was the toughest thing he had done in his life ... many didn't get through. He was now with 1RAR.

Next stop for my 'bro' was Vietnam.

Back on the old Southern Aurora heading back to Melbourne, we travelled in uniform and sat in compartments of six, sitting up all night. It always reminded me of the interior of a western stage coach, three either side facing each other.

We had boarded the train at 4pm. It was around 10 that night, my mates were still having a few drinks, and some were trying to catch a little sleep.

There were two luggage racks in each cabin and we would toss for them. The routine some adopted was to take a sleeping pill, down half a bottle of rum, climb up on the rack, stretch out and the next thing you know you're in Melbourne. That is if you didn't fall out ... it was a long drop.

I had scored a rack and was just contemplating my next move when I heard my name being called "Elliott ... Elliott".

"In here," I called.

Two soldiers appeared at our door "Sorry mate," one said, noticing my uniform, "we're looking for a soldier."

"Ok mate," I said. "My name's Elliott ... I've got a brother in the Army."

"Funny," said one, "Ralph's got a brother in the Navy."

"You blokes are 1RAR," I said ... "Where is the bastard?"

"Bloody hell, that's the problem," one said ... "we were all on the 'turps' this afternoon, now we can't find him. We think he might have fallen off the train."

We bolted from the cabin and spread out trying to find Ralph. Soldiers and sailors in a combined joint operation combed every nook and cranny of the train. We picked up more recruits from both forces as we searched. I got in touch with the conductor; he was in the process of stopping the train.

"Where was his cabin?" I asked his mate.

He took me there, I looked in, and it was empty. I was just about to leave and I heard a groan. I looked up and there he was, on the luggage rack; the top of his head poking out from under an Army great-coat.

"Rozzer," I yelled, giving him a shake at the same time.

He started to turn over and his wallet fell to the floor. I picked it up and stuck it in my pocket. I would give it to him later.

The conductor appeared at the door, clearly flustered. He had just about had enough of both Forces. He had been stopped just in time and was told all was OK.

"I was just told that you have found the missing soldier," he said.

"Who's missing?" Ralph asked as he climbed down from the rack.

"Doesn't matter mate," I said as I manoeuvred the conductor into the hallway.

The conductor definitely needed pacifying.

"If I have any more trouble from any of you, I will put you all off the train at the next stop, so help me," the conductor lectured.

"I've got it all under control sir," I said, "trust me".

He strode away mumbling to himself; turned around to say something else; changed his mind and walked on. All I caught was "useless bastards", then he was gone.

I turned back to the cabin; Ralph sat with his head in his hands.

We spent the next couple of hours catching up. We then grabbed a little sleep before the train pulled into Melbourne.

A bunch of us headed for the 'early openers'. The public bar was full. It was 8.30 am. I got the first shout and realised I still had Ralph's wallet. I had a sneaky look inside; there must have been about $500 in it. That was a lot of 'dough' in those days. It was to last him a month on leave.

At first I thought I would just see how long it took him to realise it was gone but the next shout came and his mate picked that up. Then someone else grabbed the next shout. Blokes began to peel off and Ralph still hadn't had a shout.

Then we decided to go ... goodbyes all round.

"Catch you after leave fellas," Ralph called to his mates.

Ralph and I headed to the station to get the train home to Dandenong.

He still hadn't twigged.

"I'll get the tickets mate, you get the cab fare home," I said.

"Fair enough," said Ralph, and we jumped on the train.

We got off at Dandenong and headed over to the cab rank.

Ralph jumped in the front, he was paying. I got in the back and we headed home.

We pulled up outside of home. I got out quick so as to give him a bit more pain before I came clean about the wallet.

I was on the verandah looking down at him trying to find his wallet and at the same time explaining to the impatient cabbie that all was OK.

I was enjoying this immensely.

He looked up at me, panic on his face ... "Col, can you fix the cab mate, I can't seem to find my wallet, it's probably in my bag. I'll fix you up when we get inside."

"Sure mate," I said, "go in, I'll fix it."

Ralph headed up the steps; by this time Mum was there to greet him. I paid the cab ... out of his wallet.

"I'll tell him when I get in," I thought, laughing to myself.

We got inside and he was going through his bag, moaning ... I thought, "I'll keep this going just a little longer."

That 'little longer' went on for three days. I shouted beers, Chinese food, the movies ... bloody hell, I even shouted him a pair of trousers ... all out of his wallet.

Ralph kept telling me how grateful he was and what a great brother I was and that he would pay me back. "I'll never forget this mate," he kept saying ... I was sure he wouldn't.

By the fourth morning I had wrung every bit of fun out of the situation. He was planning to go back into Melbourne and see the Army about money and new ID cards. I left his wallet next to his bag on his bed. It looked like it had fallen out somehow. He would think he hadn't searched the bag properly. He called me into the bedroom and started to tell me the good news ... then he looked up at my laughing face ..., the comprehension took a little while until he checked the contents ... minus $150!

I laughed so hard it hurt. We were both hysterical. I think he was laughing out of sheer relief.

When we went to bed at night for the next week we would say, "goodnight", then silence, then one of us would giggle. This was followed by inane laughter. Mum would call out "go to sleep you silly sods," then she would start to laugh. I remember that leave so well, we laughed like we did as kids.

It was good to be back together.

We spent some great time with our brother Michael and sister Wendy while we were on leave. We took them out and generally spoilt them rotten. Mum was still doing it tough. She was made to get by on the same money even with two more kids. The old man hadn't moved from the chair but we were too big for him now ... things were different.

Ralph had taken him on at sixteen. I was there when it happened. In fact it was over me. I was wearing something of Ralph's and we were arguing. The old man stepped in and went for Ralph. Ralph grabbed his shirt front. He wrestled the old man onto the lounge chair. He held him down and told him never to touch him again. It shook the old man up. His authority had been usurped. That was the last time he ever laid a hand on either of us.

He threw Ralph out.

Ralph left for a while and stayed at a mate's place.

Eventually they buried the hatchet and Ralph came back home.

Our time at home flew by; we said our goodbyes. I wouldn't see Ralph till after Vietnam. "Keep your head down mate," I said as I jumped in the cab.

I went back to Sydney and Ralph headed back to his unit.

Not long after he got back, he was called into a meeting with one of his superior officers. He was informed that he didn't have to go to Vietnam as his younger brother had already served, so he was officially exempt. The only way he could go was to volunteer. Ralph promptly volunteered and eventually left with 1RAR on HMAS Sydney in April 1968.

## DEAR JOHN ... COL

Back on board, things were much the same, a few new faces but life on a war ship was all about routine.

Sydney is a great city to explore. Apart from the obvious hang-outs like Kings Cross which most of the sailors gravitated towards; there were some fantastic shows to see.

I would go to the Motor Club in George Street and catch the floor shows. I loved the atmosphere of a big band and a show. It stayed open till 4am.

We would go straight to breakfast from there.

Sydney was full of Yanks back then, all on R and R from Vietnam. They hit town with wads of cash. The local girls loved them; they would spend up big lavishing the girls with gifts. The lowly old Aussie sailor and soldier had no chance. It was tough enough buying ourselves a drink let alone having to buy one for a girl. We just couldn't compete.

There was a certain amount of animosity amongst our blokes towards the Yanks. It wasn't unusual for a fight to break out now and then. It added to the atmosphere. It was not of the type of violence seen today.

There was a code, respect if you will. No one would kick a man. The fight would start again when he got to his feet.

Many times it ended with drinks all round and the promise of friendship for life.

We hung out in The Bognor, The Mayfair, and The Texas tavern.

All joints were packed every night.

During my time in Sydney I took out a few girls, meeting them through mates, most times just casual dates.

Shellie was dating a girl who lived in a flat with three other girls in Balmain.

We had parties there and would generally hang out on weekends. We all eventually paired off.

It got a bit serious with Dianne the girl I had hooked up with. We talked of marriage. I bought her a ring; took her home to meet the family. My sister Carol put on a small engagement party for us.

Not long after we got back to Sydney I left for overseas; we would marry when I got home.

Two months into the trip I got a 'Dear John' letter; she was in love with someone else ... so there you go ... it wasn't meant to be.

It knocks anyone around a bit when it happens, and I felt pretty bad at the time because I was overseas and felt powerless. But as they say, 'life goes on'.

Service wives are a special breed, some cope well, others not at all. I saw some strong men totally devastated from marriage breakdowns. We had to have one sailor restrained and sedated, then flown home after his wife left with his best mate while we were in the Far East.

After witnessing that I decided I would steer clear of marriage as long as I was in the Navy.

Sometimes having a serious girlfriend back home became a little hard to deal with when we were so far away. It brought out the stupidity in Thomo one of our 'oppos' (Navy jargon for 'opposite number' or mate.)

## THE MARATHON SWIM

We were in Malaysia and a few of us smuggled some rum back on board in our socks. We headed for the forecastle and settled down amongst the anchor chains for a nightcap.

As is the case with young blokes, our conversation concentrated on women and sexual conquests.

Thomo was a little melancholy and a little drunk. He was missing his 'squarie' (girlfriend). "Another five months up here," he bemoaned, "wish I was home."

"Yeah, well, it ain't gonna' happen, so them's the breaks," someone put in.

"Reckon I could swim home from here," Thomo said.

We all laughed. He stood up and straddled the guard rail waving his rum around. "I could just drop in here and start breast stroking," he said as we egged him on to jump. "Go for it Thomo," we chorused.

"Don't reckon I'd do it, do you," said Thomo keeping it going.

"Chuck the rum over here first mate and we'll see you back in OZ," Shellie yelled.

Bugger me ... the silly bastard jumped. We waited for a splash, but instead heard a loud thump ... then a groan.

We ran to the ship's side, looked down. There was Thomo in a foetal position on top of a floating pontoon that had been tied against the side, while part of the ship was being painted.

It would have been the same as jumping off a tall house. He was lucky he didn't kill himself. Both ankles broken ... but he had the last laugh. He was flown home to Australia and into the arms of his squarie.

"Told you I was goin' home," he called to us as they carried him off the ship in a stretcher.

At least he had the manners to leave the rum!

## THE FRANK E EVANS' DISASTER

We were participating in SEATO exercises (South East Asia Treaty Organization). The exercise was named Sea Spirit. It involved 40 ships from six nations. We were behind our aircraft carrier HMAS Melbourne. Our station was as rescue destroyer. These exercises were happening about 650 miles South East of Manila in the South China Sea. It was just on pre-dawn June 3rd 1969.

I was still on watch doing the last trick as starboard lookout in the middle watch.

I had been on watch for about 15 minutes, it was about 3.15 am. The sea was calm, the night clear. We had been involved in anti-submarine training exercises. The Melbourne was about to launch Tracker aircraft. The Commander had ordered the USS. Frank E Evans, an American destroyer, to take up plane guard position on the port quarter of the carrier. The Evans had performed this manoeuvre three times previously on that same night. She was at that time positioned on the Melbourne's port bow, some 3,500 yards off; travelling parallel.

The Melbourne had all navigation lights on at full brilliance. Two nights before, there was a near collision with USS Larson, so this wasn't unusual.

The Melbourne's Commanding Officer during these exercises was Captain John Phillip Stevenson. Rear Admiral John Crabb was also aboard. He was the Flag Officer Commanding the Australian Fleet.

Before these exercises started, Commander Stevenson held a dinner for the Captains of the five operating escort destroyers.

During this briefing, he emphasised the need for caution when operating with a carrier.

He even provided written instruction on how to avoid collision.

The silence was broken by emergency station alarms being sounded and announcements for all hands on deck. Our ship was knifing through the water, closing on the Melbourne.

Someone poked their head out of the bridge door ... "She's done it again, the Melbourne's hit another ship." Then he was gone.

My recollection is of our skipper telling us over the ships PA that the USS Frank E Evans has had a collision with the Melbourne; we were going in to assist. This first announcement was lacking in detail but our sea-boats crews were at the ready as we came upon the scene. We dropped our boats.

It was an incredible sight to behold. The back half of the destroyer was being tied to the starboard side aft of the Melbourne ... its whole forward section was missing. It was hard to believe what I was witnessing. Half a ship ... gone!

Some of the Melbourne's crew had jumped in the water, helping to rescue survivors. Ship's boats were picking up men and collecting anything that still floated. Helicopters were hovering. Scrambling netting had been rigged to the side of the carrier and surviving crew from the Evans was being taken on board the Melbourne. About 100 of the Evans' crew were taken directly from what was left of their ship.

The forward section of the Evans had gone straight down on impact, killing 74 men out of a crew of 273. Many of those were badly injured. One of the worst was a Signalman who had been on top of the Evans' Bridge. He had landed on top of the Melbourne's flight deck from the impact. Searches were conducted over the next 15 hours but no more survivors were found.

After our part in the rescue, we were all assembled on our forecastle and a prayer was said. Shock is not the right word to describe what we were feeling at the time! For me, it wasn't quite two years since the Forrestal tragedy. A thought came flooding back to me ... 'Join the Navy for a life of adventure'... bloody hell!

At the time there was no such thing as counselling. These events would impact on me in years to come ... but for now, it was back to work.

This was Melbourne's second collision. In 1964 she had collided with the Voyager, a destroyer, with a loss of 82 lives.

In this, her second incident, it transpired that the Evans turned to starboard instead of port and crossed the Melbourne's bow. She was cut in half.

Just prior, Captain Stevenson sent a direct voice message to the bridge of the Evans and warned them that they were on a collision course. The Melbourne then took what avoiding action it could and radioed to the Evans that she was turning to port. The Melbourne then gave two blasts on her siren. The Evans then turned hard right under Melbourne's bow.

The Melbourne was badly holed forward of the collision bulkhead and her trim tanks were flooded. In time she was shored up and able to sail unassisted to port. She had no casualties.

The Captain of the Evans, Commander Albert S Mclemore was asleep when the collision occurred. In charge were Lieutenants Ronald Ramsey and James Hopson.

Ramsey had previously failed the qualification to stand watch and it was Hopson's first time at sea. In 1999 the Captain of the

Evans claimed responsibility for the collision, stating he had let two inexperienced officers have charge of his ship.

The subsequent court martial completely exonerated Commander Stevenson. However, the ramifications of this incident ruined Commander Stevenson's career. This innocent man paid a high price!

In 2012 the Minister of Defence sent a letter to Stevenson apologizing for the actions of the RAN and the Government of the day.

## IN THE 'SHIP' AGAIN

I noticed a difference in many of our ship's company after the Evans incident and realised later, how it affected me.

I saw more blokes wandering the passageways and upper decks later at night. Normally they would be in their bunks or down in the Mess.

I got into the habit of going up to the lookouts to check on nearby shipping. All of this was done, to my mind, casually. No one mentioned anything about being a little nervous ... it wouldn't be cool.

I did this nightly, even after I had finished my own watch, no matter what time it was. Looking back I guess it became nearly obsessive compulsive. It became part of my nightly routine.

Months later, back in Australia, many of the crew had been reposted. We were on exercises in Jervis bay. I was caught checking the starboard lookout by a young Midshipman who had just joined us in Sydney.

It was about 2100 hours (9 pm). I had finished my watch at 2000 hours (8pm).

The lookout was just starting to tell me of the ships in our vicinity, when the bridge door opened.

"What are you doing out here Able Seaman," The 'Middie' demanded.

"Just checking what's about us sir," I replied.

"You're off watch now Elliott, so clear the Bridge wing," he said in his best 'power of command' voice.

"Yes sir... I just need to check ..."

"I said clear the bridge Elliott ... now," he interjected, clearly upset that I hadn't scurried away immediately.

"Yes sir, just checking the position ..."

"MOVE IT NOW SAILOR ... I AM GIVING YOU A DIRECT ORDER". He was starting to lose it. ... So was I.

At that moment I had a panic attack, although I didn't realise it at the time. I didn't even know what one was.

All of a sudden, it was of paramount importance to me right then and there to get a detailed report of the shipping that was about us. I kept yelling at the lookout, "What's out there ... What's out there?"

All the time I'm demanding this information, quite hysterically, the Midshipman is going ballistic.

The lookout turned to me and yelled "Col ... for Christ sake let him go".

It took a few seconds for me to realise I had the Midshipman pinned by his shirt front against the Bridge door. I think his feet were dangling. He was screaming blue-murder. Another sailor forced the door open, making me let go.

I was still demanding a report from the lookout as all this was happening. He gave me a hurried brief and the next thing I knew, I was sitting on my bunk wondering what the bloody hell had just happened!

The next morning I was put on Captain's report. The book was going to be thrown at me ... I could read the fine print.

What I had just done was a Court Martial offence.

I was facing charges of disobeying a direct order and assaulting a senior officer. This was serious stuff. I could be dishonourably discharged after serving time in Holsworthy, the service's prison base. Things were certainly looking grim.

My divisional officer would talk for me as my defence council.

I figured there wasn't much he could do ... I was guilty.

"Able Seaman Elliott ... Off caps," ordered the Master at Arms.

I stood at attention before the Captain as the charges were read out.

The Midshipman gave evidence. He told it how it was. He added that the situation could have escalated had it not been for the intervention of the lookout and the Leading Seaman that came out from the bridge.

The captain dismissed the Midshipman then studied some paperwork and finally looked up at me.

"What have you to say for yourself Elliott, do you agree with this evidence?" asked the skipper.

"Yes sir, I just needed to find out what was out there, sir," I replied.

I went on to explain how it was from my side, as best I could. I added that I didn't realise I had pinned the Midshipman against the Bridge door.

I was marched out of the office, the Midshipman was recalled.

I was outside for what seemed to be quite a while and then marched before the Captain once more.

It transpired that the charges were changed to 'absent from place of duty' (my place of duty being my bunk) and tardiness in carrying out a direct order. The argument being that I did leave the Bridge wing ... eventually!

Our Captain was aware of the effect the Evans tragedy had on many of our crew. In a way he was in there batting for me.

"You weren't about to strike the Midshipman, were you Elliott?" said the skipper as more of a statement than a question. All the time he was shaking his head in the negative ever so slightly.

I took up the cue.

"No sir."

He then gave me a huge bollicking and informed me that if I pulled anything like this again I would end up 'up the river'.

I also received a month's stoppage of leave and 14 days chooks.

This was the closest I got to counselling ... how times have changed!

We had a few more months left in Sydney, then the Stuart would go into re-fit at the Williamstown dockyards in Melbourne. All the Victorian natives were looking forward to it, me included.

## HERE WE GO AGAIN ... MORE 'SHIP'

In the meantime I had a letter from my brother Ralph telling me of his flight details. He had finished his tour of Vietnam and was on his way home.

I picked him up at the airport, grabbed his bag and we headed for town.

I had booked us a couple of bunks at 'Johnnies' (Royal Navy House). It was cheap accommodation for sailors. We dropped our gear in and headed for the Motor club.

We had a lot of catching up to do and we talked on into the night. I guess in a way it was good to be able to converse on a different level. We both had been through enough to understand that we would perceive life a little differently than before. We were able to relate.

As the night progressed, we once again began to laugh. We were enjoying our brief time together. Until disaster struck ... I couldn't believe it ... Ralph had lost his wallet! It was fair dinkum this time. I had to stake him. At first I thought it was payback but no... it was gone.

Early morning we headed for Kings Cross and breakfast. We headed back to Johnny's at 6am. I told the guy at the desk to wake me at 7am; my ship sailed at 8am. Ralph would get some more money from the Army offices in town when they opened and catch his flight to Melbourne mid-morning.

We awoke at 10am. My ship had sailed ... bugger, here we go again.

I woke Ralph and said I would figure something out. My ship wasn't due back till the following Monday. I gave him what money I could spare.

We said our goodbyes and I sat at a coffee shop to consider my next move.

Ah ha ... I had an epiphany.

This was crazy enough to work.

I had the key to a girlfriend's flat. I rang her at work and told her my dilemma and my plan. She gave me permission to go to the flat.

A twenty minute cab ride and I was sitting on her lounge ... part A complete ... time for part B.

In my best Cockney accent (thanks Mum), I rang HMAS Penguin the Navy Base at Balmoral. I spoke to the Officer of the day. I told him that I lived next door to where a young sailor was staying and it seems he had food poisoning or something similar. Apparently he had missed his ship, HMAS Stuart. Could someone make arrangements to have him picked up and taken to the naval hospital at the Base?

I must say that I was very impressed with the officer's manners as he profusely thanked the 'Cockney gentleman' and assured him that he would attend to it right away. I made a mental note to write to his superior officer and give praise.

I rubbed my eyes to make them as red as possible, stripped down to my jocks, got a pillow, a blanket and laid on the couch and waited.

If I could pull this off, not only would I NOT be charged for being adrift but I might even receive an Academy Award nomination.

A Navy ambulance pulled up outside. Two SBAs (Sick Berth Attendants) headed for the door and knocked.

"Come in," I said in my sickest voice.

When they appeared, I knew both of them. One was a mate from Leeuwin and the other served on the Sydney with me.

"Mohawk ... you're crook mate ... what's up?" one said.

I couldn't fool my mates, so I told them what I had done.

We laughed for a while then headed for the pub; two beers each then on to Penguin.

On the way they told me there were two cases of gastroenteritis in the base hospital and what symptoms I should display.

I was booked in, put to bed and told a doctor would be in to see me within the hour. Meanwhile they needed a stool sample as the Duty Petty officer suspected gastroenteritis.

My mates obtained the appropriate samples from the other fair dinkum patients and I awaited the Lieutenant Doctor.

I was examined and guess what ... I had gastroenteritis ... bugger ... just my bad luck I guess.

I was put on liquids so I would sneak into the galley and have a feed before the food came around.

I laid low for a couple of days but was making a good recovery by the Thursday and pronounced fit to return to duties by Friday.

I asked the doctor if I could go ashore for the weekend then report back to my ship when she returned to harbour on Monday.

"Why not," he said. "A signal has been sent to your ship ... and don't forget to take these medical reports with you."

"Aye aye sir," I replied, "thank you."

Just before I stepped ashore, I called in to the 'Pay Bob' (pay master) to get an advance on my next pay. It would get me through the weekend.

At 8am on the Monday I was at Garden Island dockyard, watching my ship tie up alongside.

I could clearly see Shellie grinning at me. He made a sign of throat cutting and kept grinning.

The gangway hit the dock; I was up it like a shot ... turned to the Quarterdeck and saluted. I then went below decks to the Coxswain's office and gave him my medical reports.

With a wry smile on his face he asked if my brother got away alright.

"Yes Chief," I said wondering how much he knew ... or was he just fishing?

"Carry on Elliott," he said, and turned back to his office shaking his head.

Shellie was so disappointed ... I didn't tell him for months ... he had such a big mouth.

133

We arrived in Melbourne, our ship went into dry dock and we were quartered on HMAS Quickmatch a Q class destroyer. She had a proud history fighting the Japanese during WW2. Ironically she was sold to the Japs for scrap in 1972.

The Quickmatch had been paid off to reserve in 1963. There wasn't much left of her but they had stuck in a few bunks.

It was winter and we had no real heating save a few bar heaters, but we only really slept onboard if we were duty ... or broke. Shellie and I slept on her quite a bit.

Shellie and I were assigned to repaint the lagging that covered the hot steam pipes and fuel lines throughout the Stuart. This entailed scraping the old flaky paint, repairing, then re-spraying ... they were all asbestos ... we were exposed to the deadly dust.

Asbestos was used in warships from the 1940s through to the early '70s.

Originally asbestos seemed ideal as it was corrosion proof and heat resistant. It has since been found to cause cancer Mesothelioma, lung cancer, pleural Mesothelioma, and pleural plaques, a precursor to other asbestos related diseases.

I was diagnosed with pleural plaques three years ago. Touch wood, it hasn't progressed. Back then we didn't know ... or they weren't letting on.

## SHORT BACK AND SIDES

It was a Friday night; both Shellie and I were stuck on board. Shellie's Mum lived in Glen Waverly forty minutes away, but we couldn't even scrape up the train fare.

I was lying on my bunk reading a Larry and Stretch Western. Shellie was playing solitaire. The Mess door opened and in walked six brand spanking new ODs ... straight out of recruit school.

They had been on a month's leave, after doing their three months recruit training at Cerberus and had been drafted to the Stuart.

"Hi sir," one said, "the Coxswain told us to find a bunk in this mess, is that OK?"

"Sure mate," Shellie said, "but we are Able seamen, not sirs. Grab a bunk where you see no bedding ... I'm Shellie and that's Mohawk over there."

They introduced themselves and began sorting out their gear.

They started talking amongst themselves.

"The coxswain says we can't go ashore till we get a haircut and we can't get a haircut till the ship's barber comes back on Monday."

I have got to say at this point that one of the sharpest minds I came across in the Navy was Dan Sheldon.

"Hey Mohawk," Shellie called, "are you cutting hair this weekend or not?"

I wasn't too tardy myself at the time and replied without hesitation.

"Not sure if the clippers are on board ... took them home last week, I think I've only got scissors."

"Never mind then," Shellie replied, milking the situation.

"Are you a barber sir?" asked their leader ... come in spinner!

"Second barber, sort of a 'spare' ... when the barber gets crook, I cut, but I've only got scissors." I said.

"Go on Mohawk, help the poor buggers out," interjected Shellie. "You've done scissor cuts before."

"We'd really appreciate it," another said.

"How much?" asked his mate.

"A buck each, but we'll have to be quick — we're just about to go ashore," Shellie replied, putting the cards away.

They were now practically begging me to give them a haircut.

I had never cut hair in my life, but hey, you have to start somewhere. For a quick six bucks I was willing to learn.

Shellie and I got changed into our 'stepping gear' (going ashore outfits), readying ourselves to make a quick escape.

We took them to an isolated passageway on the ship. There we separated them so they wouldn't see each other after we had finished the haircuts.

When I had done one Shellie sent them to different parts of the ship, that way they couldn't compare notes.

At one point I was trying to give one guy a square back, but I couldn't get it straight. I was using soap and a razor and every time I tried to straighten the line it got higher and higher. By this time the square back was nearly on the top of his head. I had started to laugh hysterically. Shellie was pacifying the young bloke telling him I was laughing at a joke he had told me earlier.

Another guy had big ears and I was shaving around them ... it looked like he had two mudguards above his ears. Another ended up looking like Mo out of the Three Stooges.

We did the last OD and made a dash ashore.

We made it through the gates and into the Williamstown pub. We were laughing so hard we couldn't drink.

One of our mates turned up half an hour later and told us that the Coxswain was after our scalps. He said he wouldn't let the ODs ashore because they all looked like clowns.

Apparently the Coxswain laughed his arse off too when he heard the full story. We were still going to pay for this one though. We would worry about it on Monday ... till then ... cheers!

We were made to pay the ODs back on payday. There were no hard feelings, but it was a running gag among the crew for a while.

"Are you cutting tonight Mohawk?" would be thrown at me, even from the officers.

Some things stick in your mind ... it must have stayed with John Nutman.

At a forty year reunion, he told the story of his first fleet haircut ... and we are still mates.

## SHIP'S DRIVER

I was twenty and still didn't have a driver's licence so I took the opportunity while we were in Williamstown to get one.

It wasn't because I was going to buy a car any time soon; there was no point. We would be heading up top after re-fit any way.

I decided to have lessons and obtain a licence after a small incident that had happened when we were still in Sydney.

There had appeared on daily orders, a notice from our Coxswain that any Able Seaman wishing to become a ship's driver should apply for the position by no later than 1600 that same day. Our normal ship's driver had been drafted to a shore Base.

It was a good 'perk' being ship's driver. When you were overseas you just ferried the skipper or our officers around and had plenty of time off in port.

While we were in Sydney the ship's jeep wouldn't be used much, as all the officers and many of the married sailors had cars.

My line of thought was, if I could get the gig I'd have plenty of time to learn to drive. There was a heap of my mates who could teach me.

I put my name down, not thinking I would really be considered. I didn't have a civilian licence, but if by some miracle I got the job, I could get a licence before we left.

Bugger me ... the Coxswain notified me that I would take over as ship's driver starting that week. I would be issued a Navy licence.

There was no mention of a Civilian licence. He took it for granted that I had one, so I didn't volunteer that information.

The Coxswain gave me a set of keys and told me the jeep was to be parked on the wharf opposite the gangway and that it was my responsibility to have it cleaned, fuelled and ready to go at short notice.

"Aye aye Chief."

I belted down the Mess and told Shellie. His eyes lit up.

"I know what you're thinking ... no way."

I said "You've got to teach me to drive that thing ... and quick."

Shellie and I drove around the Garden Island Dockyard for a couple of hours that first night after secure. I was crunching the gears constantly ...

"Ease the clutch," Shellie kept yelling — "you're bloody hopeless."

"I'll never get this," I said in desperation.

"You'll have to, how you can get out of this one?" Shellie laughed. "the Coxswain will kill you."

"We'd better take it back before it's missed," I said. "I'll have another go tomorrow night."

It was a slight improvement the next time out and by the end of the week I could actually take off in first gear without stalling ... well, probably six out of ten times. It could only get better from here on in.

Friday came around and I was called down to the Coxswain's office and informed that I would need to take the Captain and the 'Jimmy' (Executive officer) to a civic function. We would leave at 1900 hours. We would be going to the Royal Sydney Yacht Squadron at Kirribilli.

My throat became constricted at this news and I could barely breathe, or utter "Aye aye Chief."

Shellie and I slipped out at lunchtime for one more 'rub around' (lesson).

We got the map out and plotted the route to be taken ... my throat got tight again when I saw the Sydney Harbour Bridge.

I nearly succumbed to Shellie's plan of faking sickness but decided if I concentrated, I might pull it off.

I kept going over and over the clutch routine and gear sequence in my head. It was one of my longest days.

At 1900 I was standing at attention by the jeep at the bottom of the gangway.

I saluted as the skipper and the Jimmy approached. It was crunch time.

They jumped in the jeep. The skipper got in the front with me.

I looked up to the top of the gangway. Shellie stood there and gave me a 'thumbs up' for confidence. Then he made the 'O' sign for perfect ... I thought, "I hope I don't make a 'perfect balls up' of this."

For a fleeting moment I thought of confessing all but then it was gone ... bugger it ... it'll be another part of the adventure!

"You know where we are off to Elliott?" enquired the skipper. "Yes sir," I replied as I depressed the clutch and slipped the jeep into first gear. We glided away smoothly towards the main gate. Second gear crunched a little but I noticed no perceivable lapse in their conversation. Third gear was a breeze. Then I had to stop at the main gate and report to the Dockyard Cop and flash IDs. Back to first gear ... fairly smooth; not a hint of that kangaroo hopping crap that had plagued me the day before.

Once outside the gate it was a different story. It seemed to me cars were flying everywhere. I hadn't noticed this when I was a passenger.

There was a small hill and as we approached the lights changed to red. I had never executed a hill start before, but Shellie had told me about them. This was going to be interesting ... a car had pulled up behind me ... poor bastard ... concentrate Col.

I somehow managed to not roll backwards but the engine was screaming ... so was the skipper. "What the bloody hell ..."

The kangaroo was back ... bugger!

This rattled me a bit and things started turning pear-shaped pretty much from then on.

By the time we had gotten maybe half a mile down the road and had copped a fair amount of abuse by rude civilian drivers, the skipper was livid, the Jimmy was drained of all colour and the jeep had overheated, as had my passengers.

I was made to pull over and told to get in the back by myself with derogatory comments like, "Where the bloody hell did you get your licence?" and "Jesus, Elliott, you're the worst driver I have ever come across." ...a little uncalled for I thought ... very hurtful.

The skipper made the Jimmy drive the rest of the way there and back, so he couldn't drink that night. I somehow knew I would eventually pay for this sometime in the future. We arrived at the venue.

While the function was on I hung with the other 'real' drivers and did my best to fit in. There were a few raised eyebrows when the Jimmy got in the driver's seat as we left. He didn't appreciate me waving to the other drivers as we drove away.

I lost the ship's driver gig, but I was never questioned about my lack of a civvy licence. It just never came up.

There was no punishment involved, as there is no such charge in the Navy as bad driver, although the skipper said if it was up to him, I would never be allowed behind a wheel again ... ever.

## PAY ATTENTION OR DIE

After months of re-fit in Victoria, we headed back to Sydney. The Stuart would be back up top in three months. I was looking forward to getting back to sea.

In the meantime I had applied to do an eight week ship's diver course at HMAS Penguin. Maybe I could catch up with my mates at the hospital while I was there. Seriously, it was a tough, intensive course and there would be no time to socialize ... or party.

A ship's diver is not a fully qualified Navy Clearance Diver but more of an assistant to the CDs. We would train and be qualified to dive to 100 feet.

A Navy Clearance Diver is the toughest course there is in the outfit. The attrition rate is incredible. If twenty start a course, two, possibly three, will get through. The course I was about to undertake was only a fraction of the course the full time divers did. I don't know if I would have had the necessary attributes (balls) to become a CD. It's incredibly hard.

To be a Navy Clearance Diver requires huge mental and physical toughness. It is one of the highest paid branches in the RAN and they command great respect.

Shaun, (Ralph's son) is a Chief Petty Officer Diver with 20 years' service up at this writing and serving in Afghanistan. I have followed his career avidly and am very proud of his achievements. He is an expert in many areas, including bomb disposal. He has instructed all three services and is SAS qualified. (But he still calls me "Uncle Col" ... and so he should.)

The course I was about to start was physically demanding and would require full concentration on my part if I was to pass.

Our fitness was sorely tested right from the beginning. They ran our bollocks off. Seven kilometre runs before the sun came up, then a 2K swim on your back, two or three 'run jumps', then another run.

Thirty minutes for breakfast, lectures, then practical diving. We came home after dark. At the end of the day you just wanted to sleep.

A run jump was a daily occurrence and was used as a fitness tool, or if you were caught not paying attention it could also be a punishment.

"Elliott, four run jumps ... go."

Here's how it went. You would run to the end of the pier, jump off, swim half way back, where you would find a thick Manila rope attached to a spar overhanging the water. You were required to climb up the rope without using your legs, some twenty-five to thirty feet up, flop over the top, hit the water and swim to the beach, then repeat. This was all done in naval issue overalls and fins. When the overalls were wet, they felt like lead. It was a real test.

Many times I saw blokes fail to reach the top after three or four rounds, myself included. You couldn't come out till you got over. Dropping off to sleep during a lecture brought on the run jumps.

I loved the practical diving the most. Anyone who has dived knows the great feeling and the sense of freedom diving can bring. It's a different world.

The Navy was all about being able to complete work or surveys under water; mine detection, repair, life-saving ... no sightseeing, all business.

We would be tested time and time again on safety procedures. Our diving instructors were tough 'old school' boys and would not tolerate any insubordination or lack of total commitment. To them there was only one branch in the Navy. The other branches were there just to support them.

These divers considered themselves somewhat elite. We, as ship's divers, were to them only just bearable.

The Petty officer in charge of our group, of which there were seven, had a favourite saying, "Pay attention or die."

He would then give us some instruction and then we would dive.

One of the things we were taught was how to retrieve or respond if we lost our face mask or demand valve. It is a very basic procedure. We were taught from the outset that above all, the biggest enemy of the diver is panic. If you followed basic procedure you could overcome.

Hence, "pay attention or die."

The demand valve (air mouthpiece) on the Hooker gear in those days could fill with water, if they came away when diving. They were attached to the harness and once you lost and then retrieved your demand valve, you would have to hold the blurter valve on either side and in turn blow into it. It would clear all the water and you were able to breathe again.

Hooker gear has a harness arrangement that was strapped on over the overalls, with an air-line to the surface vessel that pumped the air down to you. This is all quite primitive in today's methods, but this was the apparatus of our time.

We were also attached with a signal line ... two tugs, go left ... one tug, go right, and so on.

If you lost a face mask you would not be able to see at all in salt water.

Once retrieved, it was a simple task to clear it, put it back on, put pressure on the forehead section and exhale through the nose. The pressure would clear all the water from the mask.

How the instructors would test us was by sending down an

instructor diver who would swim up behind you, rip your demand valve out and pull your mask off. They would then swim away and observe your reaction.

Some forgot all and panicked, others stuck with procedure.

On our course, we lost two to panic in the first two weeks ... I had paid attention.

Another time we dived with lead boots. These were laced on in a very special but simple way. The boot covered half way to your knees and was extremely heavy. They enabled you to walk on the seabed.

There was a steel piece almost like a skewer that went down the middle of the lace. The canvas lace criss-crossed the steel which had a round 'O' piece at the top.

If you wanted to rid yourself of the boots you would simply insert your finger in the 'O' piece and pull upwards. As the skewer came out, the laces would part and the boot would come away ... very clever ...

"Pay attention or die." We were shown how to lace the boots on, then it was our turn.

"OK, Able Seaman 'Tosser', don the lead boots and prepare to dive," said the instructor.

Of course his name wasn't Tosser. I can't remember his real name but it should have been Tosser. He was from another ship; we only had two on course from the Stuart.

This particular bloke was a bit painful; a 'know it all' type who constantly told us how good he was at ... well, every bloody thing.

The instructor had observed that he hadn't been paying attention, so he was first up.

We were diving in reasonably shallow water that day, about 30 feet.

AB T (Able Seaman Tosser) set about putting his lead boots on. He wound the canvas laces around and around his legs and even made the ludicrous statement, "these mongrels won't come off." It was a wonder he didn't cut his blood supply off, they were that tight.

Over the side he went. He reached the sea bed, was given some signals and began to respond. The Petty officer instructor had the standby safety diver enter the water a short time after AB T began his dive.

The boss had given the standby diver instructions out of our ear shot. He then turned to the rest of us.

"Who can tell me what AB T has just done?" he enquired of us.

"Stuffed up the laces of his boots," someone volunteered.

"Bet your arse he did. Like I say, pay attention or die."

"If he were to run into any unforeseen trouble down there, like air supply problems and was not in possession of a knife, he would die." said our Petty officer. With that he turned off AB T's air supply.

A short time later AB T was hauled to the surface with the standby diver buddy-breathing (sharing air) with him. The boss had instructed the standby diver to watch his reaction and then to move in and assist.

AB T was absent from the class after lunch that same day. No questions were asked and he was never mentioned or seen on course again.

Our concentration level rose considerably.

One task we were given was to dive down a buoy chain, maybe 40 feet deep. At the bottom, the chain was anchored to a large round cement block called a shot. We were given a cold chisel, a hammer and a length of cast chain and told to cut two links off each end.

The other version was a hacksaw blade and a length of pipe that had to be cut. It was an endurance exercise.

For this task we were made to dive without weight belts. The only way to get to the bottom was to pull yourself down the chain, then wrap your legs around the chain at the bottom to stop floating up.

It is hard work under water as there is no friction to assist you in these tasks, however it can be done.

My turn came and I completed it in a fairly short time. Thinking I would be congratulated on my proficiency, I headed for the surface.

"All done Petty Officer," I announced with a beam on my face.

"Too quick, Elliott ... go back and do it again," he said.

"That'll teach you to kiss arse," I thought to myself.

This time I finished the job and sat at the bottom for another ten minutes and enjoyed the passing fish parade.

We did night dives, underwater obstacle dives and free ascents. We were never down long enough to have decompression problems but we learnt about these problems in class. There was a fairly comprehensive theory set of exams to sit.

From 80 feet down we did free ascents. With an instructor diver with you, you took off all your harness and air supply and left it on the sea bed. Then we would head to the surface.

You never exceed the rate of the rising bubbles and all the way up you must continually slowly whistle. This equalises the pressure in your lungs. For every four feet you rise, you gain another litre of air in your lungs as the water pressure decreases.

The natural reaction is to hold on to your breath and if the instructor saw this happening, he would punch you in the stomach to remind you to exhale. We eventually did free ascents unassisted.

When you reached the surface you were not out of breath. I found free ascents to be quite an exhilarating experience.

My course came to an abrupt end around this time.

I was stationed as standby diver and was sent down to check on the diver below, he hadn't been responding to signals.

I dropped over the side and followed the mooring line down.

At about 50 feet I noticed the other diver's lines were warped around the chain. He couldn't receive his signals. I swam down another 30 feet and found him sitting on the bottom.

I signaled him to follow me up to show him the problem.

Instead of swimming around or slipping off his gear to buddy breathe to the surface ... He panicked, grabbed my face mask and pulled out my demand valve.

I was taking an inhale at the time and breathed in water.

I felt a searing pain in my lungs and couldn't orientate myself .... I eventually headed for the surface. God knows how I made it.

The other diver got to the surface and we both went to hospital. My course ended in disaster…Bugger.

## THE SNAPSHOTS

A bunch of us were sent to the gangway with our gasperators (Naval issue gas masks). We were told we would be demonstrating their use to a class of WRANs (Women's Royal Australian Navy); apparently they were on course as nurses.

When any sailor got drafted anywhere in my time, he had to take his gasperators with him. It was part of your issued kit. Navy rules stated that these gas masks were to be cleaned every three months with special lubricants, thereby keeping them in good operational order.

The truth of the matter was that the masks would be stowed in lockers in the Mess and never saw daylight for sometimes years at a time. I certainly hadn't had mine out of its bag since I left Leeuwin. I had taken it to Penguin with me as it was required, but it still hadn't been opened.

Six of us were lined up in front of the class of WRANs.

The Chief Bosun's mate brought us to attention and gave the order "By numbers … remove gas masks."

In unison, we opened our bags and pulled out our masks.

I was looking straight ahead and saw the nurses starting to giggle; some laughed out aloud. At first I thought someone's fly was undone …

The Chief Bosun's Mate gave an order to the WRANs in quick time.

"CLASS … ABOUT TURN".

Someone said, "Mohawk, look down" … there at my feet were a dozen or so 'dirty pictures' scattered on the ground, the kind sold to sailors in every Asian port. They were probably 1920 vintage and very explicit.

"PICK UP YOUR SNAPSHOTS ABLE SEAMAN," the Chief barked at me.

"But Chief, they ain't mine," I stammered.

"REPORT TO THE REGULATING OFFICE ... NOW!" he ordered. "AT THE DOUBLE, SAILOR."

Someone had stowed the pictures in my gasperator sometime when we were up top and forgot to retrieve them. They certainly weren't mine, but how could I prove that?

The Officer of the Day called me into the office. He had been discussing it with the Chief.

I managed to convince them that they weren't my pictures. They worked out when the Stuart had been overseas last, which in turn meant I hadn't done my regulation gas mask clean in nearly a year. See, they get you one way or the other. I was given summary punishment.

I had to work in the galley all weekend, while my mates went ashore and celebrated the completion of their course ... and they didn't even let me see the photos. There's no justice!

I came home on leave not long after this to the news that my father was in hospital with sclerosis of the liver. I went in to see him. He looked jaundiced and the doctors told me he wouldn't be coming home.

My memory is sitting by his bed and as we talked he did, in his own way, try to apologise for the life he had given us. He went on to promise me he would be a changed man when he got home. I left the hospital that day. I never saw my father again. He died at the age of 49. So sad; such a wasted life. Auntie Nobby was at home to help Mum. She took charge and she and I arranged the funeral and sorted out all the other bits and pieces.

## CHANGI

Before too long we were back up top. I was in my element, re-discovering the exotic places I had visited before. I was enjoying the different cultures once again.

Ralph had been sent to Selerang Barracks near Singapore. It was commonly referred to as Changi. The famous Changi prison is nearby.

During WW2, after the fall of Singapore in 1942, the Japanese held over 3,000 civilians in the Changi prison. It was built to hold 600.

The Japanese held up to 50,000 mainly British and Australian servicemen as POWs at the former British Selerang Barracks.

It has been determined that nearly 900 allied servicemen died during their incarceration there. Many more perished under appalling conditions when they were sent to the Burma Railway, Sandakan Airfield and various other labour camps.

Once again I was confronted with Japanese brutality as I explored Changi's history.

In 2000, the old prison was demolished but thanks to the Preservation of Monuments Board, the original gates were kept for posterity and their historical value. They now adorn the new Changi.

The prison now houses the most serious offenders in the country as well as death row prisoners. Capital punishment is well established. Hangings are carried out on Fridays.

Punishment by caning is also carried out twice a week at the prison. It is said that up to one hundred canings can be performed in a single week. Singapore justice is brutal, but many believe very effective. The crime rate in Singapore is one of the lowest in the world.

Ralph took my mates and me onto the Base. We ate at the Army Mess hall and couldn't believe how good the food was. I never realised how limited the menu was on a destroyer. I was in the wrong outfit if it was based on tucker.

We would go into Singapore and hang out at the famous Bugis Street. It was a real festive atmosphere in those days. Servicemen and tourists from all over the world would gather to eat, drink and carouse. Bugis street, in those days was famous for its 'Shims' (transvestites). We referred to them as 'kaitais' or 'Beanie Boys'.

I knew of many a young sailor who got a huge surprise at the end of the night. I can honestly say I wasn't one of them ... fair dinkum.

Some of these 'girls' were absolutely stunning. I would sit there with my mates and just watch the passing parade. We would mark them out of ten. There were quite a few 10s but I must admit we saw a few minus 1s as well. Some of the real girls found it hard to compete with the kaitais.

There was a standard gag we told about the young sailor in Singapore, shacked up for the night. The 'girl' kept reaching across and stroking the sailor's balls. "Why do you keep doing that?" he asked.

"Because I miss mine," came the reply.

Today the new Bugis Street is a tourist Mecca. A must for incredible shopping and dining ... all the sailors have left ... sad!

Security was high while we were in the Far East. When we were in Singapore we would post sentries while alongside at the British Naval Base HMS Terror.

When we were on duty we would have to stand guard at night armed with an SLR (self-loading rifle).

Between midnight and 4am the English guard boat would patrol the area. We never knew when they would appear near our ship. If you were not alert and didn't hail the guard boat first, you would be in big trouble. They would try to surprise the guard on duty. God help the poor sentry that didn't spot them first. A report would be lodged the next day from the Poms complaining of slack security on our part.

## WHEN IN DOUBT ... IMPROVISE

The exchange went something like this when you sighted their lights. They would be about a hundred yards out so we needed to yell -

Sentry ... "Hail Guard Boat."

Guard Boat ... "Hail Stuart" (us)

Guard Boat ... "Report Stuart"

Sentry ... "All small arms and armoury secure, ammunition secure, NBCD lockers locked". A great rambling list would be memorised and called to the 'Pommy' Guard Boat.

Upon completion the guard boat would call, "Carry on Stuart".

Then they would head to the next ship and do it all over again.

My problem was, I couldn't for the life of me remember the report I had to yell back.

I had gotten away with it every time I stood sentry. Each time the guard boat had come around, I was off watch.

One night I was on watch — it was about 2.30 am. I saw the guard boat lights ... bugger ... what was that report?

I decided to wing it and improvise ...

"Hail guard boat," I called.

"Hail Stuart"" came the reply, then ... "Report Stuart."

The rest of my report was just sounds I made up on the spot. I was hoping they sounded like words so just for effect I threw in the odd, "locker" or "ammunition" as I knew those words featured in there somewhere. It went something like this, "HAV ... NA TESSIL ...LOCKER AND GRONEG TOWER PADANGO ... SECURE AS IS AMUNITION DILTOID ROOM AND HATCH SEURE BRIDGE SENTOLL VIVOID LOCKED, CHECKED AND RIGGED TAHAFNE ... BOENYA RESISTO." I called this out with the highs and lows in my voice and with real authority ... it sounded fair dinkum even to me.

"Carry on Stuart," came back their reply. I was chuckling to myself thinking that the Poms would be thinking, "Bad speaking Aussie bastard," and then ... "Wonderful display Elliott, very entertaining," said the Officer of the Day standing right behind me. I must have jumped three feet in the air. He was lucky I didn't shoot him.

He had come out on the upper deck for some fresh air. His timing was perfect. He had watched and listened to the whole performance.

I was told to report to him the next day. He strode away.

He made me learn the correct report and recite it to him before I was allowed ashore again. He had a lot of trouble keeping a straight face as he was giving me a bollicking.

The story got around the ship quickly and I had to do the guard boat routine to the howls of laughter of all my shipmates. It got better every time I performed it.

The Officer of the Day dined out on the story in the wardroom and I was summoned to perform the routine there as well.

I have told the story as accurately as possible, but I think it might be one of those 'you had to be there' type tales to really appreciate it ...well, the Navy did teach me to improvise.

## "DON'T LET ME DOWN ELLIOTT"

Every couple of years, Ralph and I caught up overseas.

He was sent to Terendak Military Base, 13 miles from Malacca in Malaysia. We kept in touch by letter.

At one point we were leaving Singapore and were asked to take an Army cricket team back to Malacca.

Ralph had gotten into the team and knew he and his mates would overnight it on the Stuart. He kept it as a surprise.

I was in the sonar room as we left harbor. My job was to keep a sonar watch as we headed out to sea.

We had just gotten out to sea when Shellie came up.

"Hey Mohawk, there's a soldier in the Mess, he sounds just like you," he exclaimed. "He's one of the Army cricket team we're taking back to Malacca," he went on.

"Grab these headsets Shellie," I said, realising it was Ralph. I headed for the door. Shaky little bugger was in the Mess.

Ralph and his mates were eating supper.

He introduced me to his mates and we spent the next few hours on the upper decks catching up.

I got permission from my Chief for Ralph and his mate to sleep in the sonar room. It was a hot steamy night and the sonar room was air-conditioned. The next morning we anchored off the beach, just out from the Base. There was no wharf and we were sending sailors and soldiers ashore by the ship's boats.

The skipper had invoked the privilege leave rule, which meant our sailors could go ashore to play sport. They would return to the ship by eight at night as there was no accommodation for our boys on the Base.

Privilege leave is only granted to those who have not broken any rules or been on chooks in the previous six months.

I, of course, didn't qualify, but I thought if I play the 'I haven't seen my brother in ages card,' the skipper might make an exception and let me go ashore as well.

I duly put in a request to the skipper. He gave me permission to not only go ashore with my brother but allowed me to stay overnight in his barracks. He said I must be on the beach at 1700 (5pm) on the Sunday. The ship would sail an hour later. I promised the skipper I would be there.

"I am placing my trust in you, son," he said. I left with his voice ringing in my ears ... "Don't let me down Elliott".

What a top weekend we had. All Ralph's mates were party animals. We went into Malacca and hit the bars.

Sunday night found me back at the Base in the soldiers' Mess with Ralph, his mates and a group of their wives.

I was sitting on the bar holding court, beer in one hand, ukulele in the other. All the best New Nee Soon numbers were being sung and my best routines were being aired.

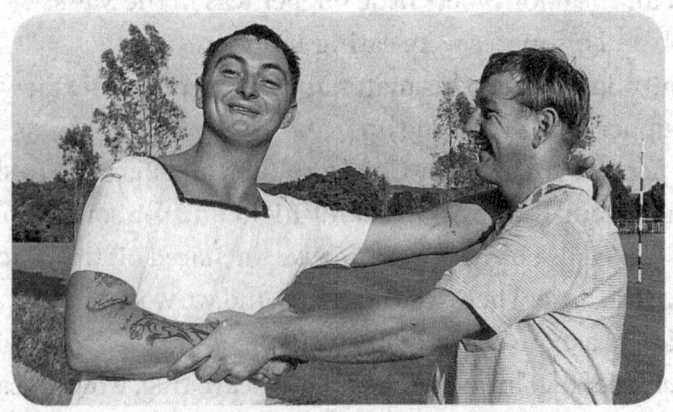

*With Ralph in Malacca ..."I'm coming Skip"*

"Hey Col," Ralph said, "time to get back to the beach ... it's twenty to five."

I swung down from the bar a little unsteadily and lurched toward the door with a chorus of goodbyes and slaps on the back. Ralph had trouble getting to his feet so I told him, "I'll be fine mate, stay there, it's just down the road."

I walked out into the bright sunlight and squinted.

I headed off down the road toward the beach, two steps forward, one step back ... making progress, none the less.

"Don't let me down Elliott" ... the skipper's words were echoing in my head. ... "I'm coming Skip."

I trudged steadily on. It seemed to be getting hotter and the foliage was becoming denser. I checked my watch, 20 past 5 ... "Oh crap". I tried running but couldn't quite pull it off ... "Maybe the boat will wait."

Just as these thoughts entered my befuddled brain, an Army jeep pulled up. "Hey sailor, where you headed?" a soldier called.

"The beach, gotta catch the last boat ... 20 minutes ago," I said, as much to myself as to the soldier.

"You're headed the wrong way ... the beach is back there," he said, pointing over his shoulder, "unless of course you're heading to the other side four days march away," he added, laughing.

I got to the beach but the boat had returned to the ship. "After all that trekking I need drink ..."

I got the driver to drop me back to the soldiers' Mess and the party continued. The Army MPs came in looking for me. The soldiers and their wives hid me under the table and reported they hadn't seen a sailor.

I was finally arrested at 2am playing pool in the rec room with Ralph.

He was told to get back to his barracks and I was put in a cell for the night.

I woke in the morning with a huge hangover and an even worse guilty conscience ... "Don't let me down Elliott."

It started to dawn on me that when it came to the booze, all my good intentions went out the window. I would eventually get a handle on it but that would be years away. Like many young people, I would experience much more before I could take control of my crazy ways.

For the moment, I only had myself to worry about but I had no excuses for the disrespect I had shown the skipper.

I had held up the ship's departure and a boat was sent the next morning to the beach to pick me up.

It didn't matter to me about the punishment, it was the mental anguish I felt. The skipper made me feel like the jerk that I was. It was as if I had personally hurt his feelings. I had betrayed his trust.

I made a promise to myself that I would re-evaluate my behaviour and toe the line. I became a saint. Shellie thought I was unstable and wanted me to get some sort of treatment. He seemed to think there was some sort of 'party medicine' that I could take. He was beside himself with worry but I was determined to change my ways.

In the coming months I studied for my Leading Seaman exams and passed with flying colours. Getting promoted was not just a matter of being qualified. It also encompassed being considered a responsible candidate with an attitude to match. I had a lot of work to do, to convince my superiors that I had changed. I did state before that it took me six years to get my four-year Good Conduct Stripe. A lot of work had to be done.

## MY FRIEND THE QUEEN

1970 saw our ship, HMAS Stuart, designated Escort Destroyer to the Royal Yacht, HMY Britannia.

Her Majesty the Queen and Prince Phillip were in Australia for our Bi-Centenary celebrations. Princess Anne was on board and The Prince of Wales attended part of the tour.

Two hundred years before, Captain James Cook had laid claim to Australia for Great Britain.

I would like to say that it was my new behaviour and attitude that was the catalyst for our ship being chosen as escort ... well it could have helped ... but no, our ship was a good choice because of a great crew and her overall look.

It was a huge amount of work for our crew, as the ship had to be in top condition. All hands were put to work.

While in company with the Britannia, we had to be in full dress uniform while on the upper deck. Imagine going to work in a mine dressed in a tuxedo ... that's how it felt.

At one point, the Royal yacht did a 'sail past'. We lined the deck and gave a hip, hip, hooray while rotating our caps in the full Navy tradition (clockwise).

Her Majesty stood at the rails and waved ... then I am sure she smiled directly at me. I have convinced myself of this.

The weather was a little rough at one point in NSW and the Royal yacht couldn't get in, so it was decided to pick up the royal party and divert them to our ship for tea and bickies with our skipper and the officers. They would then rejoin the Britannia when the weather settled.

Imagine the buzz I got when I was told by my Divisional Officer that I was assigned as the bowman on the transfer boat that would deliver the royals to our ship. I would get up close, (but not personal).

It was a huge honour and the thought that I had been chosen because of my now exemplary behaviour was making me prouder by the minute.

Just as I was bathing in this reflected glory, my DO (Divisional Officer) interrupted my reverie by telling me that I must wear my Vietnam medals. He then went on to inform me that that was the only reason I got the gig ... to add a bit of colour to a normally bland white uniform as it were. Still I was proud ...bugger it.

The last time I had seen the Queen was in 1954. I was a five year old kid in Victoria. I remember lining the main road with Mum, Carol and Ralph. We all had little Flags and waved them as the motorcade went by. She smiled at me then as well ... I have convinced myself of this!

Now here I was ... 1970, standing to attention at the base of the gangway as the Queen and Prince Phillip boarded the boat.

I had been instructed previously on the do's and don'ts of being in the presence of royals.

"Speak only if you're spoken to (the DO emphasised this point to me), got that Elliott?" he reiterated.

"No problems sir, no chatting," I said.

"Exactly," he went on, "and in the unlikely event that you are spoken to, address the Queen as Your Majesty or Ma'am and the Prince as sir and do not, and I repeat DO NOT, under any circumstances touch the Queen or the Prince."

"What if she slips on the gangway sir?" I put in.

"She won't slip on the gang..." he trailed off using a rather stronger tone. "Just do what I tell you for Christ's sake," he said, becoming more exasperated.

He seemed to be under pressure.

"Aye aye sir," I said ... "no chatting and let's hope she doesn't slip."

"Bloody hell" ... he trailed off, as he strode way. I watched as he disappeared below decks, still shaking his head.

"No chatting, and if she goes down ... let her go," I mumbled to myself as I headed down to the Mess to polish up my medals.

As the royals approached, I was standing at attention, eyes looking directly ahead — well nearly. I had turned my head ever so slightly to the right so I could catch a better close up.

I was given no instruction on facial expressions so I gave the slightest hint of a smile. It was more like a welcoming glimmer than a smile.

Well, bugger me, she smiled back ... I have convinced myself of this.

I guess she recognised me. I have been a fan ever since.

P.S. She didn't slip ... God Save the Queen. (I wasn't allowed to.)

## HMAS CERBERUS

My time on the Stuart came to an end and I was drafted to HMAS Cerberus, the recruit training depot in Westernport, Victoria. I was hoping to stay at sea but orders are orders and I resigned myself to the fact that I would spend at least a year there before I could go back to the fleet.

At least I would be in my home state and close to family. I could catch up with my civvy (civilian) mates on a regular basis. The boys were still playing the local gigs.

I was still an Able Seaman and although I was qualified and due for promotion, I was, in the opinion of the skipper, "Not quite ready yet." On my last application, he made the statement that he was very aware of my newfound adherence to naval discipline but a little more penance was needed. I felt like a monk! Although he did concede in giving me my four year good conduct badge, (two years after it was due).

The Coxswain advised me not to sew it on ... he said I should use press studs. He didn't think it would "be there for long."

"Oh ye of little faith."

Still, he wished me luck and told me to keep my nose clean and the promotion would happen soon enough.

I arrived at Cerberus and was immediately put on the gangway, watch-keeping. I hoped there would be no Reserves coming into the depot to play pretends.

Didn't see any ... great!

Winter was on its way and the temperature was way down. Victoria has the reputation of being able to show all four seasons in the one day. It's not a great state for weather.

I felt the cold more than normal as I hadn't experienced a winter in years. It seemed every time it started to get cold at home I was in the Far East, and then I would come home to summer.

A mate put me on to a good trick. He would wear ladies' panty hose under his bell bottom trousers … it works a treat.

I had the thought that if the wind changed, I would become a transvestite.

At the first hint of wanting to put 'lippy' on, I would take off the panty hose. Still they did help.

I had been watch-keeping for a couple of months and one morning I received a phone call just as I was finishing my shift. I was told to go to the Administration block and report to my Divisional Officer.

When I had arrived at the depot I was given some typed information on the rules and regulations of the Base and it had informed me of whom my DO was. I hadn't met the Lieutenant but I was about to.

I supposed he had only just caught up with the fact that I was on board and it was customary to meet new personnel face to face.

Either that, or my past had caught up with me and he wanted to check out the legend that I was … and get some tips.

I found his office and knocked.

"Come in," came the reply in a matter-of-fact voice.

"Able Seaman Elliott reporting as ordered sir," I announced as I came to attention and saluted.

"Stand at ease Elliott," he said in a pleasant tone, accompanied with a welcoming smile, (not unlike the Queen's).

His manner was quite disarming as he talked about his love of ships, all the time asking me of my experiences while referring to my records. I correctly assumed that he hadn't done much sea-time but would have liked to.

He quizzed me on Vietnam, the Forrestal and the Evans tragedies, asking of my thoughts and opinions on these events.

Eventually he went on to explain how Cerberus was first and

foremost a Senior Recruit establishment and we needed to send these recruits into the fleet feeling confident in the knowledge that they would further their Naval education on board our fighting ships. He went on to explain that the men they met on those ships would mentor them and pass on more practical knowledge.

As he was telling me this, I wondered if he knew about the haircuts. As he talked I felt he was leading up to something.

"Elliott, I have noticed here that you topped your division in the seamanship exams after your year at Leeuwin."

"Yes sir," I said, showing a little pride. It was all I had; my chest expanded a smidgen.

"It seems that you have knuckled under as it were, of late. Your previous DO reports that you are very capable but sometimes a little, shall we say adventurous. It goes on to say that you finally have seemed to have taken your naval career seriously, therefore I am prepared to offer you a promotion to Leading Seaman on one proviso ... that you become a Recruit School Instructor with the next intake."

I was, probably for the second time in my life, gobsmacked. (The first time was when the Cubs knocked off my beer bottles.)

There had to be a catch. The Lieutenant went on to explain that I would need to regulate my kit (uniforms) back to original naval issue. That was it, that was the catch.

This was a tough one for me, I think the only original issue I had was my dirk (knife) and my name stamp. All the rest of my kit was tailor-made in Hong Kong with the appropriate dragon emblems on the inside of my cuffs of my dress blues. My whole kit was 'tiddly' (fancy). There were shark-skin white front shirts that were my pride and joy. I was also wearing American issue dungarees from my time in Vietnam. It was tolerated in the fleet but here at Cerberus it was strictly against the rules, especially in recruit school. Nearly all my kit had to be replaced.

It was going to cost me about $90, a veritable fortune at the time. Still, it was a promotion ... a small price to pay.

## RECRUIT SCHOOL INSTRUCTOR

I subsequently picked up my 'hook' (promotion to Leading Seaman Under Water Control) and headed for the Administration building at recruit school.

I now had a new DO and had to report to him.

He was very officious and obviously took his job very seriously, a total turnaround from the last one. I had the feeling that this guy could prove to be a little bit too 'by the book'. I would need to be on my toes.

He lectured me on sticking to the curriculum. Variations would not be tolerated.

I was given two weeks to familiarise myself with the classes that I would be teaching.

I was to teach Basic Seamanship, Naval Indoctrination, NBCD, Navigation, Ship's Husbandry and Drill using the SLR.

All by the book; no shortcuts, strict Navy.

I would take the recruits through all the same routines that I had been put through as a Junior Recruit years earlier.

Where I had maybe 6 or 7 instructors when I joined, I now had to take all classes. It was a huge work load, and it certainly felt a little daunting, but I felt a little excited at the challenge.

I headed to my cabin at the end of the recruits' donga and began to swat up on the books I had been issued with.

I was sharing the cabin with another instructor, an old mate as it turned out. Ross 'Speedy' Heazlewood was a top hand and gave me the heads-up on recruit school.

He talked me through the procedures and was a great help.

"And Mo ... one more thing," Speedy went on, "tread carefully around the DO."

"He's a little too Navy, doesn't seem to have a sense of humour."

"Thanks mate," I said. "I kind of figured that when I reported in."

My first class of recruits were certainly a varied mix of characters from all over Australia, but all out for adventure.

The one thing I noticed was that their expectations of the Navy was not quite aligned with the reality of what they were about to experience.

It took me back to my first days. I had seen so much since then and I understood what they were feeling.

Our division consisted of two classes. I had one class and Leading Seaman Robertson the other.

'Robbo' had taken a few classes through previously and knew the ropes. He was a great help in the early weeks and he had my back. We became fast friends.

In recruit school, all recruits addressed their instructor as 'sir' no matter what the instructor's rank.

I had recruits aged from seventeen to twenty-six. I was twenty-two at the time and I realised it was my job to turn these civilians into disciplined sailors. A little bit of the 'pot calling the kettle black' as it were, but still the shoe was definitely on the other foot this time. I needed to rise to the challenge but I felt I was up for this new responsibility.

Like all recruits in any service you had the odd clown of the class and Recruit Watkins was mine. He hailed from Footscray, a city boy and out for fun. If I had a nemesis, he was it.

### I DID IT MY WAY!

If there was a giggle or a disturbance in class or on the parade ground, you could bet it was instigated by this bloke.

As an instructor, the old saying of familiarity breeds contempt was never truer. I needed to sort him early, or at least I got his mates to. It happened like this.

I caught him out on parade during rifle drill, so I brought the class to attention outside the Gunnery School. I then made Watkins fall out and report to me.

I had him sit down with his back to the wall, facing the parade ground and made him light up a smoke and take it easy. The rest of the class was still at attention watching on.

I then informed the class that they would double march (run) around the parade ground with their weapons at the 'high-port' for the remaining forty-five minutes of the drill class.

I told them they could thank Watkins for this and suggested this would be the way it worked from now on. I also explained that they could sort out Watkins in their own time, as he was the catalyst of their pain.

I never heard a peep out of Watkins for the remainder of the course … or anyone else for that matter.

By the time I was past my first intake, I was revelling in the job. I felt a great sense of pride when the Chief Instructor informed Robbo and me that our division had scored the highest exam results for the past three years. We headed for the pub that night slapping each other on the back and expounding each other's virtues. I was so proud.

I thought my next PP1s (performance evaluation) would reflect these results and I would duly be praised for my great effort. It wasn't to be.

My 'un-naval' sense of humour let me down big time … it happened this way.

## D.A.D.F.A.

Our DO walked into the Instructors' tea room one lunchtime when half a dozen Instructors were there, myself included.

"Attention," the Senior Petty Officer called as our Divisional Officer entered the room.

"Stand easy men," the Lieutenant announced. "I am here to inform you all that we will be using some new abbreviations or acronyms for certain Instructors at recruit school from now on. The chosen ratings will be given new name badges with your rank and appropriate title displayed. For example Petty Officer Wilkins, you will have the badge P.O./W M Wilkins (S.I.R.S) ... that is of course Petty Officer Weapons Mechanic Wilkins Senior Instructor Recruit School. Leading Seaman Robertson you will have the abbreviation L.S./T O Robertson W.I.R.S, and that is of course, Leading Seaman Tactical Operator Robertson Welfare Instructor Recruit School.

*D.A.D.F.A ... Recruit School*

All the time this Lieutenant was giving out these new titles there was much rolling of eyes and sly looks of 'what the' between the Instructors. It was obvious that this guy had too much time on his hands and was trying very hard to be relevant. On reflection he was not unlike the character Frank Burns in the TV series MASH.

When he had got through all the assembled Instructors, I piped up and said, "Excuse me sir, I haven't been given a title, what will I be?"

I am sure I didn't have the wrong inflection but he looked at me as if I had really slighted him. It was supposed to be a light hearted comment but he took instant offence.

"You ... you will be nothing Elliott ... nothing at all," he railed, displaying his annoyance.

"Aye aye sir," I replied.

He then informed us that the name badges were being made and

163

must be worn at all times while on duty at recruit school as from the following Monday. He then left the room.

"So I guess you're nothing Mohawk," Speedy put in with a laugh.

"Well I guess I will have to have the appropriate badge made myself," I said as a mischievous thought entered my head.

On parade the following Monday, I stood in front of my class, ready for inspection, my new badge neatly displayed above my left shirt pocket, L.S./U. C Elliott (D.A.D.F.A.).

Our Commander inspected the classes followed by the Chief Instructor and the DO.

I brought my class to attention as the group of officers approached.

"Class ready for inspection sir," I said with pride.

The Commander commented on my class's good turnout and walked on.

The DO was just passing me when he spotted the badge.

"Elliott," he said under his breath, "what does that badge mean?"

I could see his brain ticking over trying to figure if, just maybe, he did give me a title.

"It's nothing sir," I replied.

"What do you mean … nothing? I didn't give you a title … did I?" he said, as more of a statement than a question.

"No sir, you didn't give me a title and the badge reflects that sir," I said with a straight face.

He mouthed the letters "D.A.D.F.A. What the hell does that stand for?" he demanded.

"Leading Seaman Elliott/Under Water Control D.A.D.F.A. Recruit School … that's D.A.D.F.A., sir … Deputy Assistant Director of Fuck all … sir," I said without a smile. It was hard … I said this in a conspiratorial voice, it was our little joke.

"Report to my office immediately after parade," he ordered as he strode away red-faced, not impressed and definitely not amused in the slightest.

*Me and Kaz*

*Kaz and Cassie on the night of Cass's graduation from Australian Dance and Performance Institute*

*Let's rock*

*Tessie Two Shoes*

*Anzac day (Ralph 2nd from left top row)*

*On my 60th*

*Marks Division Reunion*

*Jodie with "Jock"*

*Kim and "Chaffy"*

*Kaz and I on our wedding day*

*From left, Miffy, Mum, Me, Carol, Ralph and Wendy in front*

*From left, Kim, Jodie and Cassie*

*Our Grandchildren, from left, Adam, Madison, Joshua and Cody*

*"Boats of Crete", painting by Karen Elliott*

*"Country Lane", painting by Karen Elliott*

*Mum with Wendy and her husband Pete, Karen and Craigie in the background*

*"Maybe"*

*From left, Robbo, Ralph, Chief Petty Officer/Clearance Diver Shaun Elliott (Ralph's son), me and Jamie Davis on board HMAS Gascoyne*

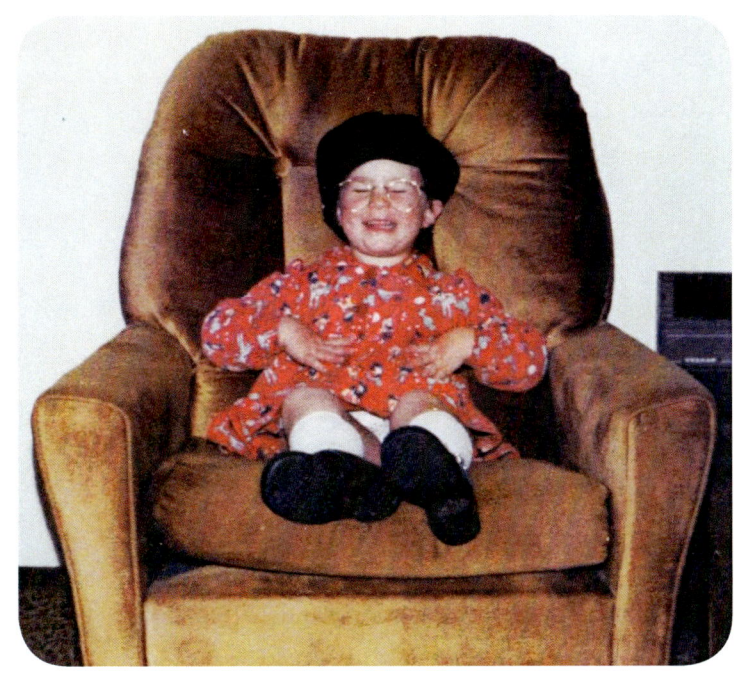

*Jodie — doing a "Benny"*

*Jodie, doing a "Chad"*

*Jan Craig, Pam Shelton and "Craigie"*

*Matilda, our latest grandchild*

*With Pete and Pam, 1972*

*My biggest fan, Mum*

*A new addition, Cassie arrives*

*He ain't heavy*

*Then there was Cassie with Seiko (the watch dog)*

*Kim, Pop and Nanna*

*Joanie doing her party piece, "Burlington Bertie"*

*With Craigie on Anzac Day (today)*

*Hari Kari,
failed Kamikaze pilot*

*Slugger Mulligan*

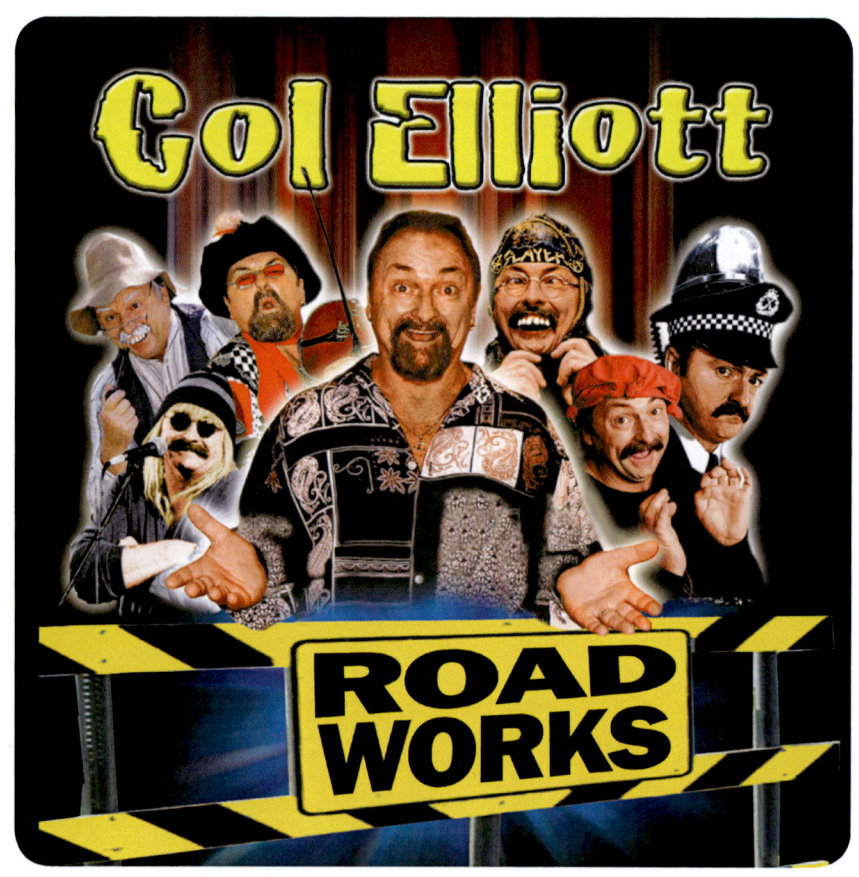

*Talk about schizophrenic*

"Bugger ... here I go again," I thought ... just as I was starting to get there.

He let me know he wasn't at all amused by my sense of humour and any more breaches of the rules would result in dire consequences.

"What did you think you would achieve by this Elliott?" he queried, arms folded.

"A belly laugh sir," I replied, "or at least a chuckle."

It wasn't the answer he wanted and he completely lost it. I was told to watch myself in future or the axe would fall!

Three weeks after this event I was told to report to his office to sight and sign my PP1s (performance evaluation reports).

"Read them now Elliott and sign them," he demanded.

I read his assessment of my performance in his presence and was not at all surprised to notice it was not a glowing report; in fact there was no discernible light at all.

Phrases like 'Adherence to rules elude this Rating', and 'More application will be needed in future to gain more satisfactory results'. That one was totally unfair.

"Sign them Elliott and get back to your class," he said with growing impatience.

"With all due respect sir, I am unable to sign these as I believe they do not reflect fairly on my performance."

I knew I had the right to refuse to sign the evaluation if I had sufficient reason to disagree ... Navy rules ... Marty taught me that.

"What are you talking about, it's my job to assess you and this is how I see it. Now sign it and get back to your class," he demanded.

"I respectfully repeat sir, that this assessment doesn't even mention the fact that our Division has had the best exam results in the past three years. This is due, in no small part to my own diligence, of which I am very proud."

"We will see what the Commander has to say about this Elliott ... is that what you want?" he replied with a smirk.

"That's exactly what I want ... sir," I replied.

He didn't want to hear that either.

A few days later I fronted the Commander.

He had read the assessment before I was called before him and gave me the right to state my case.

I gave him all the facts and topped it off with the D.A.D.F.A. episode. He made me repeat its meaning. His head went down as he tried to appear to be studying his notes. There was an ever so slight tremor happening in his shoulders. I stated that the DO had taken offence to the fact that I had tried to bring a little humour to the table and that it wasn't my intention to mock him, but I now felt it was more poor judgement on my behalf. I also stated that I had apologised to him after the incident.

I also felt it shouldn't affect my evaluation, especially with our recruit school results.

The Commander's eyes were watering when he looked up. He dismissed me only barely holding back his laughter.

"Come on 'ya' bastard ... laugh," I thought as I left his office.

The DO went in next. I sat outside as he spoke to my DO.

Half an hour later I fronted the Commander. This time my DO was with him.

The Commander asked me to read the 'new' modified assessment. Our recruit school results were recorded in this version and duly applauded.

Apparently I still needed to adjust my attitude to authority and would need to curb my tendency to bend the rules to suit myself. Overall it was the best result I was going to get under the circumstances ... I signed!

I needed to watch my back from here on. The DO would certainly be waiting for me to screw up. He had lost a little bit of face.

## THE CHIEF BREWMAKER

The Navy had changed since I was a Junior Recruit. I had signed up for twelve years' service. The recruits that I was now teaching would sign on for nine years but if they didn't like the three months initial training they could walk away at the end of it. Once they committed to the nine years they then had the option of handing in eighteen months' notice ... talk about commitment!

We were told of this legislation when we came in as Instructors and it was made clear to us that it would not bode well if any of our Recruits took the discharge option at the end of training. It was, in fact, our job to keep them enthusiastic.

All of my recruits seemed very keen and were constantly asking me about life at sea. When we had spare class time, I related some of my adventures and they sat transfixed till the end of each yarn.

In the last three weeks of their training, they received a series of lectures on the different Branches that they could apply for. I gave the lecture on Under Water Control, and at the end of all the lectures I handed out preference forms.

The forms listed their preference in order from 1 to 3. I then informed the Class Leader that he was to collect all the completed forms in a week's time. They would then front a Selection Committee a week from that date. They were all so keen and I felt that none of my boys would go for the discharge option. I would often overhear their conversations on their preferences so I thought all was well ... then one night there was a knock on my cabin door.

"Excuse me sir," said recruit Coster. "May I have a word?"

"Sure Coster," I said, "what's the problem?"

"Well sir, I have looked at all the Branches and there's nothing I want to be ... maybe I should take my discharge."

Speedy was by my side in a flash ... this was an emergency.

"Coster, I can't believe what I'm hearing," I said with surprise. "You have had a great time here and there are a number of Branches I am sure you would excel in," I said, trying to placate him.

"Well nothing seems to grab me sir, so I thought maybe I might give it all a miss," he said dejectedly.

We talked for a while longer, both Speedy and I trying to get some enthusiasm injected into the 'down in the mouth' recruit.

I finally told him to have a good re-think overnight and come back and talk to me before parade in the morning. I assured him that between us we would sort out the problem and that all would fall into place.

Speed and I headed out for the night. I gave it no more thought and thought it would resolve itself overnight.

It wasn't to be ... bright and early the next morning, Coster was at my cabin door, still adamant that there was no Branch that he felt suited him.

I was sure he just needed a little more time and that after he talked to some of the other recruits, he would find a Branch. I made a mental note to have a talk to his Class Leader. Maybe that would help. There was still a week or so before the papers had to be handed in to the Selection Board.

He then asked me if there were any papers he'd need to fill out if he were to take his discharge. I went into a kind of damage control mode and came up with a ridiculous solution for him. To this day I wonder at how my brain works and how I even dreamt this up on the spot.

"Coster," I said in a conspiratorial voice, at the same time looking from side to side so as not to be overheard, "I may just have the answer. There is one Branch that is not even listed on the form and it has been left up to me to choose a suitable recruit to fill this position. It has just become vacant in the fleet. I was going to wait for the next intake but the more I think about it, the more I am sure you might just be the man I am after ... no forget it," I trailed off ... "I will organise your discharge pap ... "

"Sir, what is it? ... I might ..."

I knew I had his interest. My mind was working overtime.

"Well, there are only four of these special people in the whole of the Navy. One has just died and left an opening but if I let you in on this, you must keep it strictly to yourself ... understood? ... totally confidential."

"Yes sir ... what is the Branch?" he said with the first hint of enthusiasm I had detected in him since our first conversation.

"Chief Brew Maker to the Fleet," I said, noticing a slight disbelief in his eyes. I kept talking ..."Just keep going," I said to myself.

"There are only four in the Navy. They are in charge of the tea we all drink at sea ... they are trained in Ceylon and go directly to the Fleet as Leading Seaman. No waiting for promotions. They are very special sailors. I nearly became a Chief Brew Maker myself, but just missed out," I said with the appropriate disappointing reflective look on my face.

## CROSSED TEASPOONS – COSTER'S CHOICE

All this time I could see he was starting to be convinced ... "Just keep it coming Mo," were my thoughts.

"You've probably seen the Chief Brew Maker yourself Coster," I said.

"He arrived from the fleet last week and has been visiting the school this week. You would have noticed his right arm insignia ... crossed teaspoons ..."

"Yes sir, I think I did see him last week sir," Coster stammered with excitement. He had convinced himself and at that point I knew I had him.

"Well, how do you feel about this Branch, Coster?" I asked.

"I'll take the position sir ... and 'mum's the word'" he said with enthusiasm.

"Right, that's a load off my mind," I said with a sigh of relief.

"Leading Seaman Heazelwood, will you bear witness to the fact that I have officially chosen Recruit Coster as our next Chief Brew Maker?"

"Certainly Leading Seaman Elliott," Speedy replied from within the cabin, his voice on the edge of collapse.

"Right Coster, report back to class and remember this is privileged information."

"Aye aye sir," he said as he marched away with a distinct swagger in his step. Speedy was hysterical when I closed the cabin door.

There was no way Coster took me seriously, he had just played along with the gag and would eventually sort out his Branch preference.

The week went by quickly with no more visits from Coster ... all was well.

My class had all passed their exams and had their results.

With only a few short weeks left in recruit school, their excitement was apparent.

When they left us they would go on leave for a few weeks and then on to their respective drafts in the fleet.

I had the class assembled in front of the dormitory at 0900.

The Class Leader would double march them to the Administration block, I would join them there. I rode a 'treadley', (Navy for bicycle). They duly assembled outside the Administration building ...

They would now front the Selection Board and be given their branches. Their excitement was palpable.

I stood them at ease and explained what was expected of them.

"You will be called before the Board individually. The Board comprises of your DO, the Commodore, the First Lieutenant, the Chief Instructor and our Civilian Psychologist. Upon your name being called you will march smartly in, come to attention, salute the Board and state your name and serial number."

I went on to explain that their aptitude would be noted and their preferences would be of priority. If they didn't get their first choice it could be sorted, once they got to the fleet. I wished them all good luck and reported my class as ready for the Board.

"Recruit Anders, report," came a voice from within.

Five minutes later Anders came out beaming. "I got my first choice sir ... Radio Operator."

"Well done Anders," I said, now double back to your block and work on your kit."

"Aye aye sir," he said proudly as he doubled away.

"Recruit Anthony, report" .... and so it went on.

"Recruit Coster ..."

They seemed to be taking an inordinate amount of time with Coster I thought ... and then ...

"LEADING SEAMAN ELLIOTT, IN HERE IMMEDIATELY," a voice from within bellowed.

I came to attention in front of the Board, next to Coster who was looking a little dejected.

The DO handed me Coster's form and demanded I explain.

I quickly looked at the Civilian Psychologist who was trying to stifle a wracking fit of laughter, clearly this guy had no discipline. It then came together in my mind ...

I looked down at the form in my hand ... Oh Jesus!

All the Branches had been ruled out and written across the top was ... CHIEF BREW MAKER AS APPOINTED BY LEADING SEAMAN ELLIOTT.

I was given a huge bollicking and the DO made the comment that "Elliott seems to think he's some sort of comedian" ... how prophetic that statement would be!

As for Coster, well, he went to sea as an Officer's Steward. At least he got to make tea for some of the fleet. He went on to serve 25 years and paid off as a Chief Petty Officer. "Well done mate ... 'ya' done me proud."

## GETTING RESTLESS

I took one more class through recruit school. Again, it was a rewarding experience but my time there was coming to an end.

A hiatus was coming. There would be no more recruits for a few months and soon it would be time for me to head back to the fleet. I awaited my next draft.

In the meantime, I was given the job of Accommodation Leading Hand, supervising the upkeep and maintenance of the ship's company dormitories; completely boring and mind numbing. Most days I had nothing really to do. I sat in the block's office watching TV. I knew I had to get some other job when I found myself getting into Days of our Lives.

I went ashore at every opportunity and spent a lot of time with my musician mates at home. They were playing local gigs and I would take my Navy mates out to watch them. I started to envy their freedom and toyed with the idea of leaving the Navy.

Mum was bringing up Michael and Wendy on her own but she had fallen into a drinking pattern with her friends in the area. It wasn't always good for the kids. We were more than a little concerned for her and the young ones. She was desperately lonely and it was sad to see.

Since my father had died, she had found a new freedom and couldn't believe the amount of money now available to her as a widow.

It wasn't that it was such a great deal of money but it was so much more than he had given her for all those years.

Legacy came to help. They are a fantastic organisation and made sure that the kids never went without. Ralph, Carol and I, were all on hand and made sure they were always OK.

I stayed weekends with Mum and got to spend time with Michael and Wendy.

Jim Craig was working as head mechanic at a local car yard and helped me buy an ex-Government Ford Falcon at a great price. $1,500 was a lot of 'bread' in those days. It was a good car and I thought it was so cool at the time.

## INSURANCE, HASTINGS STYLE

Back at the Base, things rolled along as usual. Weeknights the mates and I would head into Hastings to the pub.

Col McVeigh, one of my old Marks division mates from Leeuwin was drafted to Cerberus and we bumped into each other on the Base. He was taking out a WRAN Nurse at the time and suggested we do a double date; I would take out her girlfriend. It was all arranged. Friday night we would go to 'Hasto for a Tasto'.

During the day Col suggested he drive my car with his girl, as he was getting off earlier and that I could catch up later with my date. She had her own car and would pick me up. I had only had my brand new second-hand car for a few weeks and felt a little apprehensive, but hey ... he was my mate.

After the dinner we were all heading to Stony Point, a local parking spot for a few more 'cool drinks' as Col put it.

In fact that was Col's nickname, 'Cool drinks McVeigh'. It was his best 'pick up' line ... "Would you like to join me for cool drinks?" I think it went.

The date went well; we were all having a great time. We left the pub at closing and headed to Stony Point. Col and his girl were in my car. I was driving my date's car. We followed on a few minutes behind.

I rounded a bend in the road and saw a car in the scrub, another car head-first into a tree. People were getting out of the first car to assist those in the one smashed into the tree. The smashed car looked a little familiar. Bugger!

I raced over to my car. I could vaguely hear police or ambulance sirens.

I found Col sitting with his back to the car, his girlfriend next to him sprawled out being assisted by a girl from the other car. There were no obvious signs of blood but she was moaning in pain; she had a broken leg. The ambulance arrived and she was being attended to.

I turned back to Col.

He kept saying "Sorry Mohawk, I'll make it up to you."

"Don't worry mate," I said. "As long as you guys are going to be OK we'll be fine." "But mate," Col interjected, "forgot to tell you, I haven't got a licence"... bugger ... no insurance payout. This would hurt.

I looked over and saw a cop talking to the other driver. At that moment I had another of my brilliant ... not always well thought out epiphanies.

I quickly messed my hair up, pulled out my shirt and lay down next to Col. "Quick, tell me what happened?" I asked Col.

Col told me briefly how he lost it on the bend and swerved to miss the other car. All this conversation was happening as another cop was heading over to us.

"Just take my lead mate, I just might be able to make this work." I said to Col under my breath.

The cop approached us and nodded. He seemed to be a middle-aged guy, a veteran who had probably seen this a thousand times.

"You OK?" he said to Col in a friendly concerned tone.

"Yeah, fine thanks," Col replied, a little shakily.

"What happened?" he asked, looking at Col.

"I lost it on the bend," I interjected, even more shakily.

"Are you saying you're the driver?" he said to me.

I noticed the up inflection in his tone, so I just kept it going. "Yes that's right officer, I'm just glad everyone is going to be OK," I said in what I hoped was a concerned, 'good guy' type tone.

"I understand you boys are Navy but I will still require you to make a statement down at the station. I'll take you down there now," he said.

We arrived at the station and were taken to an interview room.

"Right, let's get started," he said, taking out his pad.

I started to create my story as he patiently listened and sagely nodded.

"You are a remarkable young man," he finally said, with a wry smile on his face.

"You managed to crash this car, while at the same time drive the third car to the scene of the accident ... that's amazing" ... bugger!

"When did you twig to it?" I asked.

"Well I got my first hint when your girlfriend told us how you came upon the accident scene and I got the second hint when I saw you mess your hair up, rearrange your clothes and then lay down next to the driver. Not exactly clever police work, but I need to know the reason. Care to explain?" he said.

I told him the truth this time and he wrote his report.

With a warning of "This time it's just a warning but remember we're not all dumb coppers ... good try though, now get out of here."

I thought to myself, "Now there's a decent chap!"

Col helped pay the car out as it was a write-off; his girlfriend was in plaster for a while but otherwise ok. Life returned to normal ... well almost.

## FRESH BREAD?

I was getting more restless and it seemed to me that when I become bored I become more adventurous and that's when the proverbial hits the fan.

It was coming up for New Year's Eve and Jim and Jan, Jim's new wife, were throwing a party at their place. All my civvy mates would be there and I was really looking forward to it.

I had managed to get hold of an old Hillman bread-van, it still had the 'Fresh Bread' sign on the double doors at the back, but pride doesn't come into it when you're desperate.

I had helped out one of my mates from Lyndale with a few bob and he repaid me with the van. It was rusting away in his dad's backyard but still had a few months registration on it. I gladly excepted it in lieu of payment and drove away with some extra bits and pieces that I would need to keep my new wheels operational ... I'll explain.

I managed to pinch one of Mum's baking trays. It was essential to position it under the sump of the van whenever I stopped to park. The tray would catch the dripping oil from the broken seal, and then it could be re-introduced to the engine via my new funnel, when I took off again.

I also kept a four gallon drum of old sump oil I obtained from our local garage (no charge). It was being dumped anyway, so old Les at the service station was glad for me to take it.

When I collected the oil after parking, it was never quite as much as I started with ... some would be lost in transition. The drum was a backup ... well it worked for me. At least it was a temporary solution.

## 'ARRY

I turned up at Mum's one Friday night and my elder sister Carol was there. It was always great to see her and she had brought Sue, my niece along. Carol had come to pick Wendy up for the weekend; although Wendy was Sue's Auntie, they were the same age so in fact they were more like sisters.

Mum had met a 'gentleman friend', through a friend and he was coming over for tea. Mum was all 'dolled up' and the house was spic and span.

She said if we were to stay and meet him, we were not to be 'silly sods', as she put it.

Carol had a wicked sense of humour and together we were a force. Carol had met this chap before and had christened him 'Dunlop' because he wore huge ripple-sole rubber shoes that were in fashion at the time.

"What time is Dunlop arriving Mum?" she asked. "Any tick of the clock and don't be calling him Dunlop ... his name is 'Arry. I'm warnin' you pair, don't be showin' me up," she said with her still strong London accent.

There was a knock at the door, Mum straightened her dress, turned to us with a 'behave yourselves' look on her face and answered the door.

I stood and shook hands with Harry. He said "Hi" to Carol and took a seat with us in the kitchen. He was wearing a suit and had his Dunlops on as Carol had predicted.

Mum was like a schoolgirl and being very attentive, offering Harry this and that and we noticed she was doing her best to put all the 'H's and T's' on her words and take the edge off her accent. She was doing her best 'toff'. Then she blew it ....

"We're having steak for tea Harry," Mum said, making sure she put the 'H' on his name, then it all went 'pear shaped' as she said, "Would you like a 'hegg' with it?"

Carol came straight in with ... "Yes Harry, have hay hegg by hall means, hor maybe hay homlette and maybe harfterwards we could have hay happle".

"Hor maybe hay horange, Harry," I followed with. We were hysterical. Harry wasn't sure if he was allowed to laugh but his eyes were twinkling.

"Take no notice of these pair of bleeders 'arry, they got no bleedin' manners," said Mum, her accent had returned!

I drove back to the Base that night but found it hard going, I couldn't stop laughing.

## THE KEYS TO THE LOLLY SHOP

Daily orders came out for New Year's Eve. I was named as Duty Leading Seaman for MUPs (Men under Punishment). I also had three blokes in cells at the gangway. It was my job to make sure they got fed and check on them periodically with the gangway staff.

It sounds sinister that there would be men in the brig but you didn't have to do much wrong in those days to end up in the slammer for a night. It could be for drunk and disorderly, or overstepping your leave by a week or two, (after seven days it was classed officially as desertion) or some other minor infraction like telling a superior to get knotted ... you get the drift.

The Navy of my day was certainly tougher than it is today.

One of our sayings in those days was, "BUT YOU CAN'T LOCK ME UP CHIEF".

"WATCH YOUR FINGERS SON" ... CLICK!

I had six blokes to supervise on chooks, plus the three in the cells to look after and it was the night of Jim and Jan's party. I was a bit dirty on the whole idea of missing it.

I was told that I must make sure the men in cells were fed and the guys on chooks must be supervised at all times. ... my mind was at work, they didn't specify WHERE they should be supervised. ...

To cut a long story short, I loaded all the men under punishment including those in the cells, into the back of the bread-van and we drove out the back of the Base near the Gunnery Range and headed for the party. It was about an hour's drive away.

All the boys promised to come back with me at the end of the night. With any luck we wouldn't get caught.

We partied into the night at Jim's. The band had a jam session and half the neighbourhood turned up. It spilled into the street and we had a ball.

One of the boys drove back just before dawn. I was out to it in the back of the van but all were accounted for. One of the lads put me to bed, locked the other guys back up and managed to do all this undetected. He should have been immediately recruited for SAS training.

Everything was now back to normal except for the fact that the prisoners were all unaccountably roaring drunk and singing.

At 8 am that morning Speedy woke me, still fully dressed in my Dress Blues; beer and food stains as an addition.

"Mohawk, wake up, you're being piped to report to the gangway ... at the double ... it's now the third time you've been called."

"Bloody hell Speed, where's the treadley?" I stammered, my head pounding. I was still 'two sheets' to the wind.

I jumped on the pushbike and headed for the gangway. I fell off twice and took the knee out of my bell bottom trousers in doing so. I felt no pain. The elbow of my top was taken out as well and I could feel the blood running down my arm on the inside ... still no pain.

I came to attention as best I could in front of the Officer of the Day, saluted and tried my best to focus on the situation.

"ALL THE MEN IN CELLS ARE DRUNK, ELLIOTT ... EXPLAIN," he roared!

I started to plead 'no knowledge' but I think my slurred speech and the stench of stale alcohol made my attempt a non-event.

Blood was dripping at his feet from my newly inflicted wounds so I was glad when the confrontation was over and I was allowed to get back to sleep. I didn't get to sleep in my own cabin though. The bed I was given was a little hard and there were bars on the window but oblivious to this I slumbered on.

## OPPORTUNITY KNOCKS

A few months earlier I had met an old shipmate in a Melbourne pub. It was great to catch up and he told me of his new work with an international oil company.

He had taken his discharge from the Navy and used his expertise to secure this civilian job. While in the service he worked in Under Water Control, as did I.

He painted a great picture of his life overseas. He was making incredible money and suggested I should consider applying for a discharge and that he was sure there was a position coming up and that he would submit my name. He would be in touch.

I didn't think any more of it, but true to his word he rang and gave me a contact to call and an interview was set up.

My work with depth sounders and graphing was what they were after and it would require some sea time. They had a preference for service men with experience. I knew my stuff and the job was mine if I could make myself available.

The money was at least ten times my Navy pay and the total package included flights back to Australia with a whole raft of benefits.

They were willing to write to the Navy with their offer if it would help me secure a discharge. I would be sent to Canada on joining the company.

I would need to be ready to start within a few months or so.

I thought long and hard for about two minutes and decided to try for a discharge. I applied through the proper channels and my request went to powers that be in Canberra. I thought they would be overjoyed at the prospect of losing me but no, my request for a discharge was denied. Obviously they hadn't heard about Jim's party yet.

It really was a great surprise to me that Canberra didn't jump at the chance to be rid of me. I somehow thought it would be a 'lay down misere' ... well I'll be buggered, they really did like me. What a turn around, I felt a little chuffed.

This refusal only made me more determined, so I respectfully applied again ... again it was rebuffed. What to do?

I had my original DO back and went to see him.

He suggested I make an appointment to see the Civilian Psychologist that worked for the Navy on the Base.

I made the appointment and she helped me with an application that suggested I needed a compassionate discharge to help my mother and my younger brother and sister now that my father had died. The new job would help me cope financially as an added benefit.

While I was awaiting an answer from Canberra I was given my new draft. I would have three weeks leave, then I was to report to HMAS Vendetta, a Daring class destroyer.

She was in re-fit in Melbourne and then would be doing work-up trials and then up to the Far East.

I resigned myself to the fact that I would be back at sea but at least this time I had a little rank. Life would be a little easier and besides I'd be back to the old stomping grounds. There was no news from Canberra all through my leave and with just a few days left I accepted the fact that I was going back to sea.

I duly reported to my new ship. I was told at the gangway to find a bunk in the Aft Mess and stow my gear.

As I walked into the Mess I was greeted by an old mate from my previous ship, HMAS Stuart.

'Stilts' Sherrin was an Able Seaman and the same branch as me; it was good to see him.

"Heard you were coming mate," he said with a big smile of welcome on his face.

"I've got you a top bunk over in the corner and they have already named you as 'Killick' (Leading Hand) of the Mess. There's a few of our old crew from the Stuart on board as well, so this should be a good trip."

Alex Sherrin was an ex JR like myself and was nicknamed Stilts because of his long skinny legs. He was a top hand and I smiled at the thought of having a few familiar faces around.

I stowed my kit bag on the bunk and headed to the 'Pay Bob's' office to sign in.

There would be some papers to sign to officially become part of the crew. I headed up to the Writer's office.

"Leading Seaman Elliott reporting," I said to the Chief Writer.

"Did you say Elliott ... Leader?" he asked.

"That's right Chief," I replied as he shuffled some envelopes in his hand.

He handed me an envelope.

"Good luck on the outside Mr. Elliott," he said with a grin, "here's your discharge papers."

# PART THREE

## BACK TO CIVVY STREET

I headed back to the Mess to pick up my kit.

Stilts was waiting. "We'll miss you mate, good luck and don't forget to keep in touch," he said.

We shook hands and I grabbed a few bits and pieces I wanted to keep out of my kit and headed for the gangway.

I looked over my shoulder as I left the Mess. My last sight was of Stilts trying on a pair of my No.8s (working jeans).

As I headed back to Mum's place, my mind was racing.

It struck me as a little disconcerting, that for the first time in seven years, I didn't have an authority in control of my life.

It would be fair to say I felt a little unsure of myself, even a little frightened. The thought crossed my mind to turn the car around and go back, cap in hand ... that wouldn't work, I'd left my cap with the kit!

I had been in the Navy all of my formative years; I was twenty-three and had known no other life since I was sixteen. It felt strange ... was I making a huge mistake?

Anyone that serves in any regimented outfit for any length of time usually becomes a little institutionalised. I have learned since, this is quite a normal outcome. Your security has been taken away and you need time to adjust.

Some can't adjust and end up re-enlisting. This happened to my brother Ralph. Two years National Service including Vietnam and there was no going back. After a short spell on the outside, he made the decision to go back to the Army. I drove him back into Melbourne on that day ... best thing he could have done, he couldn't adjust to the outside again. He needed to be with those that understood him.

I initially stayed at Mum's. I bunked in with Michael but it was a temporary solution. I would need to get into a better situation.

There was a message at Mum's from Shellie. He had gotten his discharge, married and was living in Caulfield, a few suburbs away. Mum gave me his telephone number.

I jumped into the old bread-van and headed off to catch up with Shellie. He had married a girl from Western Australia. I had met her in Sydney and briefly took out her girlfriend, while Shellie and I did our Able Seaman's course at Watson.

I was surprised at his being married, he was such a party animal and it seemed somehow out of character. Was it possible we were starting to mature? ... I had my doubts.

The bread-van was coming to the end of her life; Jim had patched her up too many times now and besides Mum wanted her baking tray back. I persevered for a little while longer, I had no choice.

Jan, Jim's wife, had christened the van Pebbles after the Flintstones character. I had taken Jan to the shops once and she could see the road through the floor. I needed a rolling start by then, so Jan suggested we stick our feet through the floor and start it like Fred did.

Jim and Jan's flat was 'party central'. We all enjoyed a drink and we had all been mates since we were kids.

I left the Navy with a basic knowledge of Bingo, I could ask for a beer in ten different languages and track a submarine.

I definitely wasn't prepared for life as a civilian but the job overseas was going to happen; I just had to survive for a few more months.

I had left the Navy with $1,500 in DFRDB (Defence Forces' Retirement Benefit Fund). I wasn't able to be in the fund until I had turned 18. That was another irony ... no money for retirement but I was OK to be in combat.

I decided to find a job so I didn't have to touch my little stash.

## THRU' A LOOKING GLASS

I landed a job at Pilkington ACI glass factory in Dandenong.

The first job I was given was as a crane 'dogman'. My job was to load the blocks of sheet glass onto the trucks from an overhead crane. I was taught never to stand to the sides or directly underneath the blocks being loaded as slivers of glass would occasionally fall from the block.

It was a huge factory; they made the glass and distributed it all over Australia and overseas.

It was owned by British Pilkington and many of the management staff were brought out from England.

They had employed quite a number of ex-servicemen, so I found common ground with many of them.

I soon settled into the factory routines but found it to be totally boring after the Navy. I wondered how these blokes coped day in and day out. Still it was only temporary; I would soon be overseas again. That thought kept me going ...

I was shifted around to different sections as part of the system and at one point I had been partnered to work with an ex Petty Officer Gunner.

His name was Joe Martin and as it turned out, I had gone to school with his daughter, Cathy. Joe and I had much in common. As we worked, we talked of our time in the service and many of the men we both knew.

Our job was to roll paper down between the sheets of glass and take out any broken sheets. These blocks of glass were on big A-frame trolleys and the task took a little getting used to as there was a knack to cutting the paper off.

Joe was a very tolerant teacher and took great pains and patience with me. He stressed how important it was to take the broken sheets out as the blocks would eventually be hoisted overhead to be loaded onto the trucks. If any sheets were broken they would fall from the block and there had been some serious accidents in the past. One bloke was sliced down the front from a falling piece. It opened him up and his intestines had to be held in while he waited for an ambulance. I had already ducked a few falling sheets when I worked as a dogman so I knew the danger first hand.

## FAST GLASS

We worked on a bonus system that had been introduced. The amount of work you did, directly related to the bonus you received. It was possible to make an extra $1 an hour ($40 a week) if you got stuck into it. The wages back then were around $80 a week, so it was possible to really boost your take-home pay. We all chased the extra money.

As I was being taught, Joe was losing bonus. I kept apologising for being so slow but he reassured me it was all OK.

The problem with this system was that some of the 'interlevers' as that was what we were known as, took short cuts and wouldn't remove the broken sheets. It slowed up the process and would cost bonus.

Glass would crack if you tried to paper it too early after it had come down from the kiln. The rule of thumb was, if the glass was still warm, don't paper it. The more sheets in a block the more bonuses could be made.

There were two Russian blokes that took warm glass constantly and didn't remove the broken sheets. They were always chasing the best paying blocks. When they were chastised for this they fell back on the 'can't speak good English' bit. This created a little tension among the other workers.

I finally got up to speed with the job and Joe and I talked as we worked. I was able to relate to this man; he was old enough to be my father; he had been through so much in his own time in the Navy.

He had taken his discharge on medical grounds after being rescued from the Voyager disaster.

## SAD TIMES

It was the first incident our aircraft carrier HMAS Melbourne had been involved in. With tears welling up in his eyes, he told me his story.

The Melbourne and the Voyager (a Daring class destroyer), were performing exercises off Jervis Bay in NSW on the night of 10th February 1964. The Melbourne was flying aircraft and the Voyager was acting as plane guard.

The collision happened when both ships had altered course to a northerly heading. The Voyager was to re-position herself as plane guard. To do this she would have to turn away from the Melbourne in a large circle, cross the carrier's stern then move along Melbourne's port side. Instead of this the Voyager first turned to starboard, away from the carrier, then without warning turned to port and came under the Melbourne's bows. The Melbourne hit the Voyager just aft of the destroyer's Bridge; she rolled to starboard and was cut in half.

82 men died that night. Joe told me of the chaos and carnage and the loss of great mates. He witnessed friends dying before his eyes. As he spoke I could feel his pain. This man needed to tell me his story. It was a cathartic experience for both of us.

We both had a history of disasters at sea and both times with the Melbourne and here we were working together. It seemed so surreal.

Joe was suffering post-traumatic stress, it was very apparent to me as I listened although I didn't know the terminology at that time. He was still trying to get his pension while we worked together. This tragedy had a huge impact on his life. I understood much of what he was going through.

There were still 35 cases from the Voyager disaster being fought for compensation as late as 2008 ... the last case was dealt with in 2009 ... much too late for many.

## SHELL SHOCKED

I got a call from Shellie asking if I was interested in sharing his flat.

"What about your wife Beryl?" I asked.

"Didn't work out ... she's gone back to Perth," he said matter of factly.

"I'll come over and we'll see," I said thinking that the novelty of marriage had worn off with him ... the mongrel hadn't changed at all.

Beryl had left Shellie with a double bed and a couch; he didn't even have a fridge. There were two girls sharing a flat below his ... he used their fridge.

One of the girls was very keen on him and he used this to his advantage.

The upshot of the deal was that I would move in. We would share the rent of $20 a week and go halves in all the rest.

I slept on the couch till I could get hold of a bed. He kept promising to get a fridge and in the meantime I rented a TV from Radio Rentals at $4 a week with an option to buy after two years, if it lasted that long.

He was also out of work, so I vouched for him at the glass factory ... worst thing I could have done.

He constantly borrowed money from me but was driving the latest V8 Ford. His immediate problem was that he couldn't keep up the payments. He couldn't even afford petrol.

He kept moving the car around so it couldn't be repossessed.

When we took out girls together he told them so many lies I didn't know where to look. He dressed like a million dollars and acted the same. The car topped it off ... a total poseur. The repossesors eventually came and got his car.

He wasn't happy going to work in the bread-van.

He told our workmates we were "doing it up to race".

One night we had met two girls at Pinocchio's night club. Shellie got up to dance with his girl. Her girlfriend then turned to me and asked me what it was like being an International Pilot and won't it be fun when we take them for a ride in our Cessna at the weekend. He had done it again! He must have spun the yarn while I was getting the drinks ... bloody hell!

After we left the club we headed for the car park. They assumed we were about to get into the Mercedes ... right next to the bread-van. I steered my date to the left and tried to keep a straight face.

Shellie went into his routine about "doing it up to race" as I helped the girls into the back of Pebbles.

We pulled up outside their flat. I helped the girls out of the back of the van.

Shellie's girl got out last and I noticed a big round oil mark on her arse from my sump oil drum. Apparently the towel I put over it wasn't enough protection. She went ballistic and needless to say we weren't invited in for a nightcap ... Just as well, I only had six days to learn to fly ...

Eventually Shellie was sacked at the factory; he took off too many days.

For weeks afterwards blokes he had befriended at the factory were coming up to me on paydays, saying Shellie said that I would give them the five or ten he had borrowed in the weeks before.

When I fronted him he swore blue murder it was a pack of lies. I came to realise Shellie was out of control and couldn't be trusted. He could never get away with it in the Navy, but Civvy Street was open slather.

I was sitting on the couch one afternoon when there was a knock on the door. We were being evicted for not paying our rent!

I had given Shellie my money every week without fail; he would then head down to pay the rent ... so he told me.

In reality he would head to a bar down the road, waste a little time then pocket the money and say, "All done mate, let's go out for a few beers ... my shout."

I'd think ... what a top bloke ...

I moved back to Mum's as a temporary measure. The new job was still a few months away.

Pebbles finally chucked in the claw (broke down) ... she was just too much of a wreck. Mum got her baking tray back and Jim and I towed her to the tip. I saw the tip scroungers going through her as we drove out. One bloke actually toed off with the drum of sump oil ... he must have had a dodgy seal.

## FAST CARS/WOMEN?

Jim came around to Mum's one night after work and told me of a trade-in he had been checking out at the car yard where he worked. It was an Austin Healy Sprite sports car; racing green and according to Jim, a steal at $400.

I bought the sporty little beast ... open top and low to the ground, it was a beauty.

With my hair blowing in the breeze, Saint Christopher on the dashboard with his hands over his eyes, I was mobile again.

I had been out of the Navy around six weeks by this time, and things looked like all was going well. I was drinking a lot on the weekends, there seemed to be parties all the time. I guess like all young people, we believed we were bomb-proof.

One Friday night some friends of ours were getting engaged and we partied into the night. Jim took me home to Mum's, put me to bed, and then went home himself, although I have no memory of this, to this day.

Apparently I woke up some time later, jumped in the Sprite and headed off to visit an old girlfriend. She told me later I got there drunk. She told me to leave, so I screeched out of her drive and headed off into the night.

I woke up in hospital three days later. I had wrapped the sports car around a lamp-post after clipping another car while going through an intersection about two miles from home.

## MR COOL

I was a mess, broken jaw, smashed teeth, fractured skull. I had 97 stitches in my scalp and I was black and blue. I hurt all over.

They had wired my jaw shut. I had no memory of any of the events leading up to this, including the party.

A doctor came in to see me; he told me how I nearly bled to death and how lucky I was to have survived.

I was sedated again and drifted back to sleep; I awoke to find Mum and the kids beside my bed. The police had come to Mum's in the early hours after the accident to inform her to get straight to the hospital as I might not make it. That was three days before.

A few days later I had a visit from the guy in the other car. I was so relieved to hear he, his wife and baby were uninjured. It could have been so much worse ... what an idiot I was!

Bob McNab was a local bloke around my own age; he was a roof tiler and was married to Carol Meyer. Her and her twin sister Susan had gone to school with me. He was so forgiving and told me we'd sort it all out when I was recovered enough.

I started to think of my predicament ... no insurance on my car and I would need to fix Bob's car as well.

The other realisation was that I had no medical insurance or dental cover. It was all covered in the Navy and I thought I wouldn't need it in the short term as I would be heading overseas.

I was feeling so sorry for myself but not once did I think that my drinking was becoming a problem. It was just a spell of bad luck.

I was told I would need to stay in hospital for a couple of weeks and then it would take a good month after that to be strong enough to resume work.

This wasn't part of my plans at all and I needed to evaluate the situation, and fast. I just couldn't afford this scenario. Bills were piling up daily.

After doctors' rounds a few days later, I found my clothes and very slowly managed to dress myself. I looked up the passageway ... all clear. I found a wheelchair outside a ward and seconded it as I wasn't walking too well at the time.

I wheeled myself out to the front of the hospital, caught a cab and had him take me to Mum's.

Mum was surprised to see me but I told her I was doing so well that I was told I could come home. I didn't want her to worry so I justified the 'white lie'. I went straight to bed, I was exhausted. This little adventure had taken its toll.

Mum woke me, very upset because an ambulance had just pulled up to take me back to hospital. I told Mum how I just couldn't afford the little holiday and somehow convinced the ambulance driver and his mate that I didn't need to go back.

My sister Carol insisted she nurse me around at her place. She took a few weeks off work and was a great help.

I was wearing a little hat like 'Gilligan' as the doctors had shaved most of my hair off. They had left one sideburn and some hair at the back. When the hat was taken off, my head looked like a road map … big homeward bounders (stitches) everywhere. It wasn't a good look. I remember exactly how many stitches … it was 97. I distinctly remember asking the Doctor if he could make it an even 'ton'. He saw no humour in this and admonished me for making light of the situation. Fair enough!

I sat around for a few days pondering my current position. I needed to make some quick decisions. To top things off, I had been notified that the job I had lined up overseas was not going to happen any time soon …. "We'll be in touch" I think was the expression.

I rang my old shipmate Marty who was now a Chief Petty Officer working in Recruiting in Melbourne. I offered my 'valuable' services back to the Navy.

After a few calls he advised me I could re-enlist and offered me a few different options. I could be back at sea with my old rank as long as I passed the physical. He didn't seem to think there would be a problem. I just needed a little time to recuperate.

Jim came around one Thursday night and asked if I would like to come and sit on the couch while they had band practice. Jim's flat was just up the street from Carol's, so she was OK with it … I had a leave pass.

I sat on the couch in my pyjamas and dressing gown and of course my Gilligan. Jan made me a cup of tea as we waited for the rest of the band to turn up. They duly arrived; Pete the drummer, Pam the singer and Bob the bass player.

## KAZ — A NEW BEGINNING

Bob turned up with his girlfriend, Lorraine. She had brought her friend Karen along for the ride. Her name was Karen Wright. She was the prettiest girl I had ever seen. We have been married 41 years at the writing of this book, but hey, there's much more to tell you yet.

Now at this point I could say she took one look at me and thought to herself "how hot is this guy" but that would be a bit too hard to swallow ... you've seen my photo. The fact is I think she probably thought I was Jim's grandfather sitting in the corner waiting to 'flash' someone.

We were introduced. I could tell she wasn't really sure about the beanie, so I took it off to complete the picture. My eyes were still yellowy black; imagine Uncle Fester after ten rounds with Mike Tyson.

Karen was twenty years old and working in the advertising department as a ticket and show-card writer at Big W in Melbourne. Karen is a natural artist.

Today she paints anything from landscapes to portraits. She is a very talented artist and her work is quite exquisite ... beautiful. It never ceases to amaze me just how someone can create such paintings.

Back to Jim's ... That night we seemed to hit it off and I figured, even though I was punching well above my weight, if she liked me now, how good it could be when I got back to a semblance of normalcy.

## MR COOL AGAIN!

I made her laugh when I told her how great my smile was. I couldn't show her now but when my broken jaw healed and I got a new front tooth she was in for a treat. Later she told me she liked my brown eyes. The rest was a mess.

A few weeks later she was throwing a party at her place. Her parents would be away and the band, I and a bunch of our mates were invited. All was going well till I dropped a cigarette on her Mum's new lounge suite and burnt a bloody great hole in the armrest. It was a great way to start a relationship. Later, when I met her folks I apologised and offered to pay for the damage. They were very gracious but it felt very awkward at the time.

A couple of years later, after we were married and had moved to our first house, Karen's Mum and Dad bought a new lounge suite and offered us their old one.

"Mum," I said "that's so nice of you but … there's a burn mark on the arm rest … could you get that fixed first?" Her face dropped, then she started to laugh …

She has told that story for 40 years … she still loves spinning the yarn … but getting back to the story.

Karen and I became an item but I was no great catch. I was now in a lot of debt, with no great prospects. I had so many adventures under my belt and she was just starting out. It was an odd arrangement to say the least. I was still battling a few demons but somehow we hung in there. I was recovering from the accident but it was a slow process. I needed to get some headway with the mounting bills.

It took a while for the dentist to do work on me; he couldn't pull one tooth at the back as it would have broken my jaw again. He said he would, instead, rebuild the tooth but it would only be temporary.

Forty years later that tooth is still in top condition after his temporary work. My dentist today still marvels at that man's handiwork.

Karen was the reason I never returned to the Navy. I was enjoying my new-found freedom and I was in love, but I knew I had to get moving again.

I had gone back to work early and the floor supervisor put me with the sweepers. The work was constant but not too demanding and the older guys looked after me. I would get tired very easily and at lunch time I would lay down on a few old sacks, they had set up in a sort of cubby hole in-between the stacks of glass. I would be sound asleep and they often let me sleep well into the afternoon. Old Jack Flower and his mates would cover for me. I have never forgotten their kindness. They were top blokes.

My strength slowly returned and I was able to get back into the main-stream of the factory. I started to earn bonus again and began to pay the bills.

Bob McNab let me pay off the repairs to his car. I would catch up with him at the pub Thursday nights without fail.

I was thousands of dollars in debt; it would be a long haul. I had made arrangements with the hospital and the dentist.

I was now boarding with Jim and Jan in the spare room of their flat. This was handy as Jim was now working as a mechanic at the Mercury outboard factory which was just down the road from where I worked. He gave me a lift to work every morning.

Jim had a Holden Ute. It had no heating and winter mornings we would have thick ice on the windscreen. One morning it was really bad, Jim was having trouble starting the Ute. While he was doing that, he asked if I could get a bucket of water to throw over the windscreen. I came out with the bucket and threw it on the windscreen ... it shattered ... I had used hot water! I thought it would speed things up. We went to work that morning and nearly froze.

Jim bitched all the way. He was astounded that I didn't know about that sort of thing. I tried to explain that it wasn't covered in the Navy hand-book. He wasn't laughing but as I said, "Could have been worse mate, could have been raining". A mile from work, the sky opened up. We laughed till we were nearly sick.

I added Jim's windscreen to my bills.

I loved living with Jim and Jan; apart from music we had a great bond.

Jan was a nurse and worked shifts. This often left Jim and me to our own devices, not always a good scenario.

## THE BREW MASTERS

One night Jim came home with all the paraphernalia to make homemade beer. I think it was payment in lieu of some mechanical work he'd done for a bloke at work.

Anyway the upshot was we worked out that we could save a fortune if we brewed our own beer in the shed.

Jan wasn't impressed because we had commandeered the bathtub to wash our collected empties but she eventually went along with it.

We thought all was going well. We had bottled and stacked nine dozen in the shed as per the instructions. Now it was just a matter of time till they were ready to drink.

We woke one Saturday morning to the sound of gunfire ... what the hell! Jim came running in the back door yelling, "Col, the grog's exploding in the shed."

We grabbed two big saucepans to put on our heads and went into the shed.

Bottle tops were blowing off the tops of the bottles and hitting the shed roof making a hell of a racket. We salvaged all we could and took them out in the yard. We hosed them down. It seemed to settle their volatility ... a good call.

"This'll be a top drop," said Jim, with a huge grin on his face.

We both figured it would be good stuff because if it was exploding now, how much kick would we get when we actually drank it. We managed to salvage around five dozen.

That afternoon we decided to try our first bottle.

We waited for Jan to come home from work and the three of us sat down. We had chilled two bottles and if it wasn't for the plain gold bottle top at first glance it looked like a bottle of Victoria Bitter (our preferred). We had kept all the old labels on our empties.

"Here goes," said Jim as he poured three glasses.

We all sipped simultaneously ... Jan gasped and spat hers out all over the back of Jimmy's head ... it was the back of his head because Jim was busy spitting his mouthful on the floor. I made it to the sink ...

There is nothing I could compare the taste to ... bloody hell it was crook!

We sat there totally dejected then Jan suggested we could maybe give it a while longer to brew. If anything, two weeks later it tasted worse.

We put the rest in the Ute and were about to take them to the tip when Jim had an evil thought.

"The stuff looks OK so let's take a few bottles at a time to a few of our parties and BBQs and slip them in with 'legit' beers. We'll know the real ones because of the tops .... should be fun," Jim said with a mischievous laugh.

We dispersed quite a few that way. We'd be at a party and hear from across the room, "JESUS! WHAT'S THIS SHIT?"

Jim and I would have tears running down our face. "There goes another one," we'd say.

We got rid of half the home brew that way, before our mates worked out what we had done. We were threatened with expulsion from all future gatherings if we didn't put on a couple of dozen of real bottles to make up for our deceit.

I was starting to settle in to a routine when Jan became pregnant with their first child. Jan was excited as they had been trying to conceive from the day they were wed. Jan now needed my room for a nursery. I would need to move out. Narelle was on the way!

## JACK MILLS

As it turned out, Jack, a friend of Pam's, the band's lead singer, was renting half a house in Dandenong. The band had been practicing there and he had a spare room. He was the boyfriend of Pam's Mum,

Lorna. They would go out together but Jack was a confirmed bachelor in his mid-fifties.

Jack Mills was from the country and outwardly he seemed a tough old bugger. I wasn't sure if he would want to share his place but I approached him.

"You'll have to do your own cooking you know, I do my washing on Wednesdays, so you can use the laundry any other time, and you'll have to keep the place spick and span," he said with a gruff tone.

"All good Jack," I said, "what's the rent?"

The place was owned by the local RSL; Jack was a life member and paid next to nothing for the place. We went halves; it was a great set up. I moved in. I had an old sideboard and a bed. I was set.

The very first morning I woke up to Jack knocking on my door.

"Scrambled eggs on toast on the table in two minutes ... don't let 'em go cold," he said in an off-handed manner.

That was how it was with Jack, he became like a mother to me. We became great mates.

If I was coming home early from the factory, I would walk in to the smell of a casserole. "Hey Col, hope you like beef," he would call out from the kitchen as I came in the front door. Jack was a top cook. He would often cook a roast for Kaz and me on band nights. I started to regain my weight.

The house was a single structure but was divided in half to make two, two-bedroom flats.

We shared a common laundry and toilet out the back with the old couple next door. The walls were very thin and our kitchen was next to theirs.

They were a strange pair. During the day they were quiet and polite but as soon as the sun went down they would start drinking. All would be OK till around 9pm then they would start fighting and abuse each other. Their language would make a sailor blush.

Jack and I would finish tea, wash up, then sit facing the dividing wall in the kitchen, beer in hand and wait for the floorshow to begin.

Sometimes she would scream "I'll kill 'ya' ... 'ya' fuckin' bastard," followed by something smashing against the wall. Now and again we would call out encouragement and would receive a torrent of abuse back from them. This would go on for an hour or so and then they would flake out.

"Well that's it for tonight Col," Jack would say "see you in the morning," and off we'd go to bed. It became part of our daily routine.

The next day I would see the pair of them out the back and they would say "hello" as if nothing had happened.

### MY 'NEW' WHEELS

John Arnott, the crane driver at the factory had a 1953 Anniversary Ford, with a Canadian V8 in it. He sold it to me for $100. It had some serious rust issues, but it was, I thought, a bargain. It didn't require a baking tray ...

I was coming up in the world.

It was a huge heavy machine with leather seats, walnut dashboard and it seemed that I could fit a football team inside.

Jim did a little work on it but said the 'rings' needed doing and that it was a big job. Apparently that's why it blew so much smoke. Apart from that it ran OK. The driver's side door was held in place by a dog collar, so I got in via the passenger side. It needed new tyres; there was steel showing through the rubber. In fact there were little pieces of rubber actually hanging off the tyres. If I'd have knocked anybody down, they would have got twenty lashes as they fell. Still the tyres were inflated, so I guess they were drivable for the time being.

There was no power steering in those days so you needed to be strong to drive it. A three point turn could be as effective as a gym workout; you would need to catch your breath before driving off again. If you were hung over it was just as easy to drive around the block.

It was green and that spooked me a little. I believed green was bad luck for me after the Sprite ... couldn't have been the booze ...

No, I was convinced, green was unlucky for me.

Even today, after I accept the fact that my accident was caused by my being smashed, I still won't, hire, ride in, or buy anything that's green.

I've kept lying to myself all these years.

## THE DESTROYER ON WHEELS

We needed to change the colour of the Ford.

Kaz and I hand painted it 'ship's side grey'.

Two tins of Navy paint had found its way into my possession. I knew they'd come in handy one day.

So here I was driving a vehicle that resembled a destroyer with wheels. There were a few more drawbacks with my latest acquisition. If I actually wanted to start it, I would need to do some serious overtime at work. The amount of petrol it went through was phenomenal.

Kaz had bought herself a brand new Datsun 1600 and we used her car most of the time, so the Ford was only being used for work.

Things were getting serious with Kaz and me. We were talking of getting married. I was still hoping for the job in Canada and we talked of getting married and then going overseas together. In the meantime, I had debts to get rid of.

Kaz and I got married six months after we met, we had our baby on the way, so we just moved the wedding forward. The job overseas didn't happen.

It was tough telling Karen's parents that she was pregnant. She was only twenty and they knew my circumstances. In hindsight it must have been really hard for them. I know how protective I am with our three girls, even today.

First we told Karen's mum. She grabbed the kitchen table to steady herself as I told her the news. She was stressing to say the least.

Karen's elder sister Annette dropped in and we gave her the news.

She was terrific; she came into the lounge room to talk to me, told me it would all work out OK. Then we waited for her dad.

He came home, said "Hi" as he walked into the lounge room with his newspaper. I gave him the news and I couldn't believe how calm and collected he was about the whole situation.

We sat around the kitchen table and talked of the ramifications we were about to face.

Karen (Kaz) and I were adamant that we would marry and have our baby.

After some more discussion Warwick (Dad) looked up to Mum and said "Well Joan, you'd better get on the phone to the relatives and tell them there's a wedding about to happen."

Karen's mum and dad were middle-class working people. Warwick, Karen's father, was a jeweller. He operated at the back of a small menswear shop that he and Mum had set up. It fed the family but basically it just made wages. They were comfortable but there wasn't a lot of cash to splash around, especially as they had just paid for Karen's sister, Annette's wedding.

We married in a church and had the reception in a small church hall. The band played at the wedding and we left on a three day honeymoon to a lake resort a few hours away. It would have been two days but Karen's dad slipped a twenty into my top pocket as we were leaving the reception. "Have another day mate, and good luck," he said with a smile. I was back at work the following Monday.

We had got hold of a one bedroom flat. It was still in the name of the bloke who vacated it. He went to board at my mother's place. He left the bond on it and I had to pay him back over a few weeks.

He wanted out of the lease and we needed a place. It was a win-win situation.

He left us with a small lounge suite, a double bed base, a two seater kitchen table and a small bar fridge. He gave us the lot for $100.

I now had assets of $200. My Navy money had long gone and I was still thousands in debt.

Kaz worked as long as she could and I got my head down and arse up at the glass factory. I was doing double shifts at least three times a week.

I had one more debt added to the list the week of our wedding. We came home from our honeymoon to find that Shellie had sold the rental TV ... Bloody hell! I couldn't for the life of me catch a break. We soon realised if we were going to make it, we would have to really knuckle down and save. Our baby was due in May.

## KIMBO ARRIVES

Kaz gave birth to Kim Louise, our daughter, on the 24th May 1973.

It was a tough labour and they had to help her out with forceps. She was nearly 9lbs. She was beautiful ... big brown eyes. The thought that I helped create this beautiful little person was overwhelming. Life changes dramatically when a baby arrives and it was no different with us.

It was a little challenging in the flat as we had no real escape. We were on the 2nd floor, so there was no backyard. Poor Kim had colic real bad. Karen was doing it tough. There wasn't too much we could do for Kim, save rock her and try and comfort her. It wasn't long before we were both sleep deprived. We took it in turns trying to pacify her at all hours of the night.

While all this was happening, I had been working on a comedy routine with the band. I had even floated the idea to Shellie to do a duo. At first he was all enthusiastic and came to the flat for our first rehearsal. He never showed up for the second so I thought I would fly solo. (Ten years later, when I was on a concert tour, Shellie rang me out of the blue and said, "OK I'm in" ... he wasn't kidding. I always liked his front.)

## IT'S ALL GREEK TO ME

In the meantime I had started thinking about how to increase our income.

There came to my attention a job being advertised within the factory. It was a job for a 'stacker'.

Now the work entailed a team of two men. The first would drive the forklift which was fitted with two huge 'grabs' with rubber pads. The driver would 'grab' the papered glass block off the A-frame barrow and then drive it down the row of stacked glass to deposit it in its allocated bay. The stacks of glass were up to 40 feet high. The second guy would be waiting there for the driver with two felt-lined spacers ready to receive the glass.

The driver had to be very precise; it was a skill that took a fair amount of time behind the wheel to acquire. The second team member, the 'runner', had to be fast. He literally ran constantly. Everyone wore padding, helmets and protective eyewear. It was all very hot and heavy gear. The team would do each job during the shift and share the time running and driving.

The money was an extra $20 a week and they always made full bonus. It was physically, the hardest job at the plant.

I applied for the job but management tried to talk me out of it. It appeared to be a job that was in fact only ever taken on by the Greeks that worked at the factory. They didn't even speak English in the section. It was like an unwritten law that it was a Greek gig.

I insisted that I wanted the job but I was warned that I wouldn't last a week. I was also told that my place in the factory would be filled if I took on the job and they couldn't guarantee me a position back in the factory when I came to the inevitable conclusion that I couldn't handle being a stacker.

You had to be super fit, half mountain goat and fast. I guess the Greeks invented the Olympics, so I guess they felt they could monopolise this section. I was insistent about the job so with a shrug of resignation the Factory Manager gave in. I was to report to Paniotis (Peter) the foreman of the section at 7am Monday morning for my first shift.

I figured if I could do a full-on Navy diving course, I could be a stacker.

All eyes were on me as I walked into the section, some just stared, some sniggered and others just shook their heads.

"What 'you' name?" The foreman asked with a thick accent.

"My name's Col," I said as I proffered my hand.

Peter shook my hand and said "Col ... this job very hard ... maybe no good for you ... eh?" doing his best at the outset to dissuade me.

"We'll see Peter, what do you want me to do first?" I answered just as determinedly.

The foreman called out to two men standing by a forklift. One guy came over and he and the foreman had a loud animated conversation in Greek. It was fairly heated and I could tell the other guy wasn't a happy camper.

"Stavros, he teach you one day ... Nick, over there, he teach you tomorrow," Peter said dismissively.

Stavros walked away decidedly annoyed, indicated for me to go with him and I followed on like a lost puppy.

Stavros spent five minutes showing me how to put the spacers out and how to set up the A-frame barrows, ready for him to pick up the blocks of glass.

Then he showed me where the different bays were located. Once that was done the fun began.

Stavros was working at full speed on the machine. I had no sooner lined the glass up on the barrow so he could come in and grab it, than he was off, hurtling down the rows of glass. I was running behind the machine, trying my best keep up.

By the time I got to the bay he was there hurling abuse at me in Greek ... "GRIGORI ... GAMOTO!!!"

Roughly translated it means 'faster you fucker' ... I got the drift and ignored it ... for the time being. This went on all day, he never let me near the machine and I figured they were doing their best to make me quit.

There were two short 'smoko' breaks and a half hour for lunch. I felt ill.

By the end of the day, I was knackered. My legs felt like jelly but I wasn't going to show them I was hurting. "See you guys tomorrow," I called cheerfully over my shoulder as I walked out of the section. My head was spinning. I brought my lunch up in the car park!

I got home to Kaz and just lay on the couch, she woke me for tea. I ached all over. I showered and went straight to bed.

It was Nick's turn to work with me the next day. He was just as fast but a little more affable. He had more patience and after two hours he said, "I give you drive, OK?"

"OK," I said with a smile of gratitude.

For the next hour Nick worked with me on the forklift. I managed to smash a fair amount of glass in that time but Nick just laughed and made me start again. The smashed glass was thrown in big steel bins, taken upstairs and re-melted.

When lunchtime came around, I asked the foreman if I could practice on the machine during the break. He gave me the OK and I did that daily from then on. Slowly my skill improved.

For the next six weeks I ran my arse off, I didn't have an ounce of fat on me and I was getting very fit.

Eventually I got the upper hand. In the end Stavros would be coming down the aisle ... I would be there perched on the mountain of glass waiting for him, shaking my head and screaming ... "STAVROS ... GRIGORI".

The first time it happened he kept a straight face and placed the block ... then sped away. I was waiting for him at the other end. "GRIGORI," I screamed ... His face said it all, he smiled and said "ASTO THIALO RE GAMOTO" (Go to hell fucker). Those in earshot laughed ... then they applauded.

I knew from that point on, I was a stacker.

For the next few weeks I worked with both men and when a new hand got a job in the section the boys actually fought over me ... I felt like a 'bitch'. The new guy was Greek ... he went with Nick.

I was invited to lunch with the Greek guys in the canteen. All of the blokes were in heavy conversation until Peter held up his hand.

"Everybody ... speak English ... Col don't understand Greek ... only when he swear." They all laughed and spoke in English every time I had my breaks with them.

I was introduced to their home-cooked Greek food; each lunchtime was a full-on smorgasbord.

"Col, you try some of this one," a voice would say ... I have never lost the taste for it. I have a great respect for the Greek people, they are so much about family and they have a great work ethic.

Stavros took me to his family for a Greek celebration one weekend. His brother, Petros, was celebrating his 'name day', which to the Greeks is more important than a birthday.

It was a huge compliment to be invited. Kaz couldn't leave Kim but she told me I should go ... I was always up for a party.

In Greece, everyone celebrates the 'name day' of the saint that bears the same name. A full-on Greek party is something to behold, I danced like Zorba, ate and drank and Stavros dropped me home ... a little worse for wear clutching two bottles of his home-made Retsina wine ... very nice.

Tasting Stavros' latest batch of wine was always a top day.

# PART FOUR
## SHOWBIZ

I was starting to do a couple of gigs with the band around Melbourne pubs. One was a Christmas break-up for a firm but they asked Jim to cut me short as the boss's wife was a little sensitive. Apparently she didn't like Navy humour.

I came to realise that I needed to remove certain words and descriptive phrases from my show like HANGIN' LOOSE, FULL OF JUICE and THROBBIN' LIKE A SOCK FULL OF GRASSHOPPERS, 'ARSE BANDITS, and the like. I would need to tweak my show if I were to move into the Melbourne floorshow scene.

It seemed I was a little before my time.

Back then there weren't a lot of stand-up comedians in Melbourne doing the type of material I was about; it was considered a fringe-type entertainment in the clubs.

The main cabaret performers were bands and singers.

At one band rehearsal Ross D Wylie came to run a few numbers down with the band. I was in the middle of doing a bit with the boys, when he walked in. He watched me finish and had a laugh.

Ross had been working the pub and club circuit and he was working with the band over a few gigs.

He had been heavily involved with TV over the years and had quite a bit of success with recording. He had a number one hit, The Star, which was later recorded as Here comes the Star, by Herman's Hermits in the UK.

I was introduced to Ross. He was a nice bloke. The upshot was that he would introduce me to a booking agent in exchange for me writing some floorshow patter for him.

Done deal. The following week I met his Melbourne agent, Shirley McLaughlin.

At the meeting she listened to some of my comedy and offered to represent me.

It was about this time that one night I was driving home from work in the old 'battleship grey' Ford.

I heard a cop siren behind me ... bugger.

The cop got out of his car as I sat pensively waiting.

He took an inordinate amount of time going around the car, looking underneath and checking what was left of my tyres.

I knew he was having trouble getting his head around the colour. He finally came to my window ...

"What the bloody hell are you doing on the road with this son?" he asked in a bewildered voice. I don't think he could bring himself to say the word 'car'.

"Just on my way home, officer," I replied with a look of innocence.

He went into a lengthy discussion about what was wrong with my car and why it shouldn't be on the road. At one point he wanted to show me a particularly bad rust spot. To tell the truth, it wasn't a rust spot as such, it was more like a piece of the car missing. I climbed out of my driver's window ... that was the clincher.

"What the bloody hell," he started to stammer.

I explained that if I took the dog collar off, the door would drop off and it was a mongrel to re-align.

He said he wouldn't book me if I voluntarily took it off the road. He followed me home and told me not to drive it again until I got it roadworthy which he pointed out would cost more than the car was worth. In his opinion I should tip it ... I was mortified, no way, and besides it would be a waste of taxpayers' money. Two tins of ship's side grey ... all for nothing.

I decided to lay low for a few days; surely it was a fluke encounter.

Two days later I was leaving the factory, walking towards my car when I saw the cop car near the main gate. I changed direction slightly and went straight to the cop car.

"What are the chances of a ride home officer?" I asked with a cheeky grin.

Thank God he had a sense of humour. After a small lecture he decided to give me a second chance ... this time I obeyed his directive.

I was still a little insecure as a civilian. I toyed with the idea of joining the Victorian Police Force. A funny thought hit me, "What if the copper that picked me up was on the selection board?" I could always say he impressed me so much I decided to join him. I wondered if the police had a sense of humour.

## LOOKING FOR AN OUTFIT

I made enquiries and was told my qualifications would be looked on favourably. I wanted to go straight into 'Search and Rescue' but was told it would be a long process and I would have to do the whole gambit of jobs and training before I could be considered. I was too impatient for that and besides I didn't fancy directing traffic, so I offered my services to the mounted police ... that was worse, someone would need to die before a job with that branch would become available.

While I was pondering my situation, it came to my attention that the Department of Corrective Services was advertising for positions as prison guards.

I rang for an appointment and was offered an interview.

I ended up sitting for quite a few exams and spent a fair amount of time with their psychologists. I had no real desire to work in that area but the thought of being part of an 'outfit' again was where my head was at. This was serious stuff really; I mean there would be no parties at Jim and Jan's for these prisoners. I made sure not to mention that episode in the interview.

At the last interview, the head prison officer tried to push all my buttons, I guess looking for a chink in my armour.

At one point he made a statement to the fact that I was the

youngest of all the applicants and asked the question why I should even be considered.

I stated that although I was the youngest applicant, (the closest to me was around 35) I had more life experiences than most. I pointed out the fact that I had been able to perform my job whilst under fire many times in Vietnam and that I had endured much physical and mental pressure during the rigorous naval training I had received over my years in the service, especially the diving course. I also outlined my work as an instructor in my last posting at HMAS Cerberus. This I felt, was proof of my credentials and suitability.

The officer seemed pleased with my answer and said that I would be informed of their decision by letter within the next few days. I thanked the board and took my leave.

The following Thursday Kaz and I were at her parent's place for tea. I picked up the newspaper and read the headlines 'Prison officer opens front door to shotgun blast'.

I received a letter the next morning congratulating me on being accepted into the Victorian Prison system. I was to report to the Mont Park Mental Institution on the following Monday to start my psychology training.

Kaz made the comment that maybe I was the replacement.

I rang the department's office first thing Monday stating it was with much regret that due to family issues, I would not be accepting the position. The chap at the other end seemed a little miffed and asked me if I could be a little more specific regarding those issues.

"Certainly," I said. "If I take this job, my wife will have me committed," ... The phone went dead.

### AND THE WINNER IS ...

I soldiered on at the glass factory. I became the 'overtime king' but it would eventually pay off.

Karen and I had been given a small black and white TV by her parents, it was the best gift and we felt so grateful for it.

Our favourite show was on Sunday night. It was a talent quest show, Kevin Denis New Faces. Many of our Aussie stars had appeared on the show over the years. John Farnham, Paul Hogan, John Williamson and many more got their first break on New Faces.

I walked out on the landing after the show that night and lit up a smoke ... then it hit me ... I'll go on New Faces and just maybe I could win enough money to buy some new tyres for the Ford. I certainly felt I was due for a break ... this could be it!

Back then, everything on TV had to be squeaky clean, so I worked on my own version of a story my mum had taught me as a kid. It was entitled 'Albert and the 'orse's 'ead 'andle'. It gave me the opportunity to tell the story as myself but swing into all the different characters.

Shirley McLaughlin knew the producer of the show, Gary Stewart, and organised for me to audition.

I passed the audition and a few weeks later was told by letter that I was to appear the following week for the first heat.

I was placed in the middle of the show; the only comedy act. It went down well with the live audience and I scored enough to win the heat and appear in the final.

I went on to win the final. It was such a buzz.

I bought new tyres and a keg of beer for all our friends.

A showbiz career for most is a long slow process. Sure, some find instant fame but for most it's like any endeavour ... you need to work on it, it's an ongoing process. I felt I had something to offer, and this was a good start.

The talent show certainly gave me some credibility especially with my agent. She had something to sell. A few gigs began to dribble in.

One of the very first gigs that came out of it was at the White Horse Hotel in Box Hill, a southern suburb of Melbourne. I was to do an hour spot to a mixed cabaret-type audience. That's what it said on the contract. I was to be paid $90 less 10% agent's commission

... basically a week's pay, how cool was that! I couldn't believe how much I was being paid. It felt like I'd hit the big time.

Steve and Chris Mika came with Kaz and me that night. Steve and I were at Leeuwin together; we're still great mates today. Steve still comes to my gigs; I figure he's a masochist.

## THE HONORARY BIKIE

That night we arrived at the pub and I noticed a huge amount of Harley Davidsons in the car park. In fact, that was all that was in the car park.

The main lounge of the pub looked like a 'bikie' convention ... bugger. That explained the fee!

The Manager sidled up to me and thanked me profusely for actually turning up; obviously he had been let down before.

There was a three-piece band in the corner churning out classic 'rock 'n roll'.

I went with the manager to meet the band. I could tell they were a little edgy. This didn't look good. The crowd of bikies were drinking out of jugs and the noise was incredible. Bikies and their girlfriends were lurching from table to table. My mind went back to the description on the contract ... 'mixed Cabaret audience'. Mixed was the key word ... who knows what they'd been mixing.

I could smell the pungent aroma of 'jazz tobacco' (marijuana) as we walked in ... I had to somehow get a positive spin on this. A thought crossed my mind ... the leftover smoke floating in the room would probably help me through the night ... there it is, the only positive I could think of.

The band said they would do a short bracket and would announce that I would be on after the break.

They said they couldn't give me a 'play-on' as they would be taking their guitars and amps off the stage in case of damage. The manager gave me a quick nervous smile.

The band went on to explain that the last act they had at the pub, nine months before, was when they were pelted with food and empty jugs and that they had smashed an amp ... so "Good luck mate," the lead guitarist said.

"I'm sure you'll kill 'em," the manager said before scurrying away.

I had left Steve and the girls at the back of the room ... it didn't feel safe and I asked Steve to take them out. Karen and Chris insisted they wouldn't leave.

I was wearing the three piece suit that I had gotten married in ... clearly the wrong feel.

I whipped off my jacket and rolled up my sleeves to expose my Navy tattoos ... well I thought it might help ...

I looked up and coming towards me was the biggest bikie I had ever seen in my life, he must have been six foot six and built like a mountain.

He looked down at me and a huge grin appeared on his whiskered face ...

"G'day mate ... I saw you on 'telly' ... 'gees' that was funny," he said as he shook my hand vigorously.

He sat at our table and told the girls not to worry, they would be fine ... in fact he wanted to 'intro' me ... "And don't take any crap from this lot Col...give 'em heaps ... it'll be cool," he offered. The band had disappeared and we headed to the stage.

The big bloke walked up, grabbed the mike and screamed ...

"'Righto' you bastards, shut 'ya' 'guts' ... we've got a really funny bloke comin' on, he was on New Faces and he won ....so 'youse' better laugh 'cos' I like him," he said with a full jug of beer in his hand. "OK ... here he is, COL ELLIOTT." I walked on to a few desultory claps.

I expected the big bloke to leave the stage but no, he just stood next to me. I went into some stand-up and got a few one-liners out to mediocre reaction then someone yelled out in the crowd and the big fella started to react ...

"It's OK mate," I said to my offside, "I know what it was like when I had MY first drink" ... The crowd roared ...

My heckler tried to recover with a 'get stuffed' type line.

"Settle down mate," I said ... "there's no school tomorrow." Once again the crowd broke up ...

He tried again, but I had the mike. I got over the top of him quick ... "Christ, mate, the last time I saw a mouth like yours it had a fuckin' hook in it". The heckler broke up and clapped me ... from then on they were mine.

I didn't take any prisoners. I did an hour, plus an encore, all the time my big mate stood next to me and with each laugh I received, he'd give me a slap on the back. I was nearly crippled by the time I had finished. He even did a little jig when I picked a ditty on my banjo ... I guess it could have been a little reminiscent of that famous scene from the film Deliverance ...maybe that's where they got the idea.

After I left the stage the big fella put a beer carton by the 'mike' and told the room ... "All tips in 'ere and don't be 'scungie'" ...

Ten minutes later he returned to our table with the carton ... $40 odd in notes and coins, two 'joints' and a half cask of wine.

I gave the wine and 'joints' to my new-found friend but he insisted I keep one joint for 'on the way home' ... 'cos I deserved it. Who was going to argue?

The manager paid me and asked me back the following week. I thanked him and said my agent would be in touch. I figured I wouldn't push my luck. We left the pub with much back slapping and teary hugs from my new best friend for life ... he was a true 'support act' in every sense of the word.

Another gig I got directly as a result of New Faces was on Channel 7, The Penthouse Club. It ran on Saturday nights for three hours. They transmitted the harness racing live and would cross back to the station in between races.

The studio was set up like a club with a live audience sitting at tables with drinks and nibblies.

Mary Hardy and Mike Williamson, two very popular and well known personalities were the comperes and would do live commercials and celebrity interviews with the odd comedy sketch thrown in. Live variety acts would be presented in-between the races.

Mary Hardy was a natural comedienne. She had won eight gold Logies for her television work. She was famous for her uncanny ad-lib ability and she was totally irreverent. Mary was also famous for being the first female to drop the 'F' word on Australian TV.

One time when she had to present a prize to the female owner of a winning female greyhound, she said "to which bitch do I present the prize?"

Sadly Mary committed suicide in 1985.

The Penthouse Club was a steep learning curve for me. On some nights a race might be due to start in four minutes and you had to bring down your routine exactly on time, ready for the live cross. It could go the other way though, with the floor manager frantically standing in front of you giving you the 'stretch' sign. The other was the 'cut to the chase' sign. In any event we always kept one eye on the floor manager. On the odd occasion you would be cut in the middle of a gag.

## ACTORS' EQUITY

It was 1974 and I was to appear on my very first show. That night I became a member of Actors' Equity, not that I had joined of my own accord ... Mary Hardy paid my initial fee ... it happened like this.

I had arrived at the station as required, an hour before show time. I met the producer and was told to report to 'make-up'.

After that I was told I could relax with all the other performers and staff in the Green Room.

There were a few people in there I didn't recognise and I made myself a cup of tea. Grog was available but I couldn't trust myself. Mary came into the room with the producer discussing scripts for the show. Mary was a whirlwind and swore like a drunken sailor ... she was real and I knew I liked her from the start.

I stood up as she came over "Hi Col, glad to have you on tonight, you'll kill 'em, you're just what we need on the show."

"Thanks Mary, it's great to meet you," I said, a little overawed.

"Just relax for a while and I'll introduce you to Mike when he gets here ... just got a few bits and pieces to do first," she said as she re-engaged with her producer.

She made me feel so welcome and important, I liked her immediately.

A few more people drifted into the room and before too long there was a crowd.

The room went a little quiet and I looked up to see the producer in earnest conversation with a definite effeminate-looking guy in an immaculate three-piece suit.

Surprise ... they came over to me.

"Col, are you a member of the Musicians' Union or Actors' Equity?" the producer asked.

"What's that?" was my dumb reply.

"Not sure what you are you talking about ... never heard of them," ... and I hadn't.

I was ignored for the moment as the producer and the Actors Equity rep went at it 'hammer and tongs'.

Mary had walked in and heard the fuss, just as the rep was threatening to pull the entire band off the set and disrupt the show. It was 15 minutes to air time.

"If you try and put a non-union member on, we will black ban them. ..." He never finished.

Mary was hitting the roof. "DON'T YOU COME IN HERE WITH YOUR PISS-WEAK THREATS, YOU LITTLE SHIT," she screamed ... she then shoved a $20 note in his top pocket and patted it, but really it was more like an assault. "TAKE THIS AND JOIN HIM UP ... I NOMINATE ... DO IT RIGHT NOW AND THEN, FUCK OFF."

You could have heard a pin drop. She left the room ...

"How do you spell your last name Col?" the rep asked me sheepishly.

"Elliott ... two Ls ... two Ts," I spelt out, trying hard not to smile.

He took down my address and promised my membership card would be out the following week. He then left the green room very quickly.

As a footnote to this story, Actors Equity has since made me a Member for Life as reward for 38 years without missing my fees ... thanks Mary ... R.I.P.

## MY HERO

I was booked to do the Melbourne cup breakfast at the Southern Cross Hotel in Melbourne. It was an event run every year by the Carlton Football club and was considered a very prestigious gig.

Everyone on the show was a star ... I was the only one there that I hadn't heard of ...the then Prime Minister, Malcolm Fraser, Bob Hawk, plus all the major sporting stars of the day. Television stars were coming out of the woodwork. Some serious egos were being stroked everywhere in the room. It was a veritable smorgasbord of who's who and who's up whom for the rent.

Shirley McLaughlin, my agent, came over to tell me who was there that I might be able to use ... She was rattling off names and then mentioned sir Douglas Bader and kept talking. I cut in, "Shirley, did you say Sir Douglas Bader?" I asked.

"Yes, she said. He's a war hero from Eng ..."

I cut her off ... "Sir Douglas Bader was my boyhood hero," I exclaimed excitedly.

Shirley pointed him out in the crowd. From that point on, as far as I was concerned, everyone else in the room paled into insignificance.

When I was about twelve I was given a book about the life and times of Douglas Bader. The book was 'Reach for the Sky'. It was later made into a movie in 1956 starring Kenneth Moore.

It's an incredible story of endurance and bold determination.

Douglas Bader had lost both of his legs in a flying accident in 1931; he went on to become a very highly decorated Wing Commander and ace fighter pilot During WW2. He had over twenty kills to his credit and many more probables. He was known as 'Tin Legs Bader'.

He bailed out over German occupied France in 1941. Even with this disability, he attempted escape on a number of occasions and was eventually imprisoned at the famous Colditz Castle till war's end.

The German Luftwaffe had so much respect for him as a pilot that they allowed a British bomber safe passage over occupied territory to drop a spare prosthetic leg for him. His other leg had been damaged when he was shot down.

I have met many famous people in my career but this, to me, was one out of the box.

I was introduced to the stage and went into some patter, which received a reasonable response. I worked on a couple of the personalities in the room and then focussed on Sir Douglas.

I figured he was a serviceman so I guessed he would have a good sense of humour.

I had the spotlight on him and briefly told of his exploits to make sure that anyone who hadn't heard of him now were well aware of whom I was talking ... covering bases.

"Sir Douglas I began. May I have your permission to tell a story of a little known exploit of yours, that only a few know about? It has only just come to light because the freedom of information limit has just kicked in."

"By all means," he called out, right on cue.

"Thank you sir," I said, and began my story.

"In the latter part of WW2, Sir Douglas, along with five other fighter planes were sent on a propaganda mission over occupied Europe. They took off just on dusk and headed out over the English

Channel. Their mission ... to drop 100 thousand leaflets a piece, on the occupied territories. The leaflets told the Germans to surrender before it was too late ... they could not win this war ... Britain and her allies would prevail ... Surrender!"

Four hours later the anxious men at the airbase heard the distinctive drone of the fighter planes returning, Fortescue Smythe, Sir Douglas's batman stood beside the runway straining to see his superior's plane. One by one they all made a perfect landing ... all except Sir Douglas. No one knew of his whereabouts.

Every night for three months, the ever faithful Fortescue Smythe wandered down to the runway in the faint hope that Sir Douglas would return.

One night there was a message from Radar that a lone fighter plane was heading back over the channel ... Smythe stood anxiously by the runway. The plane made a perfect landing and Sir Douglas clambered down from the wing ...

"Hello chaps," he said jauntily.

Fortescue Smythe raced to embrace his hero,

"Sir, three months ago you and five others were sent on a propaganda mission to drop 100 thousand leaflets each, over occupied Europe ... you were the only one that went missing."

"Oh," said Sir Douglas, "Did you say DROP them. I thought you meant ... SHOVE THEM UNDER THE DOORS."

The room broke into thunderous applause and laughter...

"Welcome to Australia sir," I said and left the stage.

I sat at my table and poured a coffee, I looked up and Sir Douglas was standing in front of me. We shook hands.

"Sir Douglas, I feel so honoured to meet you," I said, a little overawed in his presence ... I'll never forget his response.

"One day, I'll be able to say ... I met Col Elliott."

In 1982 Sir Douglas died of a heart attack, aged 72.

## DEBT FREE AT LAST!

Kaz and I finally paid off all the debts and actually had $700 in the bank. I felt I was getting somewhere and we put the deposit on our first house. It was in a little outer suburb called Cranbourne, on the outskirts of Gippsland.

House and land was $14,200. I was able to get a war service loan for $12,000. Karen's parents, Warwick and Joan, took out a $2,000 bank loan that I could pay back weekly.

It was a real help as I had no credit rating. I paid it back religiously and it was soon under control.

I was starting to get 'smoko' (men only) gigs on Sundays at the local football clubs. They were rough and ready affairs which suited my style. The cheapest fee I got back then was $10 and all I could drink. It was the Dandenong football club, my home town, so how could I refuse. I mean I knew all of them and besides they said Ralph could drink for free as well.

Smoko's were usually comprised of a comedian and a couple of strippers, with a chook raffle thrown in.

My reputation started to build, but I was a long way from turning pro.

Every now and then a cabaret floor show would come in and I would have to clean up the act. I now had two distinct shows I could trot out.

(A) Wasn't that nice? and (B) Can you believe what that bastard just said? At least I was versatile ...

One of the problems I was facing was the fact that I often got free grog at these turns; it wasn't helping. I still had no control and it was becoming harder to manage. I knew deep down I had to address this sooner or later but I kept shelving the situation. I had left the Navy with this drinking culture and it hadn't gotten any better. I guess I felt that I deserved a drink. I figured I was working so hard it was my right.

I never really knew when I would bust out but my selfish attitude let me down so many times. You would think that I would have worked it out by now. My father dead at forty-nine, I had nearly died in a car accident ....all due to booze.

I have come to realise how insidious alcohol is, but back then I was running amok and couldn't quite get a handle on it.

When we first moved into our house I stained the wooden floorboards by hand. It was a temporary solution till we saved up for carpet.

As it happened the week they were to lay our new carpet, Karen was taken to hospital with severe gall bladder problems. She had been in tremendous pain one night and I had called a doctor out to the house. I had come home late from a gig and surprised her with a hamburger. Other blokes would have brought flowers; I bought a hamburger ... with the lot!

We sat and ate the late-night meal together as I recounted the night's highlights. All of a sudden she collapsed in agony. I immediately rang our doctor.

He arrived and gave her a morphine injection; she went straight out to it.

The next day we went in for X-rays and she was diagnosed with gal stone problems and scheduled for the operation. In those days it required a ten day stay in hospital.

Karen's mum and dad would look after Kim during the week and I would take her back on the weekend.

Kaz had been operated on and was on a drip in the recovery ward, and I would go in to visit late afternoon.

Pete Shelton came over to help me move the furniture for the carpet-layers.

Pete was the band's drummer and had married Pam the lead singer; we often hung out together and Pete and I weren't to be trusted.

That day was no different, Pete bought over some beer.

The carpet-layers came and went, we kept drinking.

I did the unthinkable; I put my daughter in the car and drove to the hospital. Thank God I arrived without incident. I walked into Karen's ward with Kim on my hip. Karen was so upset but managed to take the keys off me. Her parents took Kim and a doctor tried to pacify me. I was ranting and raving; an obnoxious drunk. I have no excuse for what I did; the truth is I don't remember any of it.

I left the hospital and managed to get hold of Pete. He was as bad as I was but drove down to pick me up.

We went back to my place and continued drinking. Pam arrived and took Peter away with much yelling and berating. I fell unconscious on the lounge room floor. I woke to the telephone ringing early the next morning.

It was Joan, Karen's Mum. She was concerned for me and then reassured me Karen and Kim were OK. She told me of the aftermath of my hospital visit. The staff had moved Karen to another room. They felt sorry for the embarrassment I had caused her and maybe a little concerned about security. Clearly she was married to an arsehole … (I said that, Mum didn't.)

Karen's mum is a very gentle lady and we talked quietly about my drinking problem; she reassured me it would be alright in the end. We have always been good friends and that day she had a right to get stuck into me but she didn't. Maybe she should have …

## THE REP

I eventually left the glass factory and managed to get a job as a sales rep.

Jan's cousin Rod got me an interview at Warner Lambert, where he worked.

They marketed Listerine mouth wash, Schick razors and blades and a variety of shampoos and hairsprays. I had no experience but during the interview, the sales manager, Don Roberts, decided to take a punt on me.

I was given a brand new, second-hand Ford Falcon station wagon. I felt so proud. I actually got to wear a shirt and tie and we decided to sell the old Ford.

It was a shame really, there was still good tread on the tyres thanks to the talent show. The 'copper' would have been proud. I got $60 bucks for her and Kaz and I went out to celebrate.

I loved the work as a sales rep but there was no such thing as overtime so I managed to score a part-time job at the local pub. It was owned by the Kelly family and they were great people to work for.

It's not 'what you know, it's who you know', as the saying goes and I got the job because of one of our mates, Allan Stocks. Allan had married the publican's daughter and was co-running the pub.

I worked as a barman in the back bar and the bottle shop and drive-through.

They were really flexible when I needed to do a gig. It was a good set up.

I got a little extra on Saturday nights because I had no problem cleaning up the toilets after closing.

When I first started the job we would take it in turns to clean. It was a dirty job with the stench of vomit and mess everywhere and the other guys would bitch and complain any time it was their turn.

I made the proposal that if I was paid an extra $5 each night I would do the job permanently. 'Doc' Kelly, the publican's son, even said he would pay me the extra himself, as long as he didn't have to listen to the other guys constantly whinging. It truly didn't bother me as I had spent quite a bit of time at sea cleaning up after seasick sailors and as far as the other, my old Chief on the Sydney had taught me that shit didn't bite. It was a classic win-win situation as far as I was concerned.

In the early 70s you could feed a family, including milk, meat and bread for under $10 a week, so $5 was a huge incentive.

Thursday nights we would have tea with Karen's folks and her grandfather, Ted Dixon. He got me another job at the Nottingham

Hill pub near their place. It was owned and operated by Kath Byers. Kath ran the pub till she was in her nineties. She was a local legend. Poppa Ted was a master builder and had helped build the hotel. It seemed I was well connected.

The routine was to drop Kaz and Kimbo off at her parent's then work the bottle shop till closing at 10 pm. Then I would pick them up and get my supper before heading home.

## GROG

Shellie would often drop in to home with his latest girlfriend; he was still full of it and would never bring any food or drink. He eventually married an Italian girl and moved to Perth.

Shellie never got the civilian thing and he ended up back in Melbourne, single and broke. I would get the inevitable phone call.

I was still a lunatic on the grog, I had no real tolerance but I kept practicing. I never drank on a daily basis, I was working too hard for that but I still had a problem with it. I would bust out every few weeks or so, sometimes with dire results.

Jan's cousin Rod and I were good mates. We had a lot in common. We both worked for the same company and Rod had served in the Air Force, and of course, we both liked a drink. We were 'tarred with the same brush' as they say.

Rod's brother Neville, had served in the Navy a few years before my service. He and his wife Jenny lived on a farm and our whole gang would have weekend parties.

Karen was pregnant with Kim at the time. When I look back at those photos of her I can't help but feel a sense of guilt. She was just a kid herself and here she was lumbered with a bigger kid. I was clearly out of control and still not able to get it all together.

There was a certain competitive rivalry between Rod and myself. We were forever jockeying for the best sales results at work and many times we managed to break National sales figures. Don Roberts, our boss, loved the results of this but some of the other reps weren't all that impressed.

A deputation of them came to us at a sales meeting to tell us to slow up ... we were making them look bad.

I told them that we were only doing our job and maybe they should lift their game. We strained a few friendships that day.

## GEE UP

I found a new running mate in Rod, he was as crazy as I was and we were forever going over the top.

We were out the back of the farm one night when I spotted a black horse by the fence.

"Nice looking animal," I casually said in between sips.

"Yeah, but you couldn't handle him," he said trying to bait me.

"I have ridden him but you wouldn't be able to," he said, pushing my buttons.

"That's crap ... I've ridden more horses than you've had baked dinners and you know it," I said, half taking the bait.

"OK, prove it ... bare-back, no bridle," Rod said.

I walked towards the horse shaking my head. I grabbed a handful of grass as I approached. I guessed he was around 15 hands and was a gelding. He was a little nervy but he let me pat him. He tentatively nibbled on the grass I held out.

I grabbed a handful of mane and swung up onto his back.

He took off down the paddock at a full gallop. I hung on and went with the flow. He rounded the paddock and started to slow ... by the time I was within a hundred metres of Rod he was trotting. I slid from his back and gave Rod a 'Told you so dickhead type look'.

Rod had a ride and we ended up getting the bridle from the shed.

Rod in front and I was behind him doubling up. We were laughing when Rod took him to the back of the house; the party was in full swing … till we rode the gelding in the back door and into the lounge … End of party … and nearly the end of two marriages.

Like two children, there was a concerted effort to keep us apart. A good call!

## THE RAG TRADE

Kevin Paterson and his wife Marg lived across the road from us; they were a lovely couple and had two young kids.

Kev had a business putting out St Vincent de Paul bags.

He would select an area, put the bags in the letterbox and three days later collect them, full of unwanted clothing.

They would be sold for rags to factories and a percentage would go to the charity. This is how it worked before they had the big charity bins of today.

Kev offered me a job distributing the bags. I would receive $1 per 100 that I put out. It wasn't much but I could do the job early morning before I hit the road as a rep, and it wouldn't interfere with my hotel shifts. Anything to make a buck.

I would start at 4 or 5am, do three or four blocks in a designated area and then go to work. Kev would pick up the full bags three days later.

One night after tea I got a call from Kev.

"Come over mate, I'm just sorting through this last lot we did and there's a beaut pair of shoes here that are 9s … your size. Don't know why anybody would want to throw them out, plenty of wear left in them, maybe it's the colour, sort of custard colour … but come over."

"Thanks Kev, I'll be there in a minute." I said.

Sure enough they were my size and really comfortable. They were a cross between a desert boot and a sandshoe.

## THE PANCAKES

I thanked Kev and took them home. Kaz said they looked like pancakes.

They were very 'comfy' and I thought they looked rather cool.

There was a little black mark on the right shoe, it looked like a defect, but apart from that, they were fine. I wore them all week.

On Friday I went to our monthly sales meeting. Before we filed into the board room I stood chatting to my sales supervisor, Pete Anderson. I happened to look down and I noticed he had a pair of the exact same shoes on. He noticed me looking and looked down as well.

"Aren't they great shoes Col?" he said, "I got mine on a bargain table outside a shoe shop in Ferntree Gully where I live. They were so cheap, and in fact they were seconds. I bought the last two pair. The other pair had a black mark on them so I only wear them at h...." His voice trailed away as he noticed the black mark!

"Which street in Ferntree Gully do you live in Pete," I asked, as if I didn't know.

He told me his address as I was taking off his shoes ... Yep, we had collected from his street. As I did this, Pete rang his wife to confirm she had thrown out the shoes. She hated the shoes and was sure he wouldn't have missed them.

Pete was trying to get me to keep the shoes and I insisted he take them home to teach his wife a lesson. We were laughing so hard it hurt.

I addressed the sales meeting in my socks and told the story.

I have it on good authority the story is still being told today ... I drove home in my socks.

It still does the dinner table circuit in my family ... "Dad tell them about the pancakes."

Every time I hear the Joe South hit from 1970, I am reminded of that day ... you remember the song, Walk a mile in my shoes!

My work as a rep was going well but I needed more freedom for my showbiz aspirations. I was getting a fair amount of work, especially the smokos but I wasn't established enough to take a chance on a full-time career.

I was called into Don Roberts's office one Friday. He was being head-hunted by a pharmaceutical firm in Sydney and he offered me a position as a sales supervisor with him. We would need to re-locate to Sydney. It was very flattering but as I explained I still needed to do this 'comedy thing' as he called it.

## THE CURSE OF ASSUMPTION

Just before Don took off for Sydney I met Graham Garner, a friend of Rod's. He and his wife were at the farm for one of our impromptu parties. I got the guitar out and did my thing.

He told me how much he enjoyed my humour and we got to talking.

He owned Peter Garner carpets along with his brother Malcolm. The 'Peter' was bought out, or dropped off somewhere along the way. They had come out from the U.K. a few years before and had four large showrooms.

They had been in the carpet business all their lives and had come out from England to work for Victoria Carpets, a huge manufacturing company in our area. After a couple of years with the firm they branched out by themselves.

Graham offered me a job selling carpet and said he would give me the flexibility that I needed to work my comedy. It was a perfect solution and I made an appointment to meet with him the following Monday. I took up the offer of the job.

I took a dive in pay but the set-up was just the ticket.

Once again I enjoyed the selling process, the interaction with the customers. It was selling after all; the only difference was the product.

As well as carpet, we sold curtains, tiles and vinyl.

Once the curtains were quoted we offered an installation deal on their completion.

Dennis, the manager of the showroom and I teamed up and would fit the curtains after work and on weekends. It was great extra income and top money at $7 a track. I was able to stop the rag-bag run and do less pub work.

We would have sales targets set and there was a healthy competition between the salesmen.

We worked Friday nights till 9pm and 9am till midday on Saturday. There was no overtime. It was a set wage, but a bonus could be achieved once you cracked your sales target.

On Friday nights we would have pizzas delivered and in the winter we would huddle in the office to eat. The showroom was huge and unheated, hundreds of displays and rolls of carpet everywhere.

There were six of us in the office one cold night, huddled around an old bar heater. I was drinking a coffee. There was an old man walking around the showroom, picking up bits and pieces and checking out the displays. He must have been in his late seventies at a guess and was dressed in workman's clothes. He was the only customer. One of the boys made the comment that he was probably after a carpet remnant for his car.

"Let him go ... it's too cold to leave the office ... he'll be OK, he'll probably piss off in a minute," he said.

They all agreed he wasn't important enough to serve.

I felt a little sorry for him and walked over, coffee in hand.

"She's a cold one tonight," I said in way of introduction.

"Sure is," he replied.

"I've just made this brew, would you fancy one?" I asked knowing it would be rude of me to keep drinking it in front of him.

"That would be beaut if it's not too much trouble," he said. We introduced each other and shook hands, his name was Tom Randal.

As we walked over to the coffee station I asked what he was after.

"Something that's not too dear and wears well is what I'm after," he said.

"OK Tom, what sort of area do you need to cover?" I asked half thinking it would be a back bedroom or maybe his lounge. I was already thinking of some off-cuts we had out the back that I could do cheap for him. He looked like he could use a good deal.

"Well I've got this plan you could look at," he said as he pulled it out of his back pocket. It's the whole house and I'll need all the wet areas done in vinyl as well." he went on.

"Oh, right, then," I said, hoping that he hadn't picked up on the surprise in my tone.

We sat on a roll of carpet sipping our coffee and I did a quick estimate of his needs. I figured it was close to a full roll for the house but I'd need a bit more time to give him an idea for the rest.

"That's a full roll of carpet Tom," I said "so I'll be able to do a better deal on it, depending on which one we go for."

Tom and I walked all over as I explained the different qualities and brands. He settled on a carpet we had on special at the time. It was a bulk-buy line and an exclusive deal that Graham had done with Victoria carpets. To this day I still remember the name of that carpet ... it was called Inspirations. What came next really inspired me.

As we inspected the vinyls, he asked about curtains and blinds.

"Sounds like a new house Tom, if you're doing curtains as well, I'll have to keep my pencil sharp," I said with a laugh.

"It is a new house Col, in fact there will be 15 in the first stage and 20 odd later on in the year spread over some big estates. About 12 different designs, some bigger than others but I can get the plans to you on Monday."

I nearly choked on my own tongue "Fu'... fantastic. Forget these prices Tom, were talking a whole new deal here," I stammered.

Tom went on to explain he owned the building company. His two sons were builders and his daughter ran the office. He didn't do any physical work anymore but would organise the fit-out; they built display houses and had been doing so for many years. They had a heap of staff and he said he would get bored if he retired. They had built many homes in and around Melbourne but felt he had been taken advantage of by some of the other interior firms.

He wanted reliability above all else and went on to say, "Everybody must make a profit but we all need to be fair."

I got the appointment book and made arrangements to come to his office, first thing Monday.

At his office, I was introduced to his eldest son and his daughter. He told them, "Col will be organizing the floorings and curtains, so you'll both need to keep in touch ... he's doing us a top price."

I hadn't even given him a price at that point; he walked with me to the car park and gave me a bunch of plans.

"I'll leave it to you Col. Give me a call when you're done ... I won't be getting any more quotes."

"So I'm 'it' then," I said, more to myself than him.

"You gave an old bloke the time of day son ... but it was the coffee that clinched the deal." He laughed and strode back to the office. I made a whole year's figures with just one customer.

It was a lesson I've never forgotten ... never assume.

I got great mileage out of that night. Friday nights we'd be in the office and I'd comment, "ooooh look, there's a customer, but don't serve him, he's probably just after an off-cut for his car ...."

I worked with Tom and his family right up till I left Garners and became a full-time entertainer. They would often come to my shows when I toured the area.

Tom would laugh the loudest. But really, I had the last laugh on that Friday night.

I enjoyed the curtaining side of the business and learnt as much as I could about the different qualities and types of fabric available. I would amuse the other staff by doing my best 'John Inman' impression while flouncing around the showroom with swatches and fabric.

I did an over the top high camp character and was caught out one Saturday morning.

I had just finished my little act when I was tapped on the shoulder by a 'chap' wanting to be served. I must have been totally convincing ... he wanted to meet for coffee. I quickly showed him a picture of my girls; I could see the disappointment in his eyes. From then on, I made sure there were no customers around when I went into 'John'. You remember the TV show, Are you being served? ... I nearly was that day.

## JODIE

Jodie Lee, our second daughter came along on 23rd July 1976. She was so beautiful ... more big brown eyes.

She was so placid and no colic, she was such an easy baby; Kim absolutely doted on her.

## THE CRAYFISH

I got my first overseas booking ... Tasmania.

I was booked to do three concerts to help promote Miss Tasmania. Although they were essentially raising money for charity I was paid a small amount and given airfares for Karen and myself.

We were very excited; it was our first holiday since our three day honeymoon.

The first show was in Dover, the second southern-most town in Australia, about 80 kilometres southwest of Hobart. It's a beautiful spot with a population of around 500. It has a great history. In 1804 it was used as a convict settlement.

It eventually became a working port and fishing village. They harvest crayfish, abalone and salmon.

I was to do a show at the local pub and we were staying there as well.

Kaz and I arrived and Thelma, the publican and her husband Dan, showed us to our room. She was a lovely lady and apologised for the room being a little on the small size. It had a double bed and a small washbasin in the corner, that was about it. It was clean and we were quite happy.

Thelma took me down to show me where I would be performing. It was a typical old-style dining room with an upright piano in the corner. I figured they could put fifty people in with a squeeze. I was to be the first show they had actually had at the pub and they were very much looking forward to the event.

Thelma said the town was buzzing. I felt very important.

The room was a sort of L-shaped and people would have to look around the corner to see me. I suggested we creep along the wall a bit to overcome the situation. She agreed and went on to say that they had acquired a special PA system for the night from a friend of theirs. She held out the contract and ticked that requirement off. Her friend would be bringing it in on the night. I thought the PA wouldn't want to be too big ... I would only be ten foot from the end of the room, but I felt it was more polite to say nothing.

"It says 'spotlight' on the contract Col ... don't think we have one of those," she said with a concerned look on her face.

"It's OK Thel, I've got one of those at home," came a voice from the back of the room.

Thelma introduced me to George.

"You the comic from the mainland?" George asked as we shook hands.

"Yeah that's right mate," I said, "nice to meet you."

George went on about how he'd rig up the light over my head and how it was his pleasure and ... "It's no trouble at all young 'fella'."

"Well that's about it then Col," Thelma said as another voice came from nowhere.

"Wouldn't expect too many tonight Thel. ... 'Satde' nights they come to listen to me at the RSL," said the voice in a taunting manner.

253

"That's old Stan," Thelma said, keeping her voice down. "He plays piano every other week down at the RSL. He's got his nose out of joint, because the town are all excited about tonight."

"Yeah, 'righto' Stan, we'll see," Thelma called as we moved into the bar.

It was mid-afternoon and Thel said the cook wouldn't be on till that night but if Karen and I got a bit peckish we could go into the kitchen and help ourselves to the pantry and the big double door freezer.

"Whatever you fancy love, help yourself," she said.

Thelma went back to work in the main bar and I headed up to the room.

Kaz was lying on the bed reading a magazine and we decided to have a little rest. It had been a long day. It wasn't long before Kaz had fallen asleep. I was really hungry so I headed down to the kitchen to rustle up a sandwich. I opened the freezer and saw half a dozen crayfish, five small and one huge one. ... Yes!!!!

Dover is renowned for crayfish and I happen to relish them. I figured I would offer to pay for one so I picked the biggest. It was huge; it should have had a leash. I took it to the table and broke it down. Salt and vinegar, bread and butter, — my mouth was drooling.

I sat in the pub kitchen and 'pigged' out. On reflection I was sure I saved some for Kaz but she is adamant I ate it all by myself. I'd say her memory of this event is better than mine. I guess she hasn't lost as many brain cells as I have so we'll go with her version.

How selfish was I? Bloody hell it was nice!

Just before the show I went down to the room to check out the 'sound'.

At first I wasn't sure what I was actually looking at.

Thelma's friend had set up a kind of pulpit, something like a preacher would use. It was decorated with plastic flowers and had a small microphone nailed to the top. Running off that was a small thin wire to a very tiny speaker that needed to be held by hand and pointed to the audience as you spoke.

I wondered what I would do when I needed to use the banjo ... maybe tuck it under my arm ... I would figure it out on the night. Thel and Dan were doing their best and were such lovely people. Above the sound arrangement was George's spotlight shining down.

The night began; people were crammed in and rearing to go. The Miss Tasmania entrant made a short speech and thanked everyone for their support.

She talked of the door prizes and raffles that would be held on the night and told them about me 'the special comedian from the mainland'.

I was introduced by Thelma to a great round of applause. They were a wonderful audience and in no time I was enjoying myself. Thelma even held the speaker when I picked up my banjo. As I went into the first few bars of, 'Gotta give the grog away', a new song I had just written, I heard the distinctive sound of a piano. I looked over my shoulder and there was Stan playing along with me. He yelled out, "Come to give 'ya' a hand." ...

I found out later, no one had turned up at the RSL. ... If you can't beat 'em join 'em!

I had been on for about forty minutes and I started to feel a little faint. I was sweating profusely and my eyes were running, in fact my right eye felt kind of swollen. I stopped for a break with the promise of coming back on. I headed for the toilet to wash my face. When I looked in the mirror my face was crimson red, my lips were swollen and my right eye was nearly closed ...

George had put his wife's portable sun-ray lamp above my head. He told me after that he thought I would only be under it for a few minutes and anyway the only reason he had lowered it on a pole was because the ceiling was so high and he wanted to make sure I got enough light on my face. I got enough light alright ... ten minutes more I could have re-made the 'elephant man'.

When I came back in the room, Thelma asked if I could draw the raffle ... no worries. Just then her husband sidled up and said,

"Some bastard's eaten the raffle Thel ... there's crayfish shells in the kitchen bin." Bugger!

I 'fessed' up and Thel told the room, to great rounds of laughter about my raid on the pantry.

She replaced the prize with wine and wouldn't let me pay for it.

About ten years after this event I was doing a gig in Rockhampton Queensland. My promoter Billy took me to my motel, No 98, in the heart of the city. We went straight to our room as he said he had already checked us in.

Inside the room Bill asked me if I could get him a drink from the fridge. I opened the fridge and there was a huge crayfish on a plate with salad and dressing. There was a note on the cray. It read 'Enjoy Col and welcome ... this one ain't in the raffle.'

There was a knock on the door and there stood Thelma and Dan.

## DYING GRACEFULLY

I was doing late night spots in the Melbourne night club scene. It was a tough call. I would go on at midnight do a twenty minute spot and repeat it at 1.30am. The clubs like The Top Hat could trade through till 3am if they put a supper on and a floor show.

The club was full of Italian, Greek and Chinese restaurateurs who had just finished work themselves and wanted to unwind. It was also a hangout for some shady characters that did business that time of night. It was a life unto its own.

I received $35 a spot, less commission. Sometimes I did three or four clubs in and around town on the same night if I could work it. On those nights I could pocket reasonable bucks after fuel and my agent. I would get home early morning then off to work. It wasn't too shabby. I would try and catch an afternoon 'kip' after work. The gig itself was hard.

You would be introduced by the band leader but the noise in the room never changed ... they just kept on talking, you were just background noise to them. You went on to no applause, just the sound of your own feet ... if you could hear it.

They took absolutely no notice of you. A table two feet away would be in heavy discussion and wouldn't even bother to look up.

I was taught a very valuable lesson early, on how to handle this situation by an Irish musician and comedian. His name was Tim Conner and he had a semi-regular gig on TV with Mike Willesee's Current Affair show.

On Saturday nights in the clubs, they would put on a 'star' act. On that night I would become the support act.

I had just finished my first spot. Tim was on next after the break. He watched me from the sidelines as I died a thousand deaths. I walked off into the dressing room feeling so dejected and embarrassed that he had watched me self-destruct.

We shook hands and he could tell what was happening in my head.

"Col, can I give you a tip son, there's a way to handle this ... it's called DYING GRACEFULLY." (He said this in a thick Irish accent.)

"Let me explain," he went on. "This place is full of people who will not only NOT understand my humour, but they would be pushed to just understand my brogue. Now I'm on in a minute and I want you to watch, pretend there is no sound and watch what I do ... you'll understand at the end."

Tim was announced by the band leader ... to no applause. He went straight into a gag ... no response. If you were looking at him you would swear he was killing them. "OK, HERE'S ANOHER ONE YOU'RE GONNA LOVE ... ALRIGHT I'LL DO A SONG ..." this went on and on. He wasn't fazed in the slightest; he was sailing through it as if he had them in the palm of his hand.

He even gave himself an encore ...

"ALRIGHT... JUST ONE MORE, THEN I REALLY HAVE TO GO."

He walked into the dressing room "See Col, it's called 'DYING GRACEFULLY', I was great ... the audience were crap. It's a tough business Col and you need to develop 'Teflon skin'. Put this one behind you and don't do too many post mortems."

Many years later I was being interviewed on Sydney radio and I told the story ... the phone line lit up ... a thick Irish voice came on the line, "COL ME 'BOYO' ...YOU REMEMBERED!!!!"

## TOURING

My agent, Shirley McLaughlin, sold her business to a musician, he, by default, became my new agent ... for about a week. On our first meeting he told me he wasn't into comedy ... or tact as it turned out.

I was on my own!

I rang every agent and told them I was available. The work started coming in and bit by bit I was making inroads.

Wally Bishop, Johnny Chester's manager, got in touch and asked me to go on a six week tour, The Greyhound Country Music Express.

'Chess' had a huge following and it was a full-on show; Cash Backman, Donna Fisk, Jigsaw and myself as compere. These performers all had hit songs and were doing television. It was a big break for me at the time.

Wally had managed The Hawking Brothers and brought them to national prominence. He had taken them to America where they appeared on 'The Grand ole, Opry' in 1975. Wal was a top operator; I was chuffed to get the opportunity to work with him.

Chess had had a great career with national hits like World's greatest Mum, She's my kind of woman, Shame and Scandal, and many more. He had a swag of awards and had worked in radio and television.

In 1964 he had toured Australia and New Zealand with the Beatles.

In 1965 he had been the associate producer on the television show Komotion, the same show Ralph's band, The Swinging Margate's had appeared on.

Wally and Chess had teamed up to tour and were a great combination.

I was quite excited about this tour. We would do on average six gigs a week and I would be paid $100 per gig ... a veritable fortune. The experience I would gain would be invaluable.

## TURNING PRO

I went to tell Graham about the tour. I was devastated when he informed me that if I took the tour he would have to let me go.

I couldn't believe what I was hearing, I was totally blindsided. I reminded him of our agreement. He agreed that he had said I could come and go with my showbiz commitments but he thought it would be the odd weekend or maybe a week at the most.

I was doing good business for him and he didn't want to be that flexible. He had a business to run and I guess I could understand his side of things but I was forced to confront the problem.

I left his office and told him I would let him know the following day.

I came home that night and discussed it with Kaz. I rang Wally mainly to get some reassurance. He told me he could probably give me up to twenty weeks work with Chess over the coming year but the final decision would be up to me.

I left Garners the next day. I was now a professional entertainer, for better or worse. I felt very vulnerable ... especially with the responsibility of our kids ... I bit the bullet and went for it.

## WALLY

Wally had lined up Greyhound buses to tour us, complete with a driver. It was a national promotion and would run on and off all year. Our first tour would be Victoria, NSW and Tasmania.

Wally was a great teacher; he gave me some invaluable lessons in backstage announcing and compering. I always felt he had a natural flair with comedy. He is a wonderful raconteur and has a great sense of timing. He was also a tough taskmaster when it came to touring.

Barry Roy was the lead guitarist in Jigsaw and a master musician: We became great mates. A few years later he was to play on, as well as produce my album, Hey you bloody Mug.

But more of that later.

We had been on the road for a few weeks when we hit Wrest Point Casino in Hobart. It was a top showroom and all the best performers of the day played there.

On the last night of our show it was our 'roadie's' birthday. The next day we were to drive to Launceston, about two hours away and do the show at the Tasmania hotel.

We all had a few drinks with 'Drizzle'. He was nicknamed Drizzle by Wally who said he sometimes acted a little wet.

We all eventually went to bed; we were to be in the foyer at 0830 the next morning to head off to Launceston.

At 0815 I was in the foyer ... so was Drizzle. He hadn't been to bed and was totally 'off his face'.

By this time he was into 'my father didn't love me' phase of his drunkenness and needed consoling or locking up, but this wasn't Navy so I consoled ... till everyone else arrived.

We packed his gear and I volunteered to take his place and drive the truck with him, by this time unconscious, in the passenger's seat.

I assured Chess and Wal it was no trouble and we all headed off to Launceston.

I was about twenty minutes behind everyone else but finally arrived at the hotel. I walked into the lounge area to find Chess and the band lined up, having a drink at the bar. The room was half full of people eating their counter meals.

### FREE MEAL?

Chess met me halfway across the room and shook my hand.

"Thanks for that mate, I really appreciate it," he said.

We were standing by a table and on it was a crayfish dinner and a pot of beer.

With a gesture towards the meal, Chess said "What do you think of that?"

"It looks fantastic Chess ... thank you," I said, and pulled up a seat.

"Enjoy," said Chess and turned to go.

"What a top bloke," I thought and took a long draught of the beer. I started in on the meal. The boys raised up their glasses in salute.

All of a sudden I looked up and noticed a 'truckie' in a blue Jackie Howe singlet standing beside me, legs apart, hands on hips. "WHAT DO YOU THINK YOU'RE BLOODY DOIN' MATE?" he demanded.

"Sorry," I said in confusion, still munching on the cray.

"I can't believe this ... I go for a piss, come back and some bastard's eating my lunch," he said to the room as much as to me.

I nearly choked on the mouthful of crayfish as it suddenly dawned on me that I had been 'set up'. I looked towards the bar ... Chess and the boys were gone.

With profuse apologies and explanations I quelled the storm. The truckie laughed long and loud as I re-ordered his lunch. While all this was happening Chess and the band were watching from behind some partitions at the end of the room.

Barry Roy in particular nearly had a fit watching the proceedings, and has never let me forget the episode.

Later when we all sat around laughing and retelling the story Chess made the statement, "Well Col, I only said what do you think of that, and enjoy. I didn't actually say I had bought you lunch now did I?"

Here we go again ... never assume!!!!!

Wally and I shared a room for part of the tour. One night I was a little restless, and was tossing and turning.

"What's up Col?" Wal enquired.

"I can't sleep mate ... bit too close to Christmas," I said in way of reply.

Well it must have been one of those 'you had to be there' type situations because for some reason, whether it was the inflection I used or the silliness of the statement, Wally broke up and was laughing hysterically. His laughter is incredibly infectious and I was away as well. We couldn't stop. Every time we started to settle, one of us would start up again; it went on for hours. It was like two little boys camping out.

Once a year ever since that time, around 35 years ago, I will ring Wal. It could be 2am or 2pm any month or day ... "Hey Wal, can't sleep ... getting too close ...," then I hang up when I hear that great laugh. It's tradition with us now.

The shows were going well; everybody was in high spirits when Wal broke some news to us. Chess had accepted an offer to host a new country music show, Country Roads, on the ABC.

We were all out of work. We had half a dozen shows left and that would be it. No one could blame Chess as it was a good break for him but it left all of us, including Wal, high and dry.

It was close to Christmas and I couldn't generate any income at short notice. I had knocked so much work back with the football clubs because I thought I would be tied up with touring. The dates had all been blocked out. We had a little money put aside but it would soon run out.

With $250 left on bank card credit I wasn't sure what to do next. I had never been out of work since I was a kid and I needed to do something and fast. I felt backed into a corner. I remember feeling a kind of shame because I had got us into this predicament. Kaz was so supportive and we looked at our options.

We grabbed the local paper and circled a heap of jobs.

I had one gig on my books. It was for Bernie Stahl's agency in Geelong. It was for New Year's Eve, 1978. Wal had booked that one.

## OUT OF WORK

First thing Monday I went to see the people at the unemployment benefits. I had no choice in this, my pride was hurt but I needed to take care of my girls.

I sat down and waited my turn to be interviewed. I looked around and felt a deep empathy for many of the people there. There was a tension in that waiting room ... no conversations at all. I wondered what their stories were.

I was called into an office. A middle-aged woman introduced herself and looked at my application. I gave her a brief rundown of my circumstances. She was very sympathetic and made sure she told me that this safety net was why I paid taxes. She told me this was my entitlement and there was no shame in asking for assistance.

I was told a cheque would be sent out the next week and if my circumstances changed I would need to inform them.

That night my sister Carol turned up at our place with a box of groceries ... that's when I lost it.

The next morning early I had a series of appointments ... International Harvester, the glass factory, Susan Day Cakes (delivery driver). I had lined up two more interviews for the next day, a Sales Rep job and a job in the curtain trade.

The guy who interviewed me at International Harvester had seen me on TV and wanted to talk more about comedy than giving me a job. I finally said I would really appreciate it if he could tell me if I had a shot at some employment. He said that the job on offer was a conveyer belt situation and that it was really for 'New Australians', to give them a start and that I would hate it and leave within a week. I explained my situation and said I would even sign a contract to say I would stay for any amount of time that he deemed would be appropriate, if he could just find his way clear to employ me.

He asked me if I had any other jobs to chase. I told him of the other interviews. Then he took the weight off my shoulders.

"If you don't have any luck with the others Col, I'll have a job here for you."

"You're a life saver mate," I said, shaking his hand, "thank you … thank you so much."

The glass factory were wanting people to start after Christmas and Susan Day said they would let me know within the week.

I drove home feeling more positive.

On the way home I passed some market gardens. People were in the fields digging a potato crop by hand. On a whim I slowed and drove in the gate.

"Understand the process?" the boss asked.

"Pretty much," I said, with as much conviction as I could muster.

I didn't have work clothes with me but was five minutes from home. He said if I came straight back I could start.

I raced in the front door calling to Kaz as I headed for the bedroom to get changed. I told her of the day's events.

"We're gonna be fine," I yelled as I headed back out to the car.

It took the boss about five minutes watching me in action to realise I knew nothing about potatoes. I explained that I was a fast learner and would work the first hour for nothing till I got up to speed. He laughed and as we talked I noticed a young kid in the next paddock messing around with a beautiful Welsh Mountain pony.

"A Welsh Mountain Pony … a beautiful breed," I said off handedly, indicating the pair.

"Do you know horses?" the farmer asked.

"Yeah, I grew up riding," I said.

"Tell you what," he said, "if you can give my son a few pointers I'll pay you to do that instead."

"You're on," I said as we walked over to the boy.

I worked the rest of the day with his son, a boy about twelve and not a complete novice.

With a crisp $20 note in my pocket, I drove home with the promise of some more lessons to come … I was on a roll.

The next day I was interviewed for a Sales Rep job with a tool manufacturer. I felt the interview went well and was told I would be contacted if my application was successful.

## ARE YOU BEING SERVED?

I then went to apply for a job in the curtain department of a manchester group of stores. The owner, Mr. Rosenthal did the interview himself.

He had a European accent and I noticed a Star of David on a chain around his neck. He was casually dressed and was friendly enough but cut straight to the chase.

After the introductions he asked almost by rote, "Do you know how to measure, quote and sell curtains?"

"Yes I do," I said, hoping I didn't sound too cocky. "I also have a good knowledge of fabrics and linings."

"You do?" he said with a little more interest in his voice.

He pushed a pen and pad over to me.

"If I have a window 6ft wide x 7ft deep, how much fabric do I need?" he asked, almost as a challenge.

"Is it a plain, shantung, print, or maybe a velvet and I'll need to know fabric width or does it have a pattern match?" I asked. He looked puzzled and didn't answer, so I carried on.

"It would be one and a half drops per side if it's centre-closing on a standard fit, no pattern match. You would need 8 yards and a bit more for tiebacks. Some people like them a bit fuller, this depends on the fabric but for the exercise let's go with one and a half drops. The backing depends on the fabric and where in the house it would be fitted. I was in my element ... I knew curtains. I did this calculation off the cuff. It was basic and I didn't need to use pen and paper ... I tried not to sound too smart arse.

He quickly pulled a wad of messy worksheets out of his desk drawer.

"Could you look at these for me?" he asked with a look of desperation on his face. "The chap who has done this job doesn't really know too much and we have been left with a mess by another fellow who has gone overseas. Things in the work room aren't good. We have a good business but quite a few jobs are coming back to the workrooms because of ... I don't know what."

It was almost like it was a confession and I was the priest. It seemed that he needed to unload this information.

I started to sort out the sheets he had given me.

Heading sizes were wrong, overlaps not included, no returns. I explained I needed clean, new work sheets if I were to work it out. But if they were this wrong I would, if I were him, do a re-measure on the job.

"It will only be right if the measure is spot on," I explained. There were so many variables like fabric drop, flooring, if the windows had sun exposure. I would need all this information before it went to the make-up stage. He sat there and shook his head. As I explained to him, it's not rocket science but there was no real room for error. Mistakes would cost. In many cases that money could not be retrieved.

As I re-did his worksheets, he had a coffee brought in.

Twenty minutes later I handed back the completed sheets.

He offered me the job on the spot and talked of conditions like company car and how I would head the department. However, I would need to teach the other chap, David, who was struggling with the job at the moment.

I drove with him to his workrooms. Six women curtain-makers were hard at it. At the end of the room was an office and inside a young bloke hunched over some paperwork.

I had a look at his latest problem which was a dye-lot catastrophe. Apparently he had made up a set of lounge room drapes and three quarters the way through ran out of material. He ordered more fabric in but couldn't match the dye-lot. I couldn't save that one but he might still be able to salvage them to another job.

In stock, store fabric needed a simple system of a running stock-take, introduced to overcome this and I explained this to David.

I spent an hour troubleshooting and sorting out his immediate problems. He was really relieved and so was the boss.

I drove back to his office and again he offered me the job.

I felt a little dishonest as I hadn't mentioned my show-biz aspirations. I figured if I became an asset to him maybe something could be worked out. For the present, I had to take care of my family. I put it in the back of my mind for the time being.

It was Friday and I would start at 8.am on the following Monday. I came home with the news to Kaz. We were both so relieved.

Just after tea the phone rang, it was Graham Garner. I don't know how, but he knew of the new job. He came straight out and asked me to come back to work for him again. He told me honestly that he didn't want me in opposition and that this time I could come and go when I liked and that this time he wouldn't renege on the agreement.

He was very persuasive but I would need time to talk it through with Kaz.

I needed another shot at my comedy or was I kidding myself.

I hung up with the promise of a call back within the hour.

We agreed I should go back to Garners. I felt so guilty when I rang Mr. Rosenthal and told him that I couldn't start.

At first he thought I was fishing for more money. I assured him that it wasn't the case. He was upset because he had been so relieved. He thought he had finally found an answer to his problems. He wanted a better explanation and I didn't really have one. I didn't want to lie, so I told him about Garners.

He gave me a 'spray' over the phone and blasted me for wasting his time ... he hung up in my ear ... I deserved that. The next morning I rang David, his curtain guy and offered to still help him.

I could hear the relief in his voice. A few days later we met in a cafe in Brighton. I got him to bring his worksheets in and I worked on them with him. I wrote out some simple instructions for him to follow.

Occasionally we met after work. I gave him my home number as well.

Over the next few weeks I taught him a lot of what I knew. Every now and then he would ring me at work with a problem. I guess I did it out of a guilty conscience but in the end it felt good to help him. He was a nice guy.

One morning out of the blue I got phone call from Mr. Rosenthal.

"I am ringing to thank you ... you're a good person. If you ever want a job, you call me." ... then he hung up.

David ended up managing all four stores.

As a footnote, a week after I went back to Garners, a cheque arrived from the unemployment department. It was for $70. I rang them and told them I was OK now, but thanks. (I kept the cheque.)

I also got offered the Susan Day Cake delivery Job and the glass factory wanted me back. Maybe they were short of stackers. I heard Stavros was beside himself ... Grigori!!!

## GETTING STRAIGHTENED OUT

True to his word, Graham gave me the time off to go on the road and do shows and some acting work.

Wally Bishop was helping where he could and was lining up work in Sydney for me.

In the mean time I worked for Bernie Stahl quite a bit.

He took me on the road to support Lucky Star, Col Joy, Jade Hurley and the odd rock band. Bernie and I seemed to click.

We talked about the business and we touched on management. Bernie was touring local and overseas stars on a constant basis and was fearless when it came to taking chances. He had a great love for the business and was a classically trained musician himself. Bernie set the syllabus for the Conservatorium of Music in Victoria. He performed in his early years as a guitarist in a flamenco band. He also taught music. I also had to constantly explain gags to him ... he just didn't get it ... still doesn't.

Bernie was heading off to the States and would be back in a month. We made arrangements to talk further.

I was starting to get small acting roles and was going to workshop classes on weekends. It was a great advantage to lock into accents.

Over the next few years I worked in TV series like The last Outlaw with John Jarrett. I have a two minute piece in that movie and stood around for three days to deliver three lines in an Irish accent. No wonder these movies go over budget.

I was a cook in the Henry Lawson Series, a drunk in Locusts and Wild Honey, an auctioneer in the ABC's All the Green Years, a shady car salesman in Twenty Good Years and a slimy character on Prisoner.

There were TV commercials and other bits and pieces but my impatience kept me from pursuing acting full-time.

At one time I was offered ten weeks' work on the Sullivans but I had to knock it back because I was on tour with Matt Monroe, (he had the hit, Born Free). Michael Caton got the gig ... he rode it to the end. He is one of my favourite Aussie actors.

Wally had convinced Ted Quig, a Sydney agent to give me a few gigs in Sydney. I was booked to do the Sunday concert at the Auburn RSL.

Lucky Grills was the star act, there was a girl singer, a juggler and myself.

Lucky was a regular on the Mike Walsh Show and was a great character actor. He was probably best known for his TV series, Bluey, in which he played a street-wise detective.

At this time I had not even met Lucky, so I was looking forward to working with him. In later years we became great mates.

This show was the last time I ever had another drink.

This is how it unfolded ...

Kaz came with me for the weekend. When we got to Sydney we were picked up at the airport by Rick Anderson, my Navy mate from Leeuwin and the Hobart.

We had arranged to stay with Rick and his wife Lynn.

Rick had gotten out of the Navy after contracting diabetes. He was 'insulin dependent' and would have to inject every day. The Navy had been his life and it was a tough transition for him to re-establish himself as a civilian. He was importing furniture at the time but was still up for a drink ...

Rick came with me to the gig, the girls stayed at home. We would have supper with them later that night.

Rick and I were early, the first of the acts to arrive. I saw the Duty Manager and he showed us back stage. He also asked if we could use a drink ... a bad mistake as it turned out.

Five minutes later a jug of beer came back stage with two glasses ... we thought, why not?

Slowly but surely the other acts arrived, and the Show Room started to fill up. I was being paid $200 less club booker, less agent and airfares. I had one other gig the night before which went down well so the weekend would yield about $40 for the effort ... not a lot but I was trying to expand my work into Sydney and at least Kaz had a break.

I had made a rule to myself that I wouldn't drink at gigs but I was feeling 'cocky' after the night before and I dropped my guard.

They brought two cooked chickens back stage for the acts. All the salads and cutlery came with it. The juggler was too nervous to eat and the girl singer was in the other dressing room ... no doubt with her own chook.

Rick made the remark that if Lucky doesn't eat any chicken, we might be able to take them home for supper.

Another jug arrived while the juggler was on and another when the girl singer was belting out 'Those were the Days my Friend', that should have rung some warning bells for me ... I was singing along to the chorus and I hate that song.

Then it was interval and the compere announced my imminent spot before the star of the show, Lucky Grills. There were great rounds of applause and whistles at the mention of his name.

Lucky arrived during the interval, introductions all around then Lucky asked me if I would mind swapping spots on the show as he had another engagement to go to later on.

"It would really help me out mate," Lucky said.

"Whatever you say mate, you're the main act. They're here for you," I said with a slight slur.

The compere was told of the change in format and he duly introduced Lucky to thunderous applause. I stood on the sidelines whistling and cheering as well, caught up in the moment and with a slight glow beginning to show.

Lucky was working well and he did two encores ... Rick and I did two more jugs.

Lucky came off to shouts of more, more ... Rick was shouting the same thing but he was talking about the beer. Lucky said a quick 'good bye' and was away. The compere went straight into my intro.

"And now ladies and gentlemen, all the way from Melbourne, his first time in the club, please welcome a very funny guy, Col Elliott," ... I was on.

"G'day," I said as I staggered across to the centre mike.

"Sssspute ta be 'ere," I slurred. The crowd roared ... this was the best drunk act they had ever seen. Then I tripped and did a header, arms out like a swan-dive, right down the middle of the Board Member's table. There were ten at the table, all the men in their green Club jackets, their wives all looked beautiful ... but not for long ... drinks, food, in fact everything went before me. I cleared the whole table as I slid to the opposite end and crumpled on the floor.

I got to my feet, chaos all around, people were a little upset ... that is definitely an understatement but you get the drift. Someone relieved me of the mike and I scurried off back to the dressing room...

"That was quick," said Rick.

"I think we'd better lock the door mate ...let 'em settle a bit. Pass us over the jug." We sat in the dressing room for at least another forty-five minutes. We waited till all seemed quiet, and then made our move.

I picked up my clothing valise, it felt a little heavy.

"I got those two chickens in there mate ... we're right for supper," Rick said as we staggered to the door.

"Seems quiet mate, now might be the time to leave," I said trying to find my feet.

We appeared on the stage and there before us was the manager, hands on hips and a definite scowl on his face.

I can't remember his exact words but it went along the lines of how I'll never work the club again and something about being a disgrace to the profession ...

I was about to apologise when the two chooks hit the floor and rolled off the stage. I was having a terrible time trying to pick them up. They were sliding along the parquetry floor.

I finally got them both in my arms and holding them like twin babies I said to the on-looking manager, "Tell you what, I won't charge a fee for the show ... you keep the cheque, I'll keep the chooks."

"GET OUT!" he screamed, pointing to the door.

"A little harsh," Rick remarked as we made our exit.

Rick and I woke up sitting in his car at 2am, cuddling a chook each.

We drove back to Rick's place. Kaz and Lyn were not impressed; even the chooks did not appease them.

I woke up late next morning with a huge hangover and the full impact of what I had done hit me.

I rang Wally Bishop ... he already knew and gave me the biggest spray.

I got the lot, he had put his reputation on the line for me, and I had let him down big time. His advice, "Get back in the Navy". Drunkard's remorse set in.

I tried to ring Ted Quig, the agent ... he wouldn't take my call.

I wasn't game to tell Kaz the full story.

## THE WOWSER

It's all in the timing as the saying goes and my getting off the grog was certainly no different. My brother Ralph had given it away six months earlier.

He came around home one night with a mate of ours, Billy.

Billy was one of the guys we had grown up with. He and Ralph flatted together when Ralph had his short stint as a civilian after Vietnam.

Bill was a little guy and had been in my class at school. He was being bullied one day in the school yard and I had stepped in and saved his arse as he put it ... his words not mine.

Now he said it was time to repay the favour.

Bill and Ralph talked with me into the night.

I decided to give the grog away for a fortnight and see how I felt.

I haven't had a drink since then ... thirty-five years ago at this writing.

It wasn't all 'beer and skittles' as they say, there was initially the withdrawal symptoms to deal with. I was warned of this but didn't think it would apply to me.

Alcohol is like any drug; your body has to adjust to not having it.

I had aches and pains, night sweats, irritability and headaches. I had been told that alcohol would take at least six weeks to get out of my system.

Probably the toughest part of getting off the drinking merry-go-round was the peer pressure I had to face. People who drank with me before, distanced themselves from me. I was so much a part of their existence and as long as I drank, it gave legitimacy to their own behaviour. Some people have a deep distrust of anyone who doesn't drink and this mentality still amazes me today.

That's not to say every one of my friends backed off but definitely those with a problem had trouble dealing with my decision.

Many would not accept the fact that I was trying to change my ways and constantly tried to get me back on the booze.

No more could I blame the grog for things going wrong in my life. I was now back in control. I had to do this thing for me. This sounds very selfish but it's the truth. If I could get my own life together, all those close to me would benefit.

The alcoholic affects so many people around them. Relationships, business, family breakdowns, children suffer; the list goes on. Alcohol is such a destructive force.

Everyone needs a rock bottom to hit before tackling their addiction. Mine was that weekend. Not the car accident, not my old man's death, not the many times I had embarrassed my wife … no, probably my ego was dented and it made me take a good hard look at myself.

I had been to see a psychologist after the catastrophic hospital visit with Kaz.

He had told me I just needed self-control and that I was a peer drinker. He said I was a social drinker just over-doing it a bit.

He was way off the mark. His assessment of me could not have been more wrong. I was an alcoholic and that's the simple truth of it.

When I admitted that to myself, a great burden was lifted from my shoulders … I finally knew what I was and I would have to learn how to deal with it on a daily basis.

It took me so long to actually enjoy myself on social occasions. All the mates getting into it … the partying continued. The more they drank, the more they came at me to give me their slurry opinions on not only me but my 'ridiculous' attempt to straighten out. And how, in their opinion, it wouldn't work.

Some apologised after, some didn't remember. Eventually, after a time most accepted the fact that I no longer drank.

While all this was happening, I was dreading the fact that I would be back on tour in a few weeks. All my drinking mates were going.

Cash Backman and Norm Tyrrell had gotten together and put a show together to tour Tasmania for a fortnight.

Both these guys and the rest of the band had done some serious drinking with me in the past and this would prove to be very testing.

I had been told to keep out of the places I normally drank while I working on my sobriety ... fat chance, I worked in those places.

Norm was our bass player, Cash the star act. Donna Fisk at seventeen was our female singer. Norm was managing her. We all kept her safe, like big brothers.

She was the only other straight person on the road.

We had toured Tasmania once before on the strength of Cash's hit, My girl Bill.

We had to fly in to this tour as we had been banned on the Princess of Tasmania last trip. We had tossed the barman for drinks and cleaned him out. We left him drunk and asleep behind his bar ... we had partied too hard. The powers that be told us not to come back.

This tour was a disaster from start to finish.

The first day Cash and Norm were messing around wrestling, they rolled down a slope and Norm broke his leg.

He stayed on tour, leg in plaster, playing at night propped on a stool.

We all thought the leg seemed to be set at an odd angle. This proved to be right. When he eventually got back home the leg had to be re-broken and re-set. If this hadn't been done he'd still be walking in circles today!

On the road the boys came to me, booze in hand "Hey Col, let's have a drink."

"No thanks fellas, I won't today ... maybe tomorrow but I'll give it a miss today," I would say. This ruse only worked on them for a day or so.

Basically the tour started with a bang ... BANG ... that was what we heard when Davo our drummer hit the power lines in Burnie with a huge kite. It had blacked out the town ... we raced to the hotel window to see Dave running away.

We were escorted out of Queenstown by the local cops.

After a day's drinking in the local pub things went pear shaped.

A bunch of bikies wanted to take us on in Savage River.

B.J. Capuano our lead guitarist managed to pacify them with his playing ... my stand-up wasn't working. I think I was taking the piss ... as the saying goes 'music soothes the savage beast'.

Another night, we were raided by the cops just as we were about to leave for the gig. We were searched for drugs. We didn't have any but it gave me some good material for the show that night. The whole town knew what had gone down ... I lit up a smoke on stage and announced that even if this cigarette was dope, it would be legal for me to use while working ... in fact I could claim it on tax ... put it down as transport. The cops that were at the gig were not amused.

Every night I would listen to the boys partying in one of the rooms. Invariably there would be a knock on my door ...

"Hey Col, let's have a drink."

"Not today mate ... maybe tomorrow ..."

"Bullshit ... you said that yesterday, come on ... bloody hell."

And on it went ... Sometimes I had to go out to them and settle the noise down. We had been asked to leave motels before.

It was so hard trying to talk sense to a drunk. I soon realised it couldn't be done. Was I like this on the grog? ... Of course, the answer was yes!

This tended to give me even more resolve.

The two weeks came to an end; I hadn't broken.

At that point I realised I had a chance to beat this thing ... a day at a time!

The funny part about this today is that some of the fans still tell the stories of how "Col Elliott and I stood at the bar all night and got pissed."

I hear some outrageous stories on a constant basis. When they are confronted with the fact that I don't drink and haven't done all these years, they still won't accept it ... I guess it comes with the territory.

*Kaz and I with Bernie and Sue*

*"Gotcha ... You pair of buggers"*

*Norm Tyrrell (Tour MGR) and Jack Tipler (Chief Tip Wallower/Brother-in-law)*

*Bernie and I*

*Having a fiddle*

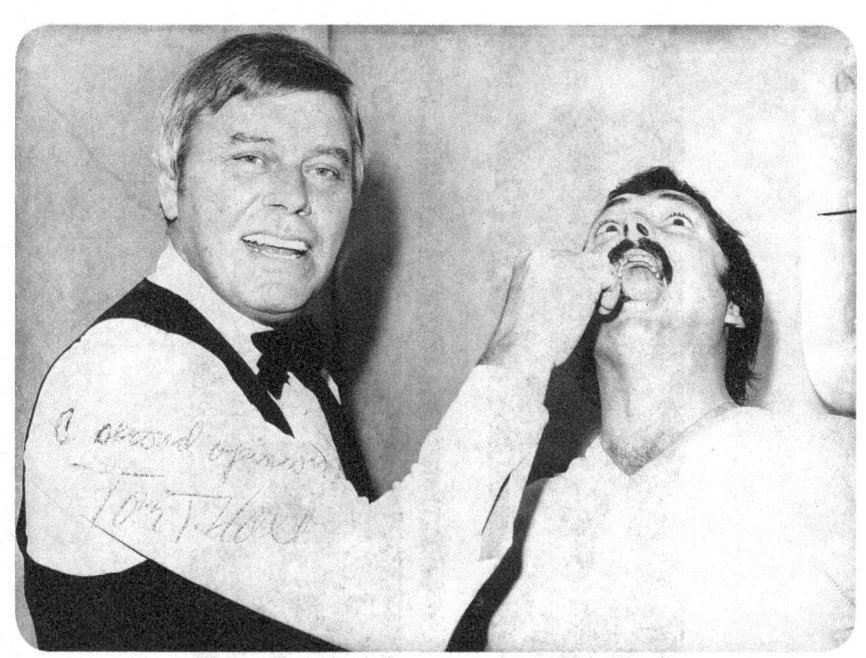

*Tom T. Hall washes out my mouth*

*"Hey you bloody mug" goes Gold*

Punjabi, the Country and Eastern Singer

With Col McEwan, alias Luigi Risotto, at The Penthouse Club.

*Chooka Dennis, king of the roadies*

*Doing a "Benny"*

*With Maurie Fields ... Our take on* Deliverance

*Guessipee doing "Hey you bloody Mug"*

*The Ernie Sigley Show*

*Tom's biggest fan*

*Kev and I strike Gold*

*On tour outback, 49 degrees*

*John Hanson, Johnny Tillotson, me and Bernie*

What often happens to alcoholics is that they replace their behavior with another. I was a pretty good worker but after giving up the grog I became a total workaholic.

I would pay dearly for that in time, but for now I was away.

## BERNIE

Bernie, Kaz and I met in a pub in Geelong and we made an agreement that Bernie would now become my manager. We clinched the deal on a handshake … that was our contract. It still applies today.

Bernie was married to Sue, his second wife. She was his secretary and ran the daily office routine. Bernie's first wife, Heather, also worked for Bernie. He's that sort of bloke. You can't dislike this man.

We set about working on the Col Elliott brand.

Bernie generated a lot of work; he had me out touring at every chance. He put me on the road with Mike 'Shirley' Williams, the floor manager from the Mike Walsh show. He in turn introduced me to Bill Wallace who booked the comedy for the show.

I got a shot at the title.

Shirley said, "You get one gig Col, if you die that's it … if it goes well, you'll be in on a regular basis, that's all I can do."

I ended up doing the Midday Show for around twelve years till its eventual demise. It was a fantastic outlet for variety acts; a format sadly missed today.

## BOOTLEGGED!!!

I had been working a lot of pleasant 'Sunday mornings' in the football clubs and some enterprising soul had taped my show. They had also taken a photo of me in full flight and were manufacturing albums and tapes for sale. I only became aware of it when I was approached to sign a copy brought to a gig by one of the punters.

I hired a mate of a mate of a mate who was a detective to track them down.

The bootleggers weren't the nicest types and had a good underground business going in the back of a strip club. Mine wasn't the only album being made.

They weren't at all fazed when I confronted them, in fact they said in broken English, "We like you Col, you funny bloke, but you make your own fuckin' records … now piss off we busy." A hand gun was flashed and it seemed more prudent to take their advice and make my own 'fuckin' records to sell.

Even when this was happening there was a positive side. They were spreading the word and more clubs wanted to book Col Elliott. Bernie was delighted and raised my price accordingly.

I decided the time was right to make my debut album. I came up with the title, You can't help laughing with Col, Vol.1. It was R-rated and definitely not for the faint-hearted.

I had them made up, a thousand at a time at Festival records and sold them at gigs for $7. They cost $1 to produce, I gave Ralph $1, (he became the 'merch bitch') and Kaz and I took $5.

It wasn't long before there was a huge demand for them. The guys from the Port Melbourne Football Club were buying them sixty at a time and selling them on the wharves. We started putting them in pub drive-through bottle shops. I even had them in a butcher's shop in Dandenong as well as all the record shops in and around Melbourne. I was selling heaps at the live gigs.

I was making more on record sales than I was at the shows.

Vol. 2 was launched and the business doubled; funny about that. I had a mate record them live on a two track tape recorder. He charged me $250 including the edit.

I recorded Vol.3 of the R-rated series at the same time that I was in the studio working on an album that was more middle of the road. I realised I needed something that could be played on radio. I would call the album, Hey you bloody Mug, after the title track.

That track was a monologue about a new Australian that had only been in the country three days and his first social outing was a game of Aussie rules football. He thought the umpire's name was 'Hey you bloody Mug' ... It would prove to be my big break ... in the not too distant future.

## HOLY SMOKE MAX!!!

I was still putting down the tracks when I went to Sydney for a few gigs Bernie had lined up. ...Ted Quig still would not accept my calls, but Wally and I had kissed and made up. (Years later I was collecting a 'Mo' Award in Sydney, when Ted came over to congratulate me. I apologised for Auburn and we laughed. He didn't realise it was me all those years before, but said they still talked about the episode and that the story had grown to the point where I had punched out the manager and the compere. Ted passed away not long after that. I was glad to finally have made my peace.

Getting back to the story ... I do go off on tangents don't I?

I was about to head to the airport on the Sunday, when I got a call from John Hanson.

"Col, I'm in a jam. Is there any chance you can do a support gig for me tonight. I've got Max Bygraves in town and the comic that does his support is crook," he said.

"Be glad to help out mate," I said, "but I'll need to change flights and tell Kaz."

That done I headed to the Penrith Leagues club with Rick in tow ... no drinking this time, at least not for me.

Max Bygraves was an absolute icon. He had been touring Australia for years and his tours were always a sell-out.

He was the consummate variety performer, singer, comedian, and actor. He had his own television show and had appeared in twenty command performances.

He had done it all and in his home country of England he was an absolute national treasure. It was a thrill to be asked to open his show.

I reported to his tour manager who had worked with Max for over twenty five years. He thanked me for coming in on short notice.

"Max is not here yet Col but I'll introduce you after the show. What I need is about a forty to forty-five minute spot, nice and clean though mate, Max's audience is a bit reserved, middle ground if you know what I mean."

"No worries Alf," I said ... that wasn't his name but he was 'Cockney' and that sounds about right.

I went on, the audience were warm and I watched my 'Ps and Qs' and walked off to a good response.

"Luvly jubbly," said Alf, "are you hanging round for Max, Col?"

"Yeah, I'll watch from the wings if that's alright Alf." I said.

"That could be 'andy," said Alf, "if you're going to be here on the wings do you think you could do a little favour for me during Max's show?"

"Sure Alf, how can I help?" I asked.

"Well," said Alf, "during the first 30 minutes of his show he does a song — Maybe it's because I'm a Londoner."

"I know the song, my mum taught me," I said, feeling very knowledgeable.

"Oh great, well there's this little smoke machine down here, it's on now," he said as he pointed to my side by the tabs.

"When you hear the opening bars of that song, could you push this button on the machine and it will push a little stage smoke around Max's feet across the stage. It gives the song a bit of atmosphere, like London smog if you know what I mean Col. Then when he finishes that song he'll go into Underneath the Arches, that's the cue to stop the smoke by touching the stop button?"

"I know that one too Alf," I said.

"Great," said Alf "So start the smoke on Maybe it's because I'm a Londoner and stop it on Underneath the Arches."

"Too easy Alf," I said, feeling very important.

Max was waiting in the opposite wings and briefly looked across at me and gave a friendly wave and mouthed the words, "Thank you" as he was introduced.

I watched from the wings as this veteran took his audience on a roller coaster ride of pure delight. He was incredible to watch.

I heard the opening bars of my cue song, I looked down towards the smoke machine ... I couldn't see a thing. All backstage lights were off. I had been looking into the light on stage and now I was blinded. It was total darkness. I fumbled round and found the machine and somehow managed to push the right button. I looked back on stage and noticed the smoke starting to form across the stage. It looked very effective and I breathed a sigh of relief.

All too soon, the song was over and Max was into the next bit, Underneath the Arches, my cue to kill the smoke.

I looked backstage and in complete darkness I couldn't for the life of me see the machine. I moved forward in panic and tripped over it, I fell heavily, I was winded, I was fighting to get my breath. My feet had landed on top of the smoke machine when I fell. I must have triggered the fast forward button or something ... it whirred into life, smoke was pouring out of the nozzle like a garden hose out of control. I tried to grab the hose that fed on stage but only managed to fall into the curtains and lose it. The hose was now firmly wedged under the drum kit on stage, smoke spewing out of it in great volumes.

I managed to find my feet and totally panic stricken I looked to the stage. All I could see was a solitary drumstick coming through the air as the band tried to keep playing ... I saw the first four rows of the audience disappear, the stage was completely gone.

I heard Max coming off stage, I couldn't see him.

He strode straight past me calling "ALF, WHAT THE BLEEDIN' 'ELL IS GOIN ON?"

I heard Alf trying to tell Max, "I think it was that bloody

comedian." There was confusion all around and I thought now was not the time to apologise ... like a rat leaving a sinking ship, I slunk away.

Just before I left I looked back at the auditorium, it was completely blanketed and 800 people had disappeared. There was an announcement that all was well, just a technical hitch and the show would continue in half an hour or so and that the air conditioners would take care of the problem. Sorry for the inconvenience!

In my defence, I suppose I could have argued that I was just trying for a realistic London fog!

Maybe twenty years after this little 'technical hitch' I was playing the Burswood Casino in Perth. I was walking across the foyer when a voice called out, "Col, over here."

It was John Hanson; he was in town on tour with Max Bygraves and was on his way over to the breakfast bar to eat with him.

John invited me to join them.

Max, ever the gentleman stood up as we approached.

We shook hands.

"I saw your poster in the foyer Col, you do get around a bit, I see you all over ... how's it goin'... all good?" Max enquired.

"Yeah, all good thanks Max," I said in response.

"I don't think we've met before have we Col?" asked Max.

"We did briefly a long time ago in Penrith," I said.

"Penrith, now that's a good club John, are we there this trip?" Max enquired of John.

"No, not this trip Max," said John.

"Shame," said Max, "good club that ... I remember one time we had to stop the show ... Alf, my tour manager got this bloody idiot comedian to work the smoke machine ..."

By this time I was starting to laugh...

Max said "Wait a bit Col, I ain't finished ... "

"I'll finish the story Max," I said, in between the laughter.

I told him how it happened. By the time I had finished my version, Max had tears in his eyes.

I met Max a couple of more times after that, the last time was at the shopping centre on the estate where we both lived.

He was in his eighties then and had emigrated to Australia. That day he was with his wife, Blossom.

Kaz and I walked up to say "Hello".

"Hello Col," he said, and then to his wife "Ask Col if he can explain the workings of a smoke machine to you love."

Max Bygraves passed away on 31st August 2011 aged 89.

He was one of the best ... I was honoured to have met him.

### THE LAND BARON

Cranbourne, where we lived was on the edge of Gippsland. Just down the road was Devon Meadows and country acreage.

I had always wanted to have a little land to run a couple of horses on. Kaz went along with my dream.

I constantly looked in the local real-estate agent's window for a property. This went on for a few years. I guess I was 'window wishing'. But one day in that window, Kaz and I found two and a half acres, just a little way back from the highway. It looked perfect. The agent took us out to look at it.

It was for sale at a bargain price, $25,000; we were over the moon. It was much cheaper than similar sized land in the area because it had an easement ... that should have rung the warning bells but hey, he was our local bloke and I trusted him.

I would learn a big lesson over this deal. You must always do your due diligence ... check out everything.

The man who had owned the land had passed away and his son put it up for sale.

We were so excited we had sold our house and were planning our new home. Our deposit was lodged and I asked the owner, through the agent, permission to clear some tea trees and form a space for our house.

While the sale was going through, we spent weekends planting new trees and plants. We had sausage sizzles with the kids and their cousins. Carol and Jack were as excited as we were. Then it rained ...

We went down to see how the easement was working and couldn't find it. Our block was a lake. Our newly planted trees and shrubs were literally floating past us. The land we were buying was the drainage point for all the acreage in the area.

I went to the council and was informed we could never get a permit to build as long as there was this drainage problem ... it wasn't their concern and I would need to consult an engineer.

We were devastated and called in Karen's sister's brother-in-law, Vass, who was an engineer. He came down and virtually told me it would cost a fortune to drain and even then it couldn't be guaranteed. The natural lay of the land in the surrounding area prevented a simple answer to the problem.

I was so angry ... the agent tried to duck me ... we had words.

The owner would not back down. It was stated that by bulldozing the tea trees I had made an 'Act of Possession' and I would have to complete the purchase. I informed the agent that I would go to jail first and I would make sure everybody knew who had sold me the land.

On enquiry we found out that no other estate agent would put the land on their books because of its inherent problems. We also found out that the father had refused to ever sell this land, knowing its problems. Apparently his decency died with him.

My solicitor fought for us. He managed to halt the sale but we lost our deposit ... and my trust in people's honesty, for a little while anyway.

We were lucky, it could have been much worse! Kaz had picked up on the 'positive' in every situation and said we could have put sand around the outside and buy in some hire boats ... it helped take the edge off things.

I caught the agent at the fence talking to a couple one day as I drove past. I pulled over and yelled to the people, "Can I have a word?" Before I got to them the agent was in his car and away... I had a quiet word to the couple!

As a footnote to this story, that land is still to this day, vacant ... just like the agent's scruples.

### "MAYBE"

One door shuts as they say... it was meant to be. Kaz and I found a beautiful little farmlet in Cannons Creek on Westernport Bay. The name out the front on a slab of wood was "Maybe". The owners had named it that in answer to their kids' questions "Can we buy it Dad?" "Maybe" ... We left the name there, it seemed just right.

It was the original farm in the area and we had four acres; beautiful grounds with sheds and old stables, weeping willows everywhere and a huge date palm in the front.

The girls were over the moon. They embraced the lifestyle, ponies, chickens even a donkey ... Isabel. She was stubborn but the kids learnt to ride on her. She became part of the family. Jodie named all the chickens ... there was Kern, Journey, Tree and Breakfast; she was such an imaginative little girl. I asked her to explain their names. Journey, went for a long walk in the paddock, Tree, always stood under the tree, Breakfast, was the first to eat. I said "Jo, what about Kern?" She said. "You know Daddy, the chicken man, Kern-El-Sandals" ... Of course, I should have known.

Kim loved the country and was on her pony Chaffey every waking moment.

Jodie had Jock, a painted Shetland. What a pair.

Kaz found a beautiful Pembroke Corgi puppy ... We called him Seiko ... he was a 'watch' dog. Life there felt good.

My sister Carol and brother-in-law Jack and their kids, Jacqui, John and Sue would stay on weekends. It was all horses and fun.

Eventually Carol and Jack bought their own place a few kilometres away.

The girls were into dancing and pony club. Kaz would hitch up the old float on weekends and she and Carol would take the kids to the meetings. Much of the time I was away on gigs but when I was home we all went … I loved those times.

## BOOTS AND ALL

We had a beautiful cat the kids called 'Boots' because he had four white socks but apart from that, was black all over. He was a very affectionate cat and would follow the kids around everywhere.

I often left my driver's side window down on the car and Boots had a habit of crawling inside my car and sleeping on the dash-board to soak up the sun.

Ralph and I were heading out one night to a gig for a football club at Fish Creek in Gippsland. It was about a forty minute drive.

The gig was being held at an old church hall. I pulled up just outside the small car park to the side of the hall.

Ralph got out the car and I went to the back to grab my guitar. Boots flew out the back and shot through between my legs. I cursed and chased him; he was obviously frightened and was very nervy. I cornered him against the hall and picked him up. The bugger bit and hissed at me. He was going berserk, I was getting scratched, and he was drawing blood. I yelled to Ralph to open the back door of the car and threw him inside. Boots was scratching against the car window and squealing.

He had never left the farm before and was terrified. We went in and did the gig. We came out to the car and Boots was still leaping around the car hissing and baring teeth. When we got in the car there was the acrid smell of cat urine.

I had just moved off down the road when Ralph screamed out … "YOU BASTARD!" … Boots had launched himself at the back of

Ralph's head and was ripping into him. He was being shredded. I started laughing. Ralph was screaming blue murder and Boots was hissing, clawing and growling.

Ralph grabbed the travel blanket and managed to cover him but not before Boots took another chunk off his forearms. I couldn't believe Boots had turned so aggressive. I made a mental note that we would make sure this cat never left the farm in future.

Ralph held tight to the travel blanket and kept Boots pinned for the rest of the drive home... Boots kept up his protest ... and pissing.

We finally arrived home, I drove in the farm gates and my headlights swept across our side entrance ... there on the back step sat BOOTS. The cat in our car was an imposter!

The best I could figure was that when I went to the back of my car to get the guitar the 'imposter Boots' must have run underneath our car and between my legs ... I just assumed he came from the back of the car. The 'Fish Creek Boots' had very similar markings to the real Boots but obviously had an attitude problem. We turned around and drove straight back to Fish Creek, we opened the door and the cat flew out the back of the car with not so much as a thank you ... Ralph had to drive home; I was hysterical.

## THE TIP WALLOWER

My brother-in-law Jack, has the greatest sense of humour and loves a good laugh. Anyone who meets Jack instantly likes him; he has that way about him. He loves people. All the kids love Uncle Jack.

He has never lost his broad Manchester accent and it adds to his character and charm.

At that time Jack absolutely loved going to the tip. It was like a big treasure hunt to him. On his little forays he had picked up some amazing stuff.

So on this day Jack introduced me to the English art of 'tip wallowing'.

Now I don't know if this was an English thing, or just Jack justifying scrounging around in a tip and making it sound a little more than what it really was … scrounging.

Either way, we headed down to the Dandenong tip one Saturday morning. As Jack pointed out, "Satee mornin's, best time son, they throw out best 'stooof' then." (That's the best I can do with his accent here.)

We were picking through bits and pieces when I spotted an old car body, it was bit of a wreck with different colored doors, not much to salvage there but I noticed a perfectly good wire roof rack on top. "Hey Jack," I called, "check this out."

Jack came over "That's the way son," he said then started to dismantle the rack. In the meantime I had gotten inside and found an old radio. What a find, I was starting to feel the buzz.

Jack took over from me on the radio and I kept unscrewing the rack. Jack emerged with the radio in hand just as I pulled one side of the rack off.

All of a sudden this old bloke was beside us "FUCK, N 'ELL" he yelled, "WHAT ARE YOU DOIN' TO ME CAR?"

He snatched the radio from Jack. The indignant look on his face set me off … I was trying to apologise and stifle a fit of laughter at the same time.

Jack was trying to put the rack back on but the old bloke was too incensed, he just kept telling us to "PISS OFF" … so we did.

We had upset a fellow 'wallower'. I think we lost a little standing in the 'Wallowers Association' that day.

## FOOTLIGHTERS

After I had created the R-rated albums the work load was huge in the footy clubs. I had left Garners after another year back with them. Bernie and I were starting to work interstate.

I had been invited to join the Footlighters Club after going along as a guest of Col McEwen's. I had gotten to know Col from my work on the Penthouse Club.

Col did a comic character, Luigi Risotto, on the show and we became good mates. Col was also a much 'in-demand' actor and was well established in the Melbourne scene.

The Footlighters Club was formed by John Newman of Tiki and John's fame, a Melbourne theatre restaurant.

Entertainers would bring guests for a luncheon on the first Tuesday of the month. Many business men would become members and would bring their clients to the show-biz luncheons as well. In a way it was a kind of networking system. I made many valuable contacts without even being aware of it at the time.

I came to know many of the entertainers of the day and went on to work with many them over the coming years.

I have some great memories of that time in my career; one of my favorite photos is of Maurie Fields and me doing a send up of Deliverance. Maurie started out as a song and dance man. He was one half of Skit and Skat and came up through the theatre era in Australia. He was one of Australia's favourite sons. We worked pantomime together at Tiki and Johns; I got to write material for his Blade Bone character.

He was a walking historian of showbiz and told me many stories of his time with Mo McCackie (Roy Rene) and many others.

Once a year in Melbourne, Tiki and John would produce the Footlighters ball. All proceeds would go to charity. There would be comedy sketches and solo performances. It was a 'must' on the Melbourne Social calendar. Tickets were hard to get and the night's event would always be recorded for radio.

Bert Newton was a big fan of Footlighters and would always be there on the night. The next day on his radio show he would play highlights.

On one occasion, I was doing a sketch as one of my characters, a priest. It was getting good laughs but there was an interjection from a heckler ... I looked across and saw Mary Hardy calling out.

She was a little 'socially excited' and people around her were trying to make her sit down. What could I do, she was my friend? I tried to ignore her and kept the monologue going ... she kept heckling. I waited for a break in her diatribe and said, "Mary ... Evil Knievel is due in Australia next week ... he's going to try and do something that has never been attempted before, he's going to try and jump across your mouth." I instantly felt bad. The whole audience were on their feet applauding. I looked back to Mary. She was applauding and whistling with them. I felt a little better.

The next day it was all anybody wanted to talk about and Bert's producer rang me for an interview.

Bert as always, never bagged Mary but highlighted the fact that it was 'bloody funny' as he put it.

I spoke to Mary a few days later, we were good ... but she didn't remember much of it.

As I became more established I found myself picking up more and more work as a compere comedian on sporting nights. They were a top way to raise funds for the clubs. There were no poker machines in Victoria in those days and the clubs were basic and always struggling. Some Victorian sporting clubs were not much more than big sheds. I've had dressing rooms called a nail!

The Sydney clubs had it all. We were poor cousins by comparison.

I was working with all the top sportsmen of the day; Max Walker, Lionel Rose, Ron Barrassi, Ted Whitten, the young Mark Jackson, Lou Richards, Dennis Lillee and many more. They were always top nights and I enjoyed them immensely.

## LITTLE BIG MAN

One of my favourite speakers on the circuit was Peter Bakos. He was an ex-champion jockey. Peter had ridden in twenty-five Melbourne Cups and had some very funny stories.

Peter was tiny, only four foot seven and a quarter. His favourite line was, "when you're four foot seven, that quarter inch is very, very, important."

He came out to 'Maybe' to pick me up one night. He was driving a huge V8 Ford Falcon. His eyes were just above the dashboard even though he was perched on top of a cushion that originally belonged on a lounge suite. He had big wooden blocks on the pedals.

My girls were amazed when this little man got out of the car … they couldn't stop staring … then Jodie turned to me and said "Daddy, can we play with him?"

## PAUL HOGAN SHOW

About this time I got a call from Johnny Ladd, he was an associate producer on the Paul Hogan Show. A friend of his, Vi Greenhalf, had a coffee show on Melbourne TV and I had appeared as a guest doing a Benny Hill impression. I did his Fred Scuttle character in a sketch. Johnny remembered me and when Paul needed a Benny Hill look-alike for a sketch on his show, he called me.

The idea for the sketch was that 'Hoges' wasn't happy that Hawaii Five O and the Benny Hill Show were on at the same time, so why not combine the two? Call it Benny Five O.

I arrived at channel nine in Melbourne and met Paul and his producers in a caravan dressing room out the back.

Paul and I shook hands but he made the comment that he just couldn't see me doing the Benny Hill impression because I had a moustache.

I turned my back on them, slipped on the beret and glasses, turned around with my hands on my hips, eyes fluttering "Good evening viewers." Hoges applauded and hired me on the spot. He offered me another $500 to shave my moustache off for the shoot.

I shaved my moustache off on the day of the shoot and went to kiss the girls goodbye. They looked around at the sound of my voice and Kim said, "Hi Uncle Ralph". The girls had never seen me before without a moustache. I had started growing it the day I left the Navy. For that matter Kaz had never seen me with a naked top lip ... "Grow it straight back." she demanded.

Every now and then they replay the Paul Hogan Shows, and there I am as Fred ... check out the lip.

I had been writing routines and creating my comic characters constantly and basically whipping myself into a frenzy with gigs.

If I could fit four gigs in on a Sunday I would. I had experienced 'broke' and I had no intention of going back there. Bernie was just as bad, neither one of us could say "no". If it was a return booking I needed new material. I was constantly working on ideas, totally immersed in the process.

Gerry Morrison, a journo mate of Bernie's was working with me on promotional material. He was so creative and we worked well together. We worked on the Hey you bloody Mug album cover and press release while I was still recording it. Gerry's input was so genuine. He was a one of those people that exuded a natural feeling of enthusiasm ... Again, another one of life's gentlemen. Gerry passed away in November 2012 ... I wish he could have read this book.

I had been trying to get some sort of record deal but was getting a lot of knockbacks. It seemed nobody believed an Aussie comedy album would work. The only comedy in the record shops were Derrick and Clive (Peter Cook and Dudley Moore) and a little Bill Cosby, that was about it.

I had approached Ron Tudor the head of Fable records. He was a pioneer and a champion of Australian recording artists. Ron had launched such acts as Matt Flinders, Liv Mason, and The Strangers. He had great success with The Mixtures and had created The Bootleg Family with Brian Cadd.

After judging John Williamson on New Faces, Ron had signed him to Fable.

John got his first gold album, Old Man Emu, with the help of Ron.

It's all in the timing as they say and Ron was a nice guy and listened to my pitch but told me to forget it … "You're up against Mondo Rock, Col, the industry is changing, I don't think this will work."

I couldn't figure out how I could be compared with a rock band. I must have missed something … I left his office dejected but not beaten. If anything it made me more determined.

I needed to be different from other comedians and I needed an edge. I enjoyed creating my characters.

'Giuseppe' did Hey you bloody Mug, I had 'Punjabi', a Country and Eastern singer with hits like, Curry with the Fringe on Top, Lipstick on your Cholera, Who's Sari Now?, I left my Harp in New Delhi. I created 'Hari Kari' a failed Kamikaze pilot who turned left at Israel and landed at the back of Dubbo, and 'Vinnie Vomit' the punk rocker. There was 'Arthur C Stalk' the gardening 'expert', 'Chooka Dennis' my roadie, 'Slugger Mulligan' the bush poet with attitude.

There is so much to comedy. I believed I needed to do more than stand there and deliver gags or one-liners.

Of course there is gag comedy and observational comedy all of which can be intertwined but I wanted more in my performances.

There were the characters, the ditties and even some straight pieces.

I have had tremendous radio support over the years with the country music story-telling side of my work like Henry Banjo and Me, Gone fishin', Zaar, I Hear a Sound. I have written and recorded with some great talent over the years, Bob Pierse (The Deltones), Lee Conway, Colin Greatorix, Allan Caswell, to name a few.

Even Kevin Bloody Wilson and I have hit gold. Kev wrote a monologue for me many years ago. We had been out one night after a gig and talking about family. He wrote the piece after I left and gave it to me the next day… It's a beautiful story and I am constantly requested to do it … It's simply titled, Hankies from Nanna.

Most people know Kev for his R-rated work but he writes some great straight stuff as well. He is a huge country fan. We also did a duo, Fair and Just, about two Coppers; no airplay but it went gold ... that's another story.

It had been suggested to me that maybe I had confused my audience by working in both areas but it seems to have worked for me over the years ... too late to change now.

I tried to make all these aspects come together. I still believe today that the comedy I do is a work in progress, it's always evolving, ever changing and that in turn I think helps keep me as a performer, more relevant.

Bert Newton was about to celebrate his 1,000th radio show at 3UZ and he invited me to perform on the show. It was to be recorded live at Her Majesty's theatre to an audience of about two thousand. Bert's show was relayed all over Australia so it was a 'biggie'.

Bert had heard me do a live version of Gotta give the Grog away and requested I do it on the day.

Kamahl, Jade Hurley, Pattie Newton, Denise Drysdale, Little River Band; it was a big line up and I felt honoured to be asked.

The performance went well and two days later I got a call from a radio station in Nambour, Queensland. The morning crew had cut my piece out of Bert's show and were playing it on a regular basis during their morning show. The morning Jock had sent it on to his mate on Sydney radio and they wanted an interview as well.

We were getting inundated with calls by the end of the week and decided to 'rush release' the album to try and cash in on the publicity the song was creating.

We couldn't keep up with the orders and we didn't have a distribution solution worked out.

Bert was promoting it and at the same time giving his listeners the names of the shops that were carrying the album.

Ernie Sigley was playing it on his show; I had worked on Ernie's TV show in Adelaide and now he got right behind it.

Gavin Wood a Melbourne Jock and a mate of mine, was also running with it ... then we got a call from EMI.

## E.M.I.

Bernie and I went to Sydney to talk a recording deal. We were to meet with their executives first thing on the Monday. We arrived Sunday night.

We felt sure it could just be the big break.

We sat down in the boardroom and were treated like long lost cousins. Placed before one of the guys was the album, Hey you bloody Mug, and Vols. 1, 2 and 3 of the R-rated series.

I had only released Vol.3 two days before and here it was in front of me in Sydney. They had obtained their own copies.

One guy spoke of markets fluctuating and of my recordings having a run on novelty value and how fickle the industry was and how tough it was out there.

I felt he was getting me ready to talk turkey.

"Let's cut to the chase fellas," one said "We are prepared to buy these albums outright ... for this". He pushed across a cheque made out for $50,000.

"So you guys then own my albums?" I enquired.

"You still get your copyright and we will sell you albums at wholesale price so you can sell them at your live gigs. You get this cheque," he answered.

"I can make that much selling these myself and I only sell them in Victoria ... in fact I've probably done that already ... you guys have the whole of Australia," I said as much to myself as to the room.

"And stop kicking me under the table Bernie." It broke the ice and we all laughed.

I had done some quick mental arithmetic and knew it wasn't such a good deal but I also figured they knew their potential.

I also wanted to own my own albums; I had created them, they were mine.

Bernie and I had done our homework before this meeting; we knew there was another system on offer, P&D (press and distribute).

We retained ownership but signed an exclusive deal with EMI to sell them nationally.

Bernie spoke to them of this system; he knew what we could expect from such a deal and he put this forward.

We all shook hands and settled on P&D.

Bernie and I walked calmly out of the building, not game to look at each other. We got down the road half a block, turned into an alley and both screamed to the high heavens … "we bloody well did it!"

## "WE BLOODY WELL DID IT!"

Our first royalty cheque was amazing. It paid out our mortgage on the farm … imagine winning the Lottery, that's how it felt.

The album went ballistic; we appeared on all the TV shows. Donnie Sutherland had me on Sounds, a rock show, singing Gotta give the Grog Away, 'Giuseppe' appeared on the midday show doing, Hey you bloody Mug.

I appeared on the morning shows and the Don Lane show. A few weeks later I was presented with my first gold album on the Midday show.

That afternoon I got a phone call from Ron Tudor congratulating me. He told me he was glad I hadn't taken his advice. I was touched by his call … what a great bloke.

I was really working on two fronts. I was getting novelty airplay on the rock stations but country music had my music on rotation as well. Nick Erby, a legendary country presenter, rang for an interview and congratulated me on my country songs. He loved Gotta give the Grog Away. I thought, "So that's what it is ….Country Music"!

The touring began in earnest, Kaz and the girls were left at home when I hit the road. There were twelve people touring with the Col Elliott show initially, support acts, band and crew. We hit every state. Over the years, I had quite a few tour managers, Norm Tyrrell (he of the Tassie broken leg) was on the road with me for about eight years, Gary Robertson did about ten years. 'Robbo' was ex-Navy. He and his wife Marie ran Axiom Entertainment and were agents and event promoters.

Robbo is quite revered in country music circles. He came up with the concept of Star-maker in Tamworth, the talent quest show which helped launch the careers of people like Keith Urban, Lee Kernighan, Troy Cassar-Daley and many more. Robbo came on the road with me simply because he enjoyed it; we had so much in common because of our Navy ties. We still hang out today. He is a walking historian of rock and roll and great to converse with. Bernie's brother Ian also went on the road for a few years.

Bernie's son Jamie toured as well as Bernie in the beginning. Brian Lloyd an ex-cop did eight years. He worked as stage manager at Seagulls club at Tweed Heads and when they folded, he hit the road with us.

We employed a few other guys in between. Eventually, I think the road wore all these people out. The attrition rate was high. It's a tough existence. I was the only constant. There's no show without Punch. We went all over. We went to places where they still vote for Menzies.

Today I go out with a great mate of mine, Jamie Davis.

Jamie can sing, yodel, tell a gag and is a top straight man.

His only complaint is ... I won't go on the road for full on tours. He missed the 'hey days'... It's all in the timing as they say.

Kaz kept the home fires burning. She held the family together. She was the one constant in the girls' lives, their stability. I was out doing country festivals and club shows. For many years I opened the Tamworth Festival Golden Guitars. I also found it hard to say "no" to charities. I have worked with so many over the years. While I was on the road I was making the money but this lifestyle was affecting us all so much.

I wanted to give my family security and in those early years I felt that this popularity wouldn't last, so I pushed the envelope. We would hit the road for a six week tour, home for a week or ten days and in that break I would do interviews and promotion for the next tour. Sometimes I would fit recording in there as well.

There was tension at home. Kaz would become the mum and dad when I was away and when I got home I felt I was in the way. I tried to fit in but it became more and more difficult.

Kaz was depressed, I was depressed. Our lifestyle was taking its toll but I would go on night after night to make 'em laugh.

There were times I wanted to give it all away. Then I would think about being broke ... I'd run a little harder.

How do you tell little girls of three and six that you have to go away, again. One time I said that I had to go and earn money so that I could get their ballet slippers.

I got in the car, they came running out "Daddy," Kim said, "you don't have to go, we've got some money" ... they were emptying out their little piggy banks on the grass ... I drove away with tears in my eyes. This scene has stayed with me all these years.

When I go interstate to do a gig even today one of the girls will pipe up, "Off to get some ballet slippers Dad?" It's funny now, but back then ...

It is not an easy life in showbiz and it was easy to see how marriages can fall apart. I missed my family so much but the life I was leading became all encompassing. It wasn't the ego of it, it was the fact that I had found something that I could do. Something that I felt I was meant to do; something that would give me a shot at the title. If I worked hard my family would never have to go without.

I have never been a 'showbizzy' type of person. This sometimes gets up Bernie's nose as I don't do the 'BBQs' as he puts it. I have even sent him off to Sydney to pick up a Mo award on my behalf because I was doing something with my family. I love performing but I don't do the 'get-togethers' unless it's for charity. This, according to Bernie, has blown a few opportunities. He's probably right but hey, I'm not good at schmoozing!

## IF IT LOOKS TOO GOOD TO BE TRUE!!!

Just after our first record deal, Bernie and Sue, Kaz and I, were offered a 5% ownership of a project called The Bay City Entertainment Centre. It was to be the home of the Wildcats Basketball Team. It would be a performance venue with radio and television facilities. It looked amazing. Some big name people were investing. We were told it was a select group. Turned out to be a select group all right ... of suckers! We went to the presentation.

Our investment was to be $100,000 between us. The guy doing all the deals was good ... very good! In fact he's still doing 'shonkies' even today. I have recently been contacted by A Current Affair to tell our story, more than thirty years after the 'sting'.

Within two months he had done a 'runner'. We were lucky, apparently some lost much more.

Kaz and I had put in half and borrowed the other half. I hit the road and started to pay the bank back. The lesson as always, 'If it looks too good to be true ... it probably is!'

## WILLY THE HILL

My tours took me to North Queensland and my promoter there is Billy the Mountain. He is, in reality Billy Ludwig, not to be confused with Bill Ludwig the State politician, although Billy has been involved in local politics. He was the Mayor of Livingstone Shire for about eight years and then went on to serve on the Rockhampton Council. In those early tours Billy would look after everything from the Sunshine Coast up. He is also a singer and gifted songwriter and we have collaborated on many occasions.

We were in Darwin doing three nights and decided to go down

town for lunch. I looked out of the window and there before me was Shellie ambling down the street. I hadn't seen him in years and ran out to catch him. He looked a little worse for wear; he wasn't in too good a shape at all. His jeans were dirty and his T-shirt had seen better days. His hair was long and scruffy. He had a pronounced limp and his left hand was tucked into his pocket. He had come off a motorbike a few years before and had lost the use of the arm.

We went back inside the cafe; I bought him lunch in between our catch up conversation. He had been living cheap in Indonesia and would come back to Australia every three months, renew his Visa and then go back.

He took us out to where he was staying. It was a real dive with half a dozen other people lounging around. There were chickens walking through the front room. It was a squat.

He was heading back to Indonesia in three days' time. I grabbed his small bag and asked Bill if we could book him in to the Casino as 'crew'.

That done we headed up to his room and between us, Billy and I got some decent clothes on him. By the time we cleaned him up he looked like a million bucks. He looked like his old suave self again. He was so grateful; it was good to see my old mate again.

He came down to sound checks; we put him with the Merch girl on show nights and made him feel important. He ambled backstage and met everyone. We took him with us to radio interviews and out to eat. We even paid him a roadie's fee.

We had lots of laughs and all too soon he had to go. He told some of the staff that he was my manager and to others he said he was my writer. I shook my head and let it go through to the keeper, at least he hadn't told them we were international pilots! A few days later we waved goodbye to Shellie as he strode across the car park. Billy had told him to keep the outfits ... our pleasure. I gave him some extra money to go on with.

When it was time for us to book out I was hit with an unexpected bill. My 'roadie' had left me with a $1,300 dollar tab. Phone calls interstate and overseas, room service, massages, the Chinese restaurant downstairs and the mini bar had had a decent work-over. Shellie had got me again, I didn't even see it comin'!

Probably two years down the track I was on the road with my old mate Terry Gordon. The phone rang — it was on loud speaker.

"Col, it's Shellie ... I need some help mate. I need a 'lend' of $800 dollars. I'll pay it straight back and..." I didn't let him finish. I went for him 'boots and all'... "No bloody way Shellie, after what you did to me in Darwin." Shellie cut in, "Yeah I know mate and I'm gonna' get it all back to you with the other money, if you could just ... "

"Shellie," I said "piss off" and I hung up. Terry sat there stunned not knowing what to make of the conversation so I filled him in on the details.

A few minutes later the phone rang again ... "What if we make it $300?" said Shellie. We nearly swerved off the road. Terry had tears streaming down his face.

Since that day, all those years ago, I will still walk into a dressing room and there on the wall written in texta are the words "What if we make it $300?" I have even had customers come up to me after a show and say that "Terry Gordon says that if I say $300 you will give me a free album". It is still happening. By the way I put the $300 in Shellie's account ... still waiting for the payback.

## TOM T HALL

I got to tour with Tom T Hall; he was a total inspiration and is an incredible country music singer/song writer. He had that huge hit, Old dogs and children and water melon wine. He also wrote the Jeannie. C. Riley hit, Harper Valley P.T.A. He has recorded eleven No.1 hit songs and 26 have been in the top 10. He is in the Hall of Fame and so many big stars have recorded his songs. I just soaked in his stories and philosophy. I loved his laid-back performances.

His story-telling style had a huge impact on my writing from that point on and I would sit and listen to his take on things as we drove around the country. I wrote, I Hear a Sound, with Tom's style in mind.

In later years when Bernie and I were in the States, we would visit Tom in Nashville. He delighted in taking us out to see some of the old dwellings and battlefield sites from the 1860s Civil War. He later sent me Civil War books and I returned the favour by sending him Banjo Patterson works that he was so very fond of.

## A NEW FLOOR MANAGER

While I was on the road with Tom, I had been booked on the Midday show. I got to the studio and went down to do my camera check.

I was approached by Jamie, the junior floor manager's assistant. He was a nice polite young bloke and always told me how he enjoyed my humour; in fact he had managed to get hold of Vol. 1 in my R-rated series and told me he loved the 'Pakistani' bits I did. I promised to leave a couple of the later volumes with Bill Wallace, the show booker, before I left that day. He was really appreciative and thanked me.

Jamie showed me my 'spot' on the studio floor and then spoke on his head set to the director upstairs.

The director had asked Jamie to ask me what my last gag would be, so they would know when to throw to the compere or commercial break or whatever. Jamie asked me the question …

Tell him my last gag will be about the bloke Chock a Block up the Bulldog!!!

I watched the colour drain from Jamie's face as I told him to repeat it to the director. He covered the mouthpiece and timidly said to me "Is that going to be OK for TV Col?"

"Yeah, should be OK mate, just tell them upstairs," I said.

"It's the one about the bloke Chock a block up the Bulldog," he repeated.

Howls of laughter came out over the PA, "Thanks Col, we'll explain it to him later." said the director.

Jamie looked at me and broke into a grin when it dawned on him that I was 'sending him up'.

"I won't forget those tapes mate," I said to him as I headed for the Green Room. I walked away and left him shaking his head.

After the show that day, I dropped into Bill Wallace's office. He was happy with the spot and said he'd be in touch for another appearance in a few weeks' time.

"Thanks mate," I said.

"By the way Bill, could you give young Jamie from the floor crew, these tapes I promised him?"

"No worries Col," he said. "I heard about the Bulldog bit. He's still laughing about it. One thing with young Jamie, he's got a good sense of humour ... he'll need it when he gets to run this place."

"I don't follow you Bill ... what do you mean, run this place?"

"Col, you're kidding ... you don't know ... Jamie? ... Jamie is Jamie Packer, Kerry's boy. His dad has him learning from the ground up; floor crew, Assistant to the assistant, camera, boom-mike operator, the lot."

Bugger ... I left the tapes.

Later that year Bernie got a phone call from John Spence, a musician and promoter mate of ours. He was working for the Packers at the time. Would Col come to do a gig for Kerry Packer at 'Ellerston' the Packer property in NSW. It was at the request of Jamie Packer; price was not an object.

'Ellerston' is north of Scone in the Hunter Valley and is the country property that Kerry Packer had set up for his passion of polo.

It boasts polo fields, incredibly huge stables, houses for his staff, a cinema, a private night club-restaurant and an 18 hole Greg Norman designed golf course, said to be one of the best in the country. Would I come to do a gig? ... Silly question!

I was flown in and everything was laid on for me.

The one thing I quickly became aware of was that Kerry Packer's staff absolutely loved the man; he had looked after his people well.

I was taken to the venue. There was to be a band on that night and I was the featured guest artist. He had flown in a South American polo team to play him and his team the next day. They would all be there. I made a mental note of not doing any South American gags, not that I knew any.

I did my sound check and had a rest in the afternoon.

I walked into the gig that night and the first person to come over was Jamie Packer. "Col, I'm so rapt you could make it. This is my mate Gynge." His young mate put his hand out and we shook.

"Can you do some Paki stuff Col?" Jamie asked.

A little while later John Spence took me over to meet Kerry Packer and his wife Ros.

I was introduced, we shook hands and before I said a word Kerry said "Col I've heard you can be a dirty bugger, so don't let me down."

Just before floor show time a huge armchair was carried into the room and placed square in front of the centre mike, three foot back from the stage. It was then occupied by Kerry Packer; I was introduced.

Within a couple of lines Kerry was laughing, thank God ... we had a top night.

A month later I was asked back to do another night for them. Thanks Jamie ... give me a yell anytime but it's not cool to do the Paki stuff anymore.

'Gynge' was David Gyngell, the son of Television pioneer Bruce Gyngell. He went on to become the head of the Nine Network. He and Jamie are still best mates.

Bernie got me the job of support to Tom Jones, it was a great opportunity. I had to get my passport in order. I had travelled the world on an ID card in the Navy. Passports were not required. I came here under the rulings in 1951. I was an Australian citizen ...

The surprise I was to get was astounding.

## I DIDN'T EXIST

When we first arrived in Australia I was just 20 months old, I was entered on my mother's papers. The law then stated that if the child was under six years old and the parents stayed for over two years, that child was automatically an Australian citizen. I had always assumed I was an Aussie.

The Hawke Government had recently changed the law, (in retrospect, from what I could work out).

I applied for my Australian passport and was told I didn't exist ... there was no record of me and if I chose to leave the country I would not be able to return.

I was not a citizen; I was now an illegal alien...this was bureaucracy gone mad.

No one would help me ... I had never really dealt with civil servants before and this was a real eye-opener. I showed them my discharge papers, the nominal role for Vietnam service; I was married to an Aussie with two daughters; I ran a business, and I had been here for thirty three years.

They didn't want to know ... "Try for an English Passport," I was told, "you're not an Aussie."

I went to the British Embassy and luckily there was a mention of me on my mother's papers ... If it wasn't for that I would be stateless.

I argued that I owed $90,000 in tax this financial year and if I didn't exist then by default the tax bill couldn't exist either, humour didn't work, the expression on their faces remained unmoving ...The boom gates were down, the lights were flashing but there were no trains coming... I tried another tack.

"And by the way, what should I do with these medals I won in combat ... who shall I send them to?" ... "Next please."

We got in touch with the press; Sydney radio picked up on it; Mike Willesee's, Current Affair, wanted to ambush the local government body.

The newspapers ran stories; great publicity but no solution. I still had the dilemma. If I left the country to go on tour with Tom Jones I wouldn't be able to come back to Australia. I was leaving in a week. I had my British passport but nothing else.

I was told that under recent rulings, my British passport didn't entitle me to permanent residency in Australia and if I wanted to come back I would need to apply for a Visa ... Time ran out and I left Australia.

The Vice Consul at the High commission in New Zealand had me waiting for three hours, he then gave me a three months Visa for back home and advised that I would need to leave the country after that. He also gave me some pamphlets on how to apply to become an Australian citizen while I was back in England.

He seemed quite amused by it all until I told him that there would be a news crew arriving shortly to get his view on this ridiculous situation ... his smile quickly vanished; he stamped my passport; gave me the papers and scurried away. He beat me out of the building.

I told the news crew that according to the pamphlets "I think I've found a loophole ... If I can get my wife or one of my daughters to adopt me, I would be OK."

I had also been told by a civil servant that I would need proof of what I had been doing on my 'stay' in Australia. I showed him my wife and daughters ... I'd been busy!!!!

After our concerts in New Zealand we flew back to Australia. I lined up with all the other visitors, quite a few of the Customs Officials recognised me and came over to tell me I was in the wrong lane ... They walked away shaking their heads. My passport was stamped for a three month visit.

The Department of Immigration and Ethnic Affairs got my call the following week, I told them where I would be touring on the date that my Visa expired and when they come to arrest me make sure to wear some make up and not striped shirts as stripes tend to strobe on TV.

A week later I got a call from a very apologetic official asking me to come into their offices 'at my convenience' and my residency would be confirmed. I now, very proudly hold a piece of paper which tells the world I am an Australian citizen.

## FALSE TEETH AND HEARING AIDS

The Tom Jones tour was fantastic, huge crowds, sometimes as in Canberra, an inside stadium of thirteen thousand people. When you hear a laugh come back at you with that type of force it's almost a physical shock.

I loved the sensation. Tom was phenomenal, with a voice that is astounding. Most nights I watched from the sides ... I was a little miffed that I wasn't asked to operate the smoke machine ... after all the experience I'd had.

At the start of the tour I had met all of Tom's touring band; many of these guys had played with Elvis and had some great stories to tell. The guys that came from the Southern States had that 'drawl' and I found that the only way they could understand me, was by me mimicking their accent. I had done this a couple of times in the Navy trying to converse with American sailors. It was a quick, easy solution when I needed to get my message across fast.

Tom's band members and backup singers would often watch me perform from the sides and hear the crowds laugh but couldn't understand my Aussie accent.

When I came off they'd say... "Hell Cole, when y'aall on stage we don' unnerstan a god dam word y'aall sayin ... people all larfin, but man we caint unnerstan."

I would reply with my 'Southern' accent ...

"Hell you say boys ..., don't rightly know what yaa'll talkin' 'bout ... I ken unnerstan' what y'all sayin'. They stood there scratching their heads.

"We unstan' you now man but when yaa'll on that there microphone is jus' diffran' is all....must be dam acoustics here," one put in.

Apparently Tom had crept up during this exchange and was beside himself. His son Mark came to my dressing room to ask me for supper with Tom after the show. He wanted me to repeat the side stage 'show'.

Tom invited me to travel with him and Mark for the rest of the tour. His Welsh sense of humour seemed to click with mine. Mark was more like a brother to Tom, they are very close. Tom was married at sixteen and Mark came soon after.

I accepted Tom's offer but it nearly killed me. I didn't realise that Tom and his management stayed up all night and slept all day. Then they would fly in to the next gig on the private jet. The band and stage crew would do daily domestic flights as I had done up until that time.

After the gig, we would have supper, go to a private function or party then head to bed around 8 am. I was wide awake because of the change in my body clock.

After one gig I was sitting next to Tom having supper, I fell asleep while chewing my entrée ... I must have been really tired ... it was seafood.

Tom, Mark, myself and management would go to the gigs nightly in stretch-limos. I had noticed there, in the limo's bar, was fresh fruit, Dom Perignon, and believe it or not CRAYFISH ... all of which, apart from the booze nobody ever touched. Of course they didn't count on the 'CRAYFISH BANDIT' ...

On a few of the nights, while Tom was on stage, the temptation was too great ... I snuck back to the limos and had a feast. All was fine until one night I fell asleep and was woken by Tom.

"So you're the crayfish thief Col?" Every night after that Tom would ask me, "Are you gonna watch me tonight or are you dining out again?"

We played the convention centre in Hobart and I got a surprise souvenir of the tour. I had noticed that when Tom performed, ladies would throw knickers up on stage. It had been going on at all the performances and I used this as part of an ad-lib this particular night.

"Come on girls," I said. "Tom's getting all the knickers — all I've had on this tour is a set of dentures and a hearing aid ... come on one set of scanties," I begged ... All of a sudden, from ten rows back came a ball of white material, as big as a soccer ball ... as it got above my head it opened out like a parachute ... it was the biggest pair of bloomers I had seen since my grandma stayed with us!

They floated down. I caught them on the end of my banjo, whirled them round and threw them to the floor as if they were alive ... I stomped on them and wrestled them ... it was the best laugh I got all night.

After the gig I had a picture taken with Tom and myself holding the drawers. I have included this photo in the book. Tom autographed the crutch ...

Years later when the earthquake struck Newcastle in NSW in 1989, I was asked for something to be auctioned at the appeal. I sent the drawers and the photo along with them ... they fetched $3,000.

## JACK MILLS MOVES IN

We had been at 'Maybe' for a couple of years when our old mate Jack Mills retired. He was bored to death so I paid him to come up to the farm a couple of days a week and do 'odds and sods' and the lawns and garden.

He loved the place and it soon became 'his' garden. I hardly dared change anything; I would always ask Jack first ... I didn't want to get into trouble. He discussed everything with Kaz and the kids loved him. He was like a grandad to them. I loved having him around.

Jack had trouble with his legs, the result of a bad car accident years before, it had forced his retirement. He couldn't always control the movement but he managed well enough once he did get moving.

I bought a ride-on mower as there was at least an acre of grounds to be mowed; it was a huge job. Jack insisted he do it all by hand.

I tried to get him to use the ride-on but on his first attempt he ran it half way up the date tree ... he never touched it again ... stubborn old bugger.

Pam and Peter had moved to Queensland and taken Lorna with them. Jack missed her so much, it was sad to see. Another blow was to come. The RSL had informed Jack that his house, the one we had shared together, was to be pulled down to make way for development.

He was going to move into a flat. He was a little sad at the prospect.

Kaz and I had a talk.

We had a bungalow next to the old stables; I had been using it as an office. It was like a one bedroom affair, all it needed was a bathroom and toilet. We decided to add these improvements. My neighbor, Phil Beesy and I got to work, he was a bit of a handyman. Before too long we had it all plumbed up and looking great.

Jack was a proud man and I couldn't let him think it was in any way, charity. I took him into the bungalow and asked him what he thought of the improvements. He thought it was fantastic and congratulated me on a job well done.

"Here's the thing Jack," I said "I go away a fair bit and I sometimes worry about Kaz and the girls ...now if you were here fulltime I would feel better about it. If you could live here in the bungalow I would consider it a big favour ... It would be your place, no rent, just do the gardens and keep an eye out for my girls," I said all this, as I paced around the bungalow.

I looked up at Jack and there were tears in his eyes ...

"Have a think about it Jack and let me know," I said as I moved toward the door ...

"Col," Jack said, "that would be fine ... thanks."

Jack moved in that week.

There were nights that Kaz and I went out, Jack would cook tea for the girls in the bungalow. He enjoyed cooking for them as he had done for me all those years back.

To get him up to the main house to have a meal with us took some planning, he was so independent. We would tell him we had cooked too much and he would be doing us a favour if he would come up to the house ... funny old bugger.

Life went on as usual for about eighteen months. One night I rang Jack to say we would be a little late and I wouldn't be calling in on him for a coffee as I usually did.

"OK mate," Jack said, "I think I'll hit the sack early ... got a bit of a gut ache."

"You gonna be OK Jack?" I asked.

"Yeah, see you in the morning," he replied.

We got home and Jack's light was still on, I wandered down.

Jack was laying on his bed in terrible pain. Kaz took him to our local doctor. After his examination and some pain treatment Jack was taken to the Dandenong Hospital by ambulance.

There was talk of a twisted bowel and when I got there in the morning they were about to operate.

I rang Jack's sister Peggy, she lived in Bendigo. I got in touch with Pete and Pam. The doctor came out after the operation and told me Jack had stomach cancer ... there was nothing they could do. They had sewn him straight back up.

A week later we got Jack home, Kaz bathed his wound and changed his dressings daily. I got a mattress and stayed in the bungalow with him. When he wasn't in pain, we'd laugh about old times and talk on into the night.

All we could do was administer the drugs and pain killers they gave us.

Lorna flew down from Queensland and stayed for a week. She found it hard to cope with his condition ... he was so ill.

His sister Peggy wanted to take him home to Bendigo and spend what time he had left. Jack agreed and we did the whole move to Bendigo about three hours away, including his parrot that complained all the way.

Within a short while Jack needed to be in hospital in palliative care.

Kaz and I got a motel near the hospital and visited him every day till a short time later he passed away.

Jack Mills was our friend.

## GOTTA GIVE THE GROG AWAY

I had been approached to make a TV comedy special for Channel Nine in Brisbane. We called it, Gotta Give the Grog Away, and we made it for less than $3,000. Basically no one got paid, only the film crew. It was comedy variety and my first venture into that area.

It went all over the country except metropolitan Melbourne and Sydney. The rest of Australia got behind it and it rated well. We were commissioned to do another two episodes. They were pretty much all written by myself and the pressure was on. All the while I was doing this, I kept touring and recording. It was ridiculous. I look at photos of me in the studio at the time… I look older than I do today… I was running on adrenaline, little else.

I was doing the Ernie Sigley show as a regular while I was making the Brisbane Specials and was offered to do my own pilot for Nine in Melbourne.

With the help of Bob Phillips, a long time Nine producer, who was an old friend, we put together a clip and a pitch for our specials. Bob had worked with them all, Graham Kennedy, Ernie Sigley, Don Lane and on Hey Hey it's Saturday. He knew his stuff and we worked well together.

Jim McKay, the big honcho at Nine in those days had caught me on Ernie's show and had approached Bob about my potential.

Ross Plap, the program director in Melbourne, had seen my Brisbane special and liked the characters. He thought I could step into the breach as Paul Hogan was winding down. He set up the pilot. He talked of a budget of $40,000 ... Bloody hell; I could even afford writers to help with the work-load. I would also have the use of a wardrobe department ... no more Saint Vinnie's for me, this was big time.

As they say, timing is everything. Ross was having a meeting with Ian Gow, the then manager of Nine in Melbourne on the Friday. He would ring me that night.

Kaz and I sat by the phone. Ross had told us it was basically a formality as the pilot had been instigated by the big boss in Sydney. Ross was just following protocol.

The phone rang. "Col the whole thing has been canned," Ross said.

"I have just walked out of Gow's office. Col, who did you tell about the series?"

I told him who knew. Ross told me I had been sabotaged big time.

"In future," he said "if you're dealing in television keep things close to your chest, there is no loyalty here, only jealousy and egos, its cut-throat."

I rang Bernie ... "It's back to the road mate."

Not long after that all the major shows were axed, there was a huge restructuring of the network.

We tried again in 1994 and were told by the then network programming head, John Stevens, that the door was shut. It wasn't going to happen.

Bob Phillips wrote in his book, 50 years of OZ TV, "It may be some consolation to Col that not many years later, the same management showed the exit door to the multi Logie award winning Rove McManus" (end quote).

Bob Phillips was adamant that one day we would win through and we kept trying. In the meantime Bob and his wife Judy Banks came up to Brisbane. Bob and I would start on my next special. Judy needed a break and would go sightseeing while we were in the studio. Judy had had a successful career herself in television. In 1969 she was the host on Fred Bear's breakfast a go-go.

The format was so innovative and was the front runner to many shows that followed. Hey Hey it's Saturday used the formula in its early years.

Judy has a mischievous sense of humour as opposed to Bob who has a quiet reserved demeanour; more the gentleman. They are a great couple.

We were staying on the 12th floor of the hotel. Bob and I walked out to the lift.

Bob, as always in his business suit and myself in jeans and sneakers. Judy came out to see us off. She was wearing her dressing gown and holding a mug of tea. It was 7am.

The lift opened up and there were four older lady bowlers in their white, starched lawn bowls uniform, complete with sun hats.

We got in the lift and Bob nodded and said a quiet "good morning" to the ladies, then we turned, as you do, to face the doors.

Judy waited for the doors to start to close and said, "Same time tomorrow night boys?" The doors closed.

The ladies didn't laugh and I waited for Bob to say "Ha ha, that was my wife," or something to that effect, but he didn't say anything. I turned my head slightly in his direction and noticed his face was crimson red ... so I said, "What do you think Bob ... she wasn't bad?"

Bob remained silent, getting ever redder in the face.

Stunned silence ... you could feel the tension, then the doors opened on the 8th floor and Bob flew out.

I went all the way down in the lift. The girls wouldn't look at me so I just kept it to myself. I could feel their eyes boring into the back of my head.

Bob flew out of the fire exit just after the lift hit the foyer.

I said, "Think of the positive Bob, a little bit of gossip just might sharpen their game."

Kaz walked into my office one morning, she had my diary in her hand, she dropped the diary on my desk. "If you add together all the time you're away in the coming year, it works out to 10 months. This is beyond ridiculous, we need to do something Col, this is no sort of life for us, or for you." She turned and walked out.

I found out later that Bernie and Sue would argue over whose turn it was to inform Kaz of an added or new date. They were as bad as I was; something had to give.

We had holidayed in Surfers on a few occasions and I loved Queensland. Kaz and the girls would come up when I worked the clubs and we would holiday as well.

Bernie and Sue had relocated to Surfers Paradise from Geelong and although they weren't the catalyst for our move, it was certainly easier if we were both in the same State. Pete and Pam were now in Queensland and Jim and Jan Craig were on the Sunshine Coast.

We put 'Maybe' on the market. Kaz and I had renovated the old farmhouse and added so much. The place looked absolutely beautiful. Kaz has a great feel for design and has often said she would have loved to be an architect.

The cold in Melbourne would really get to me and I harped on about it so much. I think I eventually wore Kaz down and we flew up to Queensland to look at properties.

We found a top horse property in Bahrs Scrub, near Beenleigh. It was a double brick homestead with wide verandas; a beautiful ten acres with stables, a tennis court, dam and irrigation. The pool was complete with waterfall. The owner had been into building swimming pools. He had spared no expense on this one. It was all in slate and the surrounds were rock and huge boulders. It looked natural and not man-made. The grounds, about an acre, were all lawns and tropical palms mixed with natives. This was enclosed with hunting post and rail fencing. It was stunning.

We bought it before we had finished the sale on 'Maybe' ... like always.

I was pushing; Kaz let me run with it.

We bridged our finance, definitely not the way to go. It's an expensive exercise and if something had have gone wrong with the initial sale of the other property I would be in trouble.

As luck would have it, 'Maybe' sold and everything fell into place.

Again there wasn't hardly any time to settle in; within ten days I was back on the road.

My sister Carol and brother-in-law Jack drove up with us and stayed on for a while before leaving Kaz on her own.

When I came back off tour, Kaz and I bought a 36 foot Ho Singh cruise boat. It was very exciting and the girls loved it.

The initial move to Queensland was a tough one for the girls. They had left their cousins and friends. There was excitement but tinged with sadness; new schools, new friends ... no close family.

I took Karen's support away from her; her parents, who were always there for backup, her girlfriends. My sister Carol loves Kaz and was close.

Now here she was, having to cope alone. She was basically a single parent.

I had no sooner ensconced my family on the Queensland property than I was away again. I was thirty-seven years old and had given my wife an incredibly hard personnel existence. I couldn't say 'no' to work ... There was little joy... just pressure.

We were in the middle of a tour of North Queensland with Billy the Mountain and we squeezed in a television meeting in Melbourne and a big charity event with the late Ricky May that same night.

When we finished the show, Ernie Sigley had organised a cab to take me straight to radio for his show. We sat there on-air eating pizza till 1.30 am then back to the hotel and sleep till 7.30 am, then off to the airport.

I then flew back to Brisbane and got a light plane to Gladstone.

I walked into a radio interview in drive time and did a show that night. We worked two more shows and were in Noosa. Our show had sold out but I was booked to do a phone interview early afternoon.

Billy's tours were always fairly intense; he never missed an opportunity for publicity which is what a promoter should do. This tour was no exception. I would do a show at night and be up early the next day for a co-host of a breakfast radio show or a photo opportunity for the local press.

We had pulled off some great front pages in our time. One of my favorites was when Bill came to tour-manage one of our Melbourne runs. We hired a cherry picker and a parachute and suspended me, dressed as Hari Kari (my failed Kamikaze pilot) 50 foot up a tree in the park outside the Herald Sun building. Bill raced in to report it and a journo and photographer came running out to get the scoop ... We called it Hari Kari's jump tours. The premise was that he would fly tourists in and push them out over the destination. He wasn't trained in landings! They ran with our scam, we got a page three ... bloody hard to pull off in Melbourne.

Back to the story ...

Bill and I had just finished breakfast radio and were at a café, eating lunch. We then headed back to the motel. Bill went up to shower while I was in the manager's office waiting for a call to do a live radio interview.

Half way through the interview I started to sweat profusely and felt sick. The Jock came on to say they were about to play Gotta Give The Grog Away and would come straight back to Col Elliott ... They started to play the song ... I spoke to the DJ, "Mate, I have to go, I feel really crook ..."

I staggered away from the phone and headed for the stairs. My room was on the next floor. I was nearly out to it. I fumbled for my key. I got into my room and tipped my travel bag upside down hoping to find an aspirin. I needed to stop this pain.

I thought I was going to pass out. I thought my chest was going to explode. I went back out to the landing and was banging on Bill's door. He was in the shower and couldn't hear me.

I somehow managed to ring down to reception and had them find Rex Harris, our band leader. Rex thought I was 'taking the micky' out of him but soon realised I was deadly serious. Rex and Lee Gorring, our other muso mate, came racing upstairs. By this time I was starting to really panic. The pain was tremendous and I knew it was a heart attack.

The boys threw me between them in the front of our truck and headed to a medical centre. We arrived shortly afterwards and they half carried me into reception. Rex was calling for a doctor. The receptionist tried to make us take a seat. The doctor had someone with her ... "Yeah bullshit," Rex said as we barged into the doctor's office. She looked up from the patient she was attending to and started to protest ... I managed to get out, "I think I'm having a heart attack". She swept her examination table clear of clutter and said "Lay him here." She ripped open my shirt and did a quick ECG on me and said "OK, hold on, you're having an attack right now but I've got you." The other patient stood there wide eyed fumbling with his pants.

I can't remember too much more but it wasn't long and I was in an ambulance heading to the Nambour Hospital. I was taken straight to intensive care and was wired up with monitors. Doctors and nurses were fussing over me. I had the feeling that I was about to die. Bill turned up and had gotten hold of Bernie; he would find Kaz and the girls. There were no mobile phones in those days; you either rang at the motel or at a public phone on the road.

The pain was subsiding; I felt so weak. I didn't want to close my eyes in case I didn't wake up again. I just needed to see Kaz and the girls again.

A doctor came over to me, "Col, I want you to just relax a little, we will be here to take care of things".

Then the Doctor gave me a feeling of hope, although he probably didn't know it at the time.

He said, "I've got a 'Hey You Bloody Mug' album at home. If I bring it in tomorrow would you autograph it for me?"

There it was ... my positive ... this guy thinks I'm going to be here tomorrow ... I started to relax.

It was Fathers' Day 1986. I had rung Kaz in the morning and sang, 'I just called to say I love you' ... I would call her back that night.

Kaz and the girls were having lunch with Pete and Pam Shelton and their girls, Christie and Amanda. Kaz and I are their Godparents.

Bernie tracked her down and told her the news.

Bernie picked up Kaz and they drove to Nambour.

She walked in ... it was emotional ... I can remember her saying, "Silly bugger, what have you done to yourself?"

The next day Kaz and the girls moved in with Jim Craig to be near me. Jim and Jan had two girls about the same age, Narelle and Kirsten. The girls had always been close and my girls were excited to see them. I am Narelle's Godfather.

I had a constant stream of visitors when I came out of intensive care and many telegrams and flowers from what seemed to be the whole show biz fraternity.

I still didn't know the extent of the damage to my heart; that could only be established by the process of an angiogram. They hadn't invented 'stents' back then so they couldn't restore blood flow as they can today. I just had to sit tight for the time being.

I was put on heavy medication to keep my heart beating and other tablets to keep its rhythm happening. There were blood pressure tablets ... I was just taking whatever they gave me ... and contemplating.

A few days after the heart attack, I felt OK so I got out of bed and walked down about four flights of stairs to the small kiosk to buy the paper. I did this every morning for a week. I got the bloke in the next room his paper too.

One morning early, two nurses came in. "Col," one said, "today is the big day, we are going to get you out of bed and walk you down one flight of stairs to see how you go."

I didn't have the heart to tell them what I had been doing all week, so I did the one flight with a nurse either side of me. When we walked past the bloke in the room next to me, he thought I'd had a relapse.

As we went past, I gave him the 'Shshshsh' sign. The nurses were pleased with my walk and gave me my 'brownie points' and a hearty "Well done". When they left I went and got our papers.

I was in the hospital ten days. Kaz and I headed for home.

The heart specialist had to wait to do an angiogram till my heart had settled as it had enlarged as well.

Three months later, all was revealed. A large artery on the right hand side of my heart had totally blocked. The heart on that side was starved of blood. This caused the intense pain. It can also cause that part of the heart muscle to die.

In my case I had lost twenty percent of my heart muscle.

It has been explained to me this way ... When a normal heart expels blood on contraction, 70% of the blood is expelled. In my case with a damaged heart, only 50% of that blood gets pushed out. My doctor told me that if my heart was a six cylinder engine I would be running on five pots ... hence all the medication, it keeps it pumping.

Twenty years later I had another episode and was saved by medical science (stents). I had a 95% closure on a major artery. Had they had not gotten to me in time I would have died, because of my already damaged heart. It wouldn't have withstood another attack.

I have ischemic heart disease and am still highly medicated today.

I had three months off straight after this first event but it wasn't long before I was back in harness.

I tried to taper it down but things began to escalate again.

Hindsight is twenty-twenty as they say, but I still hadn't learnt my lesson.

We were out in the boat one day at an anchorage called Slipping

Sands on North Stradbroke Island. At one point the bank rises straight up creating a huge mountain of sand. To climb it is not an easy feat, even for someone who is fit. I had convinced myself if I could get to the top, I would be OK.

Kaz tried to talk sense into me but I ignored her protests and scaled the mountain. I was out of breath and I guess a little out of my mind, but I didn't die ... what an idiot!

We sold the big boat and settled for a half-cabin run-about. We paid out the mortgage and life started again. We loved the boating on the Gold coast and explored all the islands. Kaz and I really came together out on the water and found a common love of boating. We still share that love today and get out every chance.

Kaz started to concentrate on her painting with some amazing results.

I had stopped smoking and kept off them for months but gradually slipped back into the road lifestyle. I did start to have some bigger breaks with work, but if you look at the old diaries we were still working hard.

I was booked to entertain on a small ship, the 'MINGHWA', 250 passengers. It was a Chinese line. It was a great holiday for the girls but I felt the pressure of having to work most nights to the same audience; a new show each performance. They certainly got their pound of flesh and I didn't really have any downtime for myself. There is no escape on a cruise. The audience is with you all the way. Still, we were all together as a family and I was happy about that.

Robbie Snowden was the cruise director and we all became firm friends for many years. Robbie had quite a few hits in the '70s; his biggest was, Nobody Really loves a Clown. In later years I would catch him at radio 4GG on the Gold Coast and then at the Gold Coast Bulletin. A great bloke and missed by us all.

Sadly Robbie passed away in 2009 aged just 60.

## CASSIE

Two years down the track and we had a big surprise! Kaz was pregnant! We told the girls and they went crazy.

Cassie Jane was born on the 19th of June 1989; some more big brown eyes and beautiful.

Our two elder girls were over horses by then, they were looking at boys and into INXS.

I would come home from a tour and find the girls hadn't ridden their horses and the tack and stables needed attention.

To be fair they had been taken away from their one true mentor, my sister, Auntie Carol. She had instigated so much with the horses and their cousins Jacqui and Sue were constantly over at 'Maybe'. Queensland wasn't the same and I think the girls had moved on. I couldn't really complain, I was away so much myself.

## QLD

Kaz wanted to get back to the suburbs; we set out to find land on water. We found an acre on salt water. It was just off the Coomera River at the northern end of the Gold Coast. We sold the Bahrs Scrub property.

Kaz and I found a builder and she designed a beautiful Federation style home. Meanwhile Bernie and I made eight half hour TV specials for the Sky Network which ran in the pubs across the country. Pay TV hadn't yet arrived in Australia. The shows were picked up in the UK and we were getting interest from record companies and had an offer to release our videos over there.

Kaz and I were renting a house on the water at Runaway Bay while our new place was getting built. I was about to have my 40th birthday and we were having a party before Bernie and I left for the UK.

The party was happening on Sunday.

## THE STRIP-O-GRAM

It was now Saturday afternoon and I was home minding Cassie. She was a month old. The girls went to the Mall to buy food for the party.

I was giving Cass her bottle when the doorbell rang.

I opened the door and there stood a young lady of maybe 20. She was in a glitzy type outfit with a young bloke behind her holding a small tape recorder.

"Hi", she said. "Are you Col Elliott?"

"That's me," I replied, still not quite sure what was happening.

"I've got a singing strip-o-gram from Mr Kevin bloody Wilson."

I laughed and told her the party was tomorrow ... I saw the disappointment in her eyes as she started to explain she couldn't come back and that she wasn't sure how the mix up happened.

I saw the worried look on the young bloke's face. Show biz is tough sometimes ... I decided to help out a fellow performer!

"Look," I said, "I've got to keep feeding my daughter and if you don't mind me doing that while you do your thing, we can still go for it."

"That would be fine," she said with the relief showing on her face.

They quickly came in; plugged the recorder in ... 'cue music' ... She sang and stripped ... the 'Full Monty' ... "Happy Birthday ... to ... youuuuu."

I couldn't applaud, I had hold of Cass, so I whistled ... I gave them a $20 tip.

They left with thank-yous and apologies all round ... I burped Cass, then rang Kev to thank him. He had the dates mixed up, but it was a great thought between mates.

The following year, on his birthday, I had arranged for a truck load of boulders to be delivered and dumped in his driveway at his home in Perth. A card was placed on top, "Happy birthday mate, hope you can use these."

He called me that day "very, very funny Col, I got a good laugh out of that ... my neighbour's not too impressed though ... they dumped them up his drive not mine, he couldn't get to work" ... bugger!

## BACK TO THE OLD DART

Bernie and I headed for the UK; we had some appointments in Los Angeles and Vegas as well. We would see what transpired.

There was a heap of meetings and I was booked to do some TV spots and live work along the way. While Bernie stayed in London I did a few gigs at the Edinburgh comedy festival in Scotland. I took the opportunity to check out the 1200 year old Edinburgh Castle.

I loved the history that I came across in the UK. It has always fascinated me that I could be sitting in a pub having a meal and that building was built in the 16th or 17th century. Australia had no European settlement till the first fleet in 1787. So it made it all the more interesting to me.

I wasn't known in England, only a few small pockets of recognition that had drifted across the oceans by ex-pat Aussies or New Australians sending back my albums and videos to the 'relo's' back in the Old Dart.

Over a period, Bernie had created a network of agents, bookers and publicity people to work with overseas and now we went to check it all out.

We worked a gig at the Aussie hangout, Deckers Down Under, in London and then on to a 'feeler' type show at a football club in Falmouth. I was quite excited about this trip as it meant we could visit Stonehenge on the way. I mentioned this to Bernie ... "The gigs at Falmouth not Stonehenge ... where did that come from?" he said.

That's when I realised Bernie wasn't a history buff.

I explained the world famous site was probably erected somewhere between 2000 BC to 3000 BC. His reply, "They'll have rocks at Falmouth mate, I'll find some ... promise."

A mate of ours, John Steel, had set this gig up for us. He was an

Aussie guitarist, living in the States and married to the lead singer, Karen Raglan, of the Sounds Of the Supremes, a very popular tribute group. Bernie had toured them very successfully in Australia.

We would work the show up from this Falmouth gig. We would play the Royalty Theatre in West End the following week.

We arrived and did our sound check. I met the manager who was very excited to have an Aussie comedian performing at his club. They had managed to sell all the tickets; I guess on the novelty value of it. The manager was riding a high with the results of the sell-out crowd.

The room filled up, the band did a set and it was show time.

The manager was originally from Manchester and had that distinctive 'Up North' accent, just like my brother-in-law Jack.

He asked me if he could do my intro. He turned to me and said "Thanks sooo mooch Col," and then went on stage.

"Ladies and gentlemen," he began, "it gives me great pleasure to introduce our very special guest comedian all the way from Australia, a very funny man indeed ... here he is ... Col Elliott." I walked on to thunderous applause ... and then in my best Manchester accent, (a virtual mimic of the manager), I said, "thanks very Mooch ... me 'coosin' in Australia told me a 'coople' of jokes about a kangaroo".

At first the audience were confused and a little stunned. I kept waffling on in my Manchester accent. Then they started booing and shouting, "geer off"... Over this I kept talking, ... "'coom' on give 'oos' a go."

John Steel and the band were in fits. I looked across at the manager and saw the panic on his face. "Now 'ang' on, you lot," I said, as people started to get a little shitty.

I waited for a lull in the abuse and then announced in my normal Aussie accent "See how you Poms are so easy to fool." The crowd broke out in applause and I knew at that point I could work to an English audience. The ability to mimic accents had given me an edge ... thanks Mum.

We arrived at the Royalty theatre with an audience just shy of a full house.

Mind you it cost us a pretty penny in advertising to make it so. There was a great mixture of English and Aussies there.

It gave me a line to use. "Thanks for coming tonight. I'll tell you a bit about myself ... I'm actually English Australian ... English by my mother ... Australian by a friend of my father's."

We had invited the press along to review us and we were excited to see a 'journo' from the Daily Mirror show up. If we could get an article in there it would be a real coup.

We had set up two flash pots on either side of the stage ready to go off on cue. They would make the explosion sound and heaps of smoke to simulate equipment blowing up.

## CHOOKA

The lights went down and the audience went quiet in anticipation.

I was behind the curtains dressed as 'Chooka' Dennis, my roadie character; I had a prop guitar that would fall to pieces in my hands when I released it.

Now Chooka's voice is high pitched and nothing like my speaking voice. The show began with a conversation between 'Chooka' and me ... it went like this.

"Excuse me Mr. Elliott, should I plug this guitar in?"

"Yeah Chook," I said, feigning mounting impatience, "the lights are down ... we've got to start the show."

"Is it the black lead I 'gotta' plug in or the red one?"

"For 'ffff' ... just plug the black one in," I stammered, impatience growing.

"Hey Mr Elliott ... what does this button do?" and then ... BANG!!

There was a loud reaction from the audience at the flashes and noise. Smoke billowed everywhere and Chooka emerged through the smoke with a shocked look on his face. The guitar fell in pieces bit by bit to the stage floor. He then did a double take and looked to the side stage. He indicated the grand piano that was on stage and said, as if he were talking to me. "Do you play piano Mr. Elliott?"... The crowd laughed and the show was away.

Chooka apologised for the disruption to the show and went on to do 40 minutes. He talked on everything from his first job to his first sexual experience ... he had trouble with both ... Chooka went over well.

The band did a number then, Hari Kari did a sketch followed by Slugger Mulligan, then interval.

I did an hour and ten in the second half as myself. It was a top night. Bernie and I couldn't be happier.

I was at the merchandise table signing albums after the show when I was approached by the guy from the Daily Mirror. He told me how much he had enjoyed the show and said he had enough 'info' on me. Then he said he particularly enjoyed Chooka, my roadie and would it be possible to have a quick word with him? Was he 'taking the micky' out of me or what?

I looked across at Bernie, he just shrugged his shoulders. He wasn't sure if this guy was for real either.

I thought I would play along with it, just to see how far it would go.

"He's out the back loading the truck but I'll be finished here in a minute and I'll go and get him," I said.

"That would be great Col," he said. "Just thought he was a natural. Maybe you could coach him; I think he'd do alright."

I went back stage and quickly changed back into Chooka.

"Does someone want me?" Chooka enquired loudly.

The journo proceeded to tell Chooka he was too good to be a roadie and should pursue a career in comedy ... he felt Chooka was a natural.

This is a completely true story ... they are out there ... scary eh?

The journo had gotten in touch with my publicist to check something out a few days later. He mentioned how much he enjoyed the roadie. He was finally put straight to the fact that Chooka and I were one and the same.

I got a phone call from him that same day and he told me he felt 'like a real Berk'. It was the best compliment I ever got.

We had television meetings with a group of producers who had quite a few successful shows on the different networks. They were calling us nearly every day. It transpired that Channel 4 had seen our video presenter and were keen to talk. We all met for lunch. The producers were very upbeat and were all over Bernie. They talked of a series and national concert tours.

They were really into my characters, especially Chooka.

One guy kept asking me to do his voice and then he'd crack up. It sounded very positive but would require me to relocate to the UK. I would really have to do some hard thinking on that.

Kaz and I would really have to weigh it all up, but for the moment I just went with the flow.

## DECISIONS, DECISIONS!

We were about to head off on the States' leg of our run. We had two more days in London.

I was going in to do a radio interview in London and Bernie was catching up with an old mate, Terry Blamey, for lunch.

Terry's a lovely bloke and was originally from Melbourne. He had run an agency there called Pace Entertainment. He often booked me for gigs and he and Bernie would often talk. He was right into computers when they first came in and helped Bernie and Sue with their set up. At one stage Terry did all the bookings for Hey Hey It's Saturday.

Bernie was the only actual manager Terry knew. One day he rang Bernie to ask for advice on what sort of percentage he should charge his new clients ... Mark Jackson, Kylie and Danni Minogue. (Terry managed Kylie all the way to the top in pop music.) That conversation is one of Bernie's favourite stories.

Just before I left our hotel I got a call from the head honcho producer we had had the meeting with a few days before.

"Sorry old mate but you just missed Bernie; he's off to lunch with a friend," I said.

"That's OK; I actually rang to talk to you Col, not Bernie."

He then went on with a whole scenario of how they wanted exclusive management rights to me … basically everything … tours, merchandise, video releases, TV, etc. He rambled on and on. I interrupted. "You will need to have a meeting with Bernie as well, he is my manager", I said knowing where the guy was going with this.

"Unfortunately if we commit to you Col, there is no real place for Bernie in this management deal. Oh, of course his agency will be able to tour you, when you go back to Australia. That would be about the amount of his involvement."

He started to go on about how big a deal this would be etc. I cut him off. "Thanks for the call, I'll have my manager ring you," I said and hung up.

I told Bernie about the call. He was more than a little surprised and I could tell he was a little hurt. He hadn't seen it coming. He looked at me and said, "It's a big opportunity Col, maybe you should think about it."

"Come on Bern" I said. "If those jerks were willing to do that to you, how long before they did it to me? Besides, we have a contract. We shook hands in the pub remember … that's binding."

## DENNY'S

I looked at Bernie and saw the emotion. We flew on to the States.

We arrived at our hotel in Encino, a district of Los Angeles. We were tired and hungry after our flight from London. It was about 11pm.

We were surprised to find out that there was no room service and we asked the desk clerk where we could maybe grab a hamburger.

"Well sir," he said "there's a Denny's two blocks down on the corner."

"That'll do," I said, "thanks mate," and we turned to go.

"Excuse me sir," the clerk said — I would advise you get a cab; they pass our hotel constantly, so you should be able to hail one fairly quickly. We have a few gangs in the area and it mightn't be a good idea to walk there."

We thanked him and walked outside. We waited a couple of minutes without seeing a cab and I convinced Bernie that as we waited we should walk slowly down towards Denny's. I figured the street was well lit and it was a main drag. We could grab a cab as soon as we saw one.

We moved off.

We chatted away as we walked and maybe half a block down, half a dozen black guys spilled onto the sidewalk in front of us. They had been sitting on the steps of a building we were about to pass.

I could see they were about to block our path. I took the bull by the horns and walked straight up to the biggest one and in my best Aussie accent I said, "G'day mate, we just got in from Australia and they told us there's a Denny's down the road a bit. What are their hamburgers like? This is a great place America. No kangaroos like back home in Australia."

I was saying anything that I could think of and tried to keep moving. They were moving with us. Then one said "We saw Crocodile Dundee ... man, that dude is so cool."

"Crocodile Dundee," I said, "great bloke, see him all the time back home."

By this time they were all joining in describing their favourite scenes in the movie. They all agreed ... they loved Hoge's knife. Before we knew it we were at Denny's. They not only ordered our hamburgers, they paid for them as well. Our new best friends! Bernie's face, through all of this had that slight panic expression, it's like a little half smile and a half 'get me outa here' look ... if you know Bernie you'll know the look ... I kept it animated.

The gang even walked us back to the hotel and said goodbye in the foyer. The desk clerk's mouth was hanging open. They left and Bernie nearly fainted.

"Paul Hogan, at this point mate, I would like to say in my best LA street talk — love you man, you're one cool dude ... thanks a heap ... you saved our arses."

The next day we caught up with Jim Wagner, long time manager of Johnny Tillotson. Bernie had been touring Johnny in Australia with John Hanson for years. Johnny has had many awards and great hits over the years, Poetry in Motion, It keeps right on a Hurtin', was another that he wrote. Elvis recorded it. He once told me that the royalties he received from Elvis from that one song bought him a new Mercedes every two years. That night we had tea with Johnny and his wife. He 'shouted'.

We checked out the comedy in town for a few days then headed to Vegas.

We had a meeting with a Jewish agent Bernie had dealt with over the years. He had a sort of 'you scratch my back, I'll scratch your's' kind of attitude.

If Bernie took one of his acts, he would help me. He took us out to some of the production shows to watch the comic relief they had to break the shows. The stand-up comics all seemed to do about 15 minutes a set, twice a night. I couldn't believe how short the spots were. My 'good evenings' took fifteen minutes.

The agent said I would have to start in the lounges, work them for a while and then he would slip me into the main-stream. I would need to 'flatten' my Aussie accent as he put it but when I gave him an example of what I could do he said I would fit in fine.

Again, I would need to re-locate to Nevada. He could fix all the legals.

We headed for Nashville. Some more meetings; caught up with Tom T Hall and then headed home. It had been hectic and we both looked forward to getting back to Oz.

In many ways Bernie and I worked well together because, being a gambler, Bernie was more likely to take a chance, where I might tend to back off. 'Let's go for it' was his favourite expression.

## THE PUNTERS

We got home from overseas just before Melbourne Cup and Kaz, Bernie and I decided to go to the Gold Coast track.

This particular day I got a glimpse of how a gambler thinks. It transpired like this ... Kaz picked the winner, I got a second and I had put $20 on the nose on a horse that was forty to one. Its name was Old Joe. Bernie told me it was the silliest bet he had ever seen. Old Joe romped home ... $800.

At the end of the day I asked Bernie how much he had lost. He said he was $50 up. I couldn't figure it. He hadn't even gotten a place, let alone a win ... this is how he explained it to me. There was a race in Sydney that he wanted to bet on, but he didn't get his bet on in time. The horse he would have put $50 on, didn't even get a place, so he said he hadn't lost his $50, therefore he was $50 up ... go figure!

When he got home Sue asked him "How did you do at the races?" He told her "I'm $50 up." ... "Well done Bernie," said Sue ... amazing.

## HOME SWEET HOME

Although we went back overseas, I never wanted to live anywhere else. Kaz would have made the move if that's where it was headed. She was very supportive but I hadn't really stopped since I was a kid in the Navy. I love Australia and I truly believe it is the best country in the world. I am so fortunate to live and work here. We are certainly blessed.

Sure, there were great opportunities overseas but my heart was here, with my family and although I was still working hard, I was quite happy to base myself in Australia. God knows I wasn't short of work.

Kaz and I built our new home, I kept making albums, DVDs and the odd TV show. We got a new puppy for Cass, (a poodle). We called her Tessie. Kim and Jo were getting bigger and the time was drawing near when they would find their own way in the world.

Before we knew it the two eldest had their own 'wheels'. Kim had my garage space. I was banished to the driveway.

It is a standard joke in the family that I would retire and buy my dream car, a two-seater sports car; a red MG. Kim said I could have my space back when the MG. arrived.

I actually got so far as to inspect one once, years before. I was tempted, till Jodie's little eight year old voice piped up, "Where will I sit Daddy?"

I looked at Kaz ... I felt so guilty ... just couldn't do it.

## STRANGER THAN FICTION

Kaz and I were invited to a friend's barbecue one night; we sat down with my mate's father, Frank Wyatt.

Frank was a WW2 veteran and had fought the Japanese in New Guinea. He never really spoke of his time there but that night he shared with me a story of mateship that was typically Australian. Frank knew that I had served and I guess he felt a certain bond because that night he opened up.

I was telling him about a book I had read by A B Facey entitled, A Fortunate Life. It is an incredible Australian story and was turned into a television movie. The author served at Gallipoli, was wounded and sent back to Perth.

While in the trenches he had been given a box that was randomly issued from well-wishers back home. His box contained a pair of socks that were knitted by the sender.

Back home, he and a mate were out on a day's leave from the

hospital and were sitting at a bus stop. Two young ladies bumped into them and said hello. One mentioned how she had sent some socks off to the front.

He lifted his trousers and said "not these ones are they?" or something to that effect and of course they were. They eventually married and were together for life.

I was telling Frank that story and it prompted him to tell me his story.

He and two other mates had joined together; they were sent to fight the Japanese. There were only about 30 in their squad and were in constant combat. It was incredibly tough terrain and the three mates stuck close. They had made a pact that if any one of the three were killed the remaining ones would look after those left back home. Frank was single, about twenty, the next mate was only sixteen and the third mate, twenty-four. He was married with two small toddlers at home; a boy and a girl.

They ran into a Jap patrol one morning. They were pinned down and things were getting nasty. They started to move forward and take the initiative when Frank's mate, Jack, the eldest, was cut in half by machine gun fire. There was nothing he could do. He told me this story with the tears starting to form in his eyes.

He then told us how the sixteen year old went home after the war and married his mate's widow and brought up his two children. He had never seen his mate from that day.

Kaz and I both looked at each other in utter amazement. We had heard this story before …

"Frank," I said "your mate's name is Doug Hocking … that little girl he brought up is my sister-in-law, Shirley … she is married to my brother Ralph."

While I was telling Frank this, Kaz was on the phone to Ralph and Shirley … 'Pa' Hocking had only just gone home, he had been around for tea. Frank and Shirley spoke at length. It was very emotional.

The next day the two old mates were on the phone for three hours.

They were both now widowers. Two days later Doug flew up to the Gold Coast. They came down to the wharf where I was working on my boat, to thank me. I had the Bulletin newspaper come down and witness their reunion. It had been fifty-five years.

Both men are now gone but there is more to this story ...

At the time of this reunion I was making a film clip as a tribute to our Vets.

Written by Colin Greatorix and recorded by my myself, the song was, What have you done for Australia.

In the clip I used some old Movietone footage of the diggers marching off to war in WW2. I also touched on Korea and of course Vietnam.

I showed my Unit and also some 'stills' of soldiers in the jungle. One of those stills is of my brother Ralph on patrol with an S.L.R.

I finished the clip and sent a copy down for Ralph and Shirley.

Ralph rang as soon as he had watched it ... He was quite taken aback ... The first piece of footage I had used from the Movietone archives showed Frank, Doug and Jack marching off to war.

A few years later I was in the middle of Western Australia doing a country festival. Two huge men sidled up to me; the biggest at six foot six introduced himself as John.

"Bet you don't know where you are Col?" he asked.

"Well as a matter of fact I do," I said, and proceeded to tell them how a fella called Facey grew up on farms in the area and if they wanted to learn some great Australian history they should get a book called *A fortunate Life* ... They both laughed.

John said "Col, A. B. Facey was my grandfather, his name is John Rose."

We are still mates.

## KIM'S POEM

I was still on the road quite a bit but things were going to have to change.

As a twenty year old, our eldest daughter, Kim, gave me this poem. It hangs in my office to this day as a timely reminder of how one life can affect so many others.

### Kim's Poem

*I wipe my eyes and blow my nose*
*cause' poor old Dad just has to go*
*we miss you heaps, when you're not here*
*you make us laugh, so full of cheer.*
*It must be hard to go away,*
*to pack your bags and leave today*
*But you'll be back in a few more days*
*Or "two more sleeps" as Cassie Jane would say*
*Although Jo and I have our own busy lives*
*We'll think of you on stage tonight*
*We're proud of you and grateful of*
*all the things you've done for us*
*Mum's so strong but she misses you too*
*hoping you'll retire soon*
*With the red MG parked out the back*
*(you can't have the garage ... you know that)*
*But I've never told you how lucky I feel*
*To have a wonderful Dad who's so unreal*
*OK, so I can't write a poem and I can't sing a tune*
*I just wanted to say ... 'chookas' for tonight*
*and we'll see you soon.*

## IN CONCLUSION

I rang home one night and had a good old chin-wag with Cass; she was about five at the time. After she told me of all her news from school she said, "Daddy, do you want to speak to Mummy?"

"Yes please sweetheart," I replied.

She called out ... "Hey Mum, Col Elliott's on the phone."

Today Carol and Jack are still on the farm; Wendy is an aerobics instructor with three beautiful children; Miffy remains a dedicated bachelor, brother Ralph retired with a swag of grandkids as well.

Our mum passed away in 2005 just a little time before her eighty-second birthday ... I can still hear her voice.

Our dear friend Jan Craig passed away in 2007. Karen and I were at her bedside along with her daughters Narelle and Kirsten when she left us.

Today, Bernie at 71 is battling bone cancer. The chemo is tough but he never complains ... the only bitch he has is because he says I don't work enough these days ... he says he has to line me up with a fence post to see if I'm moving!

Bernie and I talk every day as we have done for all these years. Once a week we have lunch and renew our contract.

I have had an amazing career and achieved more than I ever thought possible. I still feel the thrill of performing and feel privileged that people still come to my shows.

We have our three wonderful daughters and our five beautiful grandchildren. Our lives are certainly full.

Kaz says there still magic in our marriage ... mainly because I keep disappearing. She's got a great sense of humour that girl ... she needs it to be married to me!!!

I have to say that after writing this memoir it certainly has made me take a long hard look at my life. It made me re-evaluate to a point where I truly believe, in the most part, it has been a very selfish existence.

My partner in life, my wife Kaz was the one who instigated this book.

She urged me to put down all the crazy stories and adventures I had shared with her and our friends all our married life; stories from my childhood, the Navy, our life together and showbiz.

I believe to get down everything would take three volumes. Who knows, maybe there will be another one to follow.

This is more a memoir than a full-on autobiography.

I could write a book on, 'What not to do in a marriage'.

I'm an expert! But that wasn't the purpose of this exercise.

Kaz was just twenty when we had our first child, then three years later our second baby arrived. By that time my showbiz aspirations where well underway.

I gave her a roller coaster ride to say the least. She was so young and for the first six years of our marriage she had to cope with an alcoholic husband clearly out of control trying to get it together.

Then I became a workaholic entertainer that left her at home to cope as best she could while I pushed all the boundaries.

I never listened to her, it was always my agenda.

I dragged Kaz along for the ride; my ride. She had little choice but to make the most of the life I had foisted on her.

She rose to the challenge and found her inner strength but not without much emotional pain. There were nights when she'd ring Lifeline, just to get through. I was on the road, in another world.

There was a time she decided to cut back on every day spending in the vague hope that I would see our nest egg building and would cut my work load.

I could have done that but I didn't. I had my values and priorities wrong. I wasn't there for her. For that I am so sorry.

There were times when each of us nearly walked away. The pressure on our marriage was tremendous. Somehow we weathered the storm.

Not long ago, off the top of my head I asked Kaz if she would renew her vows. She answered without a moment's hesitation, "Absolutely". I'm a lucky man. We have just celebrated 41 years together.

Kaz never wanted me to give up showbiz, all she ever wanted was balance for us all.

Today Kaz and I have found that balance. We travel at the drop of a hat and get out on our boat at every chance.

After 18 years of wonderful times, we retired the 'Nauti-Col', our home cruiser and upgraded to a more seaworthy motor yacht which allows us to venture a little further afield.

We have shared many tough times together and also some wonderful memories as well.

They say hindsight is 20/20 ... our history can't change but our future can.

I say to anyone out there, cherish what you have. Time moves so quickly, make every day count and enjoy life "In-between the laughter".

Catch you at the next gig. Cheers Col.

---

*Author's footnote: Some of the names have been changed to protect the innocent... On reflection, most of the bastards were guilty!*

**A special dedication to the memory of Bernie Stahl.**
*He was more than a manager, he was a great mate and part of our family. I shook his hand for the last time on 20th November 2013.*